Debugging with GDB

The GNU Source-Level Debugger

Ninth Edition, for GDB version 5.1.1
January 2002

Richard Stallman, Roland Pesch, Stan Shebs, et al.

(Send bugs and comments on GDB to bug-gdb@gnu.org)
Debugging with GDB
T_EXinfo 2002-03-26.08

Published by:
GNU Press
a division of the
Free Software Foundation
59 Temple Place Suite 330
Boston, MA 02111-1307 USA

Website: www.gnupress.org
General: press@gnu.org
Orders: sales@gnu.org
Tel 617-542-5942
Fax 627-542-2652

Cover art by Etienne Suvasa

Table of Contents

15   Configuration-Specific Information....... 169

Debugging with GDB

Summary of GDB

The purpose of a debugger such as GDB is to allow you to see what is going on "inside" another program while it executes—or what another program was doing at the moment it crashed.

GDB can do four main kinds of things (plus other things in support of these) to help you catch bugs in the act:

- Start your program, specifying anything that might affect its behavior.
- Make your program stop on specified conditions.
- Examine what has happened, when your program has stopped.
- Change things in your program, so you can experiment with correcting the effects of one bug and go on to learn about another.

You can use GDB to debug programs written in C and C++. For more information, see Section 10.4 [Supported languages], page 104. For more information, see Section 10.4.1 [C and C++], page 104.

Support for Modula-2 and Chill is partial. For information on Modula-2, see Section 10.4.2 [Modula-2], page 111. For information on Chill, see Section 10.4.3 [Chill], page 116.

Debugging Pascal programs which use sets, subranges, file variables, or nested functions does not currently work. GDB does not support entering expressions, printing values, or similar features using Pascal syntax.

GDB can be used to debug programs written in Fortran, although it may be necessary to refer to some variables with a trailing underscore.

Free software

GDB is *free software*, protected by the GNU General Public License (GPL). The GPL gives you the freedom to copy or adapt a licensed program—but every person getting a copy also gets with it the freedom to modify that copy (which means that they must get access to the source code), and the freedom to distribute further copies. Typical software companies use copyrights to limit your freedoms; the Free Software Foundation uses the GPL to preserve these freedoms.

Fundamentally, the General Public License is a license which says that you have these freedoms and that you cannot take these freedoms away from anyone else.

Free Software Needs Free Documentation

The biggest deficiency in the free software community today is not in the software—it is the lack of good free documentation that we can include with the free software. Many of our most important programs do not come with free reference manuals and free introductory texts. Documentation is an essential part of any software package; when an important free software package does not come with a free manual and a free tutorial, that is a major gap. We have many such gaps today.

Consider Perl, for instance. The tutorial manuals that people normally use are non-free. How did this come about? Because the authors of those manuals published them with restrictive terms—no copying, no modification, source files not available—which exclude them from the free software world.

That wasn't the first time this sort of thing happened, and it was far from the last. Many times we have heard a GNU user eagerly describe a manual that he is writing, his intended contribution to the community, only to learn that he had ruined everything by signing a publication contract to make it non-free.

Free documentation, like free software, is a matter of freedom, not price. The problem with the non-free manual is not that publishers charge a price for printed copies—that in itself is fine. (The Free Software Foundation sells printed copies of manuals, too.) The problem is the restrictions on the use of the manual. Free manuals are available in source code form, and give you permission to copy and modify. Non-free manuals do not allow this.

The criteria of freedom for a free manual are roughly the same as for free software. Redistribution (including the normal kinds of commercial redistribution) must be permitted, so that the manual can accompany every copy of the program, both on-line and on paper.

Permission for modification of the technical content is crucial too. When people modify the software, adding or changing features, if they are conscientious they will change the manual too—so they can provide accurate and clear documentation for the modified program. A manual that leaves you no choice but to write a new manual to document a changed version of the program is not really available to our community.

Some kinds of limits on the way modification is handled are acceptable. For example, requirements to preserve the original author's copyright notice, the distribution terms, or the list of authors, are ok. It is also no problem to require modified versions to include notice that they were modified. Even entire sections that may not be deleted or changed are acceptable, as long as they deal with nontechnical topics (like this one). These kinds of restrictions are acceptable because they don't obstruct the community's normal use of the manual.

However, it must be possible to modify all the *technical* content of the manual, and then distribute the result in all the usual media, through all the usual channels. Otherwise, the restrictions obstruct the use of the manual, it is not free, and we need another manual to replace it.

Please spread the word about this issue. Our community continues to lose manuals to proprietary publishing. If we spread the word that free software needs free reference manuals and free tutorials, perhaps the next person who wants to contribute by writing documentation will realize, before it is too late, that only free manuals contribute to the free software community.

If you are writing documentation, please insist on publishing it under the GNU Free Documentation License or another free documentation license. Remember that this decision requires your approval—you don't have to let the publisher decide. Some commercial publishers will use a free license if you insist, but they will not propose the option; it is up to you to raise the issue and say firmly that this is what you want. If the publisher you are dealing with refuses, please try other publishers. If you're not sure whether a proposed license is free, write to `licensing@gnu.org`.

You can encourage commercial publishers to sell more free, copylefted manuals and tutorials by buying them, and particularly by buying copies from the publishers that paid for their writing or for major improvements. Meanwhile, try to avoid buying non-free documentation at all. Check the distribution terms of a manual before you buy it, and insist that whoever seeks your business must respect your freedom. Check the history of the book, and try to reward the publishers that have paid or pay the authors to work on it.

The Free Software Foundation maintains a list of free documentation published by other publishers, at `http://www.fsf.org/doc/other-free-books.html`.

Contributors to GDB

Richard Stallman was the original author of GDB, and of many other GNU programs. Many others have contributed to its development. This section attempts to credit major contributors. One of the virtues of free software is that everyone is free to contribute to it; with regret, we cannot actually acknowledge everyone here. The file 'ChangeLog' in the GDB distribution approximates a blow-by-blow account.

Changes much prior to version 2.0 are lost in the mists of time.

> *Plea:* Additions to this section are particularly welcome. If you
> or your friends (or enemies, to be evenhanded) have been unfairly
> omitted from this list, we would like to add your names!

So that they may not regard their many labors as thankless, we particularly thank those who shepherded GDB through major releases: Andrew Cagney (releases 5.0 and 5.1); Jim Blandy (release 4.18); Jason Molenda (release 4.17); Stan Shebs (release 4.14); Fred Fish (releases 4.16, 4.15, 4.13, 4.12, 4.11, 4.10, and 4.9); Stu Grossman and John Gilmore (releases 4.8, 4.7, 4.6, 4.5, and 4.4); John Gilmore (releases 4.3, 4.2, 4.1, 4.0, and 3.9); Jim Kingdon (releases 3.5, 3.4, and 3.3); and Randy Smith (releases 3.2, 3.1, and 3.0).

Richard Stallman, assisted at various times by Peter TerMaat, Chris Hanson, and Richard Mlynarik, handled releases through 2.8.

Michael Tiemann is the author of most of the GNU C++ support in GDB, with significant additional contributions from Per Bothner and Daniel Berlin. James Clark wrote the GNU C++ demangler. Early work on C++ was by Peter TerMaat (who also did much general update work leading to release 3.0).

GDB uses the BFD subroutine library to examine multiple object-file formats; BFD was a joint project of David V. Henkel-Wallace, Rich Pixley, Steve Chamberlain, and John Gilmore.

David Johnson wrote the original COFF support; Pace Willison did the original support for encapsulated COFF.

Brent Benson of Harris Computer Systems contributed DWARF2 support.

Adam de Boor and Bradley Davis contributed the ISI Optimum V support. Per Bothner, Noboyuki Hikichi, and Alessandro Forin contributed MIPS support. Jean-Daniel Fekete contributed Sun 386i support. Chris Hanson improved the HP9000 support. Noboyuki Hikichi and Tomoyuki Hasei contributed Sony/News OS 3 support. David Johnson contributed Encore Umax support. Jyrki Kuoppala contributed Altos 3068 support. Jeff Law contributed HP PA and SOM support. Keith Packard contributed NS32K support. Doug Rabson contributed Acorn Risc Machine support. Bob Rusk contributed Harris Nighthawk CX-UX support. Chris Smith contributed Convex support (and Fortran debugging). Jonathan Stone contributed Pyramid support. Michael Tiemann contributed SPARC support. Tim Tucker contributed support for the Gould NP1 and Gould Powernode. Pace Willison contributed Intel 386 support. Jay Vosburgh contributed Symmetry support.

Andreas Schwab contributed M68K Linux support.

Rich Schaefer and Peter Schauer helped with support of SunOS shared libraries.

Jay Fenlason and Roland McGrath ensured that GDB and GAS agree about several machine instruction sets.

Patrick Duval, Ted Goldstein, Vikram Koka and Glenn Engel helped develop remote debugging. Intel Corporation, Wind River Systems, AMD, and ARM contributed remote debugging modules for the i960, VxWorks, A29K UDI, and RDI targets, respectively.

Brian Fox is the author of the readline libraries providing command-line editing and command history.

Andrew Beers of SUNY Buffalo wrote the language-switching code, the Modula-2 support, and contributed the Languages chapter of this manual.

Fred Fish wrote most of the support for Unix System Vr4. He also enhanced the command-completion support to cover C++ overloaded symbols.

Hitachi America, Ltd. sponsored the support for H8/300, H8/500, and Super-H processors.

NEC sponsored the support for the v850, Vr4xxx, and Vr5xxx processors.

Mitsubishi sponsored the support for D10V, D30V, and M32R/D processors.

Toshiba sponsored the support for the TX39 Mips processor.

Matsushita sponsored the support for the MN10200 and MN10300 processors.

Fujitsu sponsored the support for SPARClite and FR30 processors.

Kung Hsu, Jeff Law, and Rick Sladkey added support for hardware watchpoints.

Michael Snyder added support for tracepoints.

Stu Grossman wrote gdbserver.

Jim Kingdon, Peter Schauer, Ian Taylor, and Stu Grossman made nearly innumerable bug fixes and cleanups throughout GDB.

The following people at the Hewlett-Packard Company contributed support for the PA-RISC 2.0 architecture, HP-UX 10.20, 10.30, and 11.0 (narrow mode), HP's implementation of kernel threads, HP's aC++ compiler, and the terminal user interface: Ben Krepp, Richard Title, John Bishop, Susan Macchia, Kathy Mann, Satish Pai, India Paul, Steve Rehrauer, and Elena Zannoni. Kim Haase provided HP-specific information in this manual.

DJ Delorie ported GDB to MS-DOS, for the DJGPP project. Robert Hoehne made significant contributions to the DJGPP port.

Cygnus Solutions has sponsored GDB maintenance and much of its development since 1991. Cygnus engineers who have worked on GDB fulltime include Mark Alexander, Jim Blandy, Per Bothner, Kevin Buettner, Edith Epstein, Chris Faylor, Fred Fish, Martin Hunt, Jim Ingham, John Gilmore, Stu Grossman, Kung Hsu, Jim Kingdon, John Metzler, Fernando Nasser, Geoffrey Noer, Dawn Perchik, Rich Pixley, Zdenek Radouch, Keith Seitz, Stan Shebs, David Taylor, and Elena Zannoni. In addition, Dave Brolley, Ian Carmichael, Steve Chamberlain, Nick Clifton, JT Conklin, Stan Cox, DJ Delorie, Ulrich Drepper, Frank Eigler, Doug Evans, Sean Fagan, David Henkel-Wallace, Richard Henderson, Jeff Holcomb, Jeff Law, Jim Lemke, Tom Lord, Bob Manson, Michael Meissner, Jason Merrill, Catherine Moore, Drew Moseley, Ken Raeburn, Gavin Romig-Koch, Rob Savoye, Jamie Smith, Mike Stump, Ian Taylor, Angela Thomas, Michael Tiemann, Tom Tromey, Ron Unrau, Jim Wilson, and David Zuhn have made contributions both large and small.

1 A Sample GDB Session

You can use this manual at your leisure to read all about GDB. However, a handful of commands are enough to get started using the debugger. This chapter illustrates those commands.

In this sample session, we emphasize user input like this: **input**, to make it easier to pick out from the surrounding output.

One of the preliminary versions of GNU m4 (a generic macro processor) exhibits the following bug: sometimes, when we change its quote strings from the default, the commands used to capture one macro definition within another stop working. In the following short m4 session, we define a macro foo which expands to 0000; we then use the m4 built-in defn to define bar as the same thing. However, when we change the open quote string to <QUOTE> and the close quote string to <UNQUOTE>, the same procedure fails to define a new synonym baz:

```
$ cd gnu/m4
$ ./m4
define(foo,0000)

foo
0000
define(bar,defn('foo'))

bar
0000
changequote(<QUOTE>,<UNQUOTE>)

define(baz,defn(<QUOTE>foo<UNQUOTE>))
baz
C-d
m4: End of input: 0: fatal error: EOF in string
```

Let us use GDB to try to see what is going on.

```
$ gdb m4
GDB is free software and you are welcome to distribute copies
 of it under certain conditions; type "show copying" to see
 the conditions.
There is absolutely no warranty for GDB; type "show warranty"
 for details.

GDB 5.1.1, Copyright 1999 Free Software Foundation, Inc...
 (gdb)
```

GDB reads only enough symbol data to know where to find the rest when needed; as a result, the first prompt comes up very quickly. We now tell

GDB to use a narrower display width than usual, so that examples fit in
this manual.

```
(gdb) set width 70
```

We need to see how the m4 built-in changequote works. Having looked at
the source, we know the relevant subroutine is m4_changequote, so we set a
breakpoint there with the GDB break command.

```
(gdb) break m4_changequote
Breakpoint 1 at 0x62f4: file builtin.c, line 879.
```

Using the run command, we start m4 running under GDB control; as long
as control does not reach the m4_changequote subroutine, the program runs
as usual:

```
(gdb) run
Starting program: /work/Editorial/gdb/gnu/m4/m4
define(foo,0000)

foo
0000
```

To trigger the breakpoint, we call changequote. GDB suspends execution
of m4, displaying information about the context where it stops.

```
changequote(<QUOTE>,<UNQUOTE>)

Breakpoint 1, m4_changequote (argc=3, argv=0x33c70)
    at builtin.c:879
879         if (bad_argc(TOKEN_DATA_TEXT(argv[0]),argc,1,3))
```

Now we use the command n (next) to advance execution to the next line of
the current function.

```
(gdb) n
882         set_quotes((argc >= 2) ? TOKEN_DATA_TEXT(argv[1])\
    : nil,
```

set_quotes looks like a promising subroutine. We can go into it by using
the command s (step) instead of next. step goes to the next line to be
executed in *any* subroutine, so it steps into set_quotes.

```
(gdb) s
set_quotes (lq=0x34c78 "<QUOTE>", rq=0x34c88 "<UNQUOTE>")
    at input.c:530
530         if (lquote != def_lquote)
```

The display that shows the subroutine where m4 is now suspended (and its
arguments) is called a stack frame display. It shows a summary of the stack.
We can use the backtrace command (which can also be spelled bt), to see
where we are in the stack as a whole: the backtrace command displays a
stack frame for each active subroutine.

```
(gdb) bt
#0  set_quotes (lq=0x34c78 "<QUOTE>", rq=0x34c88 "<UNQUOTE>")
```

```
        at input.c:530
#1  0x6344 in m4_changequote (argc=3, argv=0x33c70)
        at builtin.c:882
#2  0x8174 in expand_macro (sym=0x33320) at macro.c:242
#3  0x7a88 in expand_token (obs=0x0, t=209696, td=0xf7fffa30)
        at macro.c:71
#4  0x79dc in expand_input () at macro.c:40
#5  0x2930 in main (argc=0, argv=0xf7fffb20) at m4.c:195
```

We step through a few more lines to see what happens. The first two times,
we can use 's'; the next two times we use **n** to avoid falling into the **xstrdup**
subroutine.

```
(gdb) s
0x3b5c  532          if (rquote != def_rquote)
(gdb) s
0x3b80  535          lquote = (lq == nil || *lq == '\0') ? \
def_lquote : xstrdup(lq);
(gdb) n
536                  rquote = (rq == nil || *rq == '\0') ? def_rquote\
 : xstrdup(rq);
(gdb) n
538                  len_lquote = strlen(rquote);
```

The last line displayed looks a little odd; we can examine the variables
lquote and **rquote** to see if they are in fact the new left and right quotes
we specified. We use the command **p** (**print**) to see their values.

```
(gdb) p lquote
$1 = 0x35d40 "<QUOTE>"
(gdb) p rquote
$2 = 0x35d50 "<UNQUOTE>"
```

lquote and **rquote** are indeed the new left and right quotes. To look at
some context, we can display ten lines of source surrounding the current line
with the **l** (**list**) command.

```
(gdb) l
533                  xfree(rquote);
534
535                  lquote = (lq == nil || *lq == '\0') ? def_lquote\
 : xstrdup (lq);
536                  rquote = (rq == nil || *rq == '\0') ? def_rquote\
 : xstrdup (rq);
537
538                  len_lquote = strlen(rquote);
539                  len_rquote = strlen(lquote);
540      }
541
```

```
542        void
```

Let us step past the two lines that set `len_lquote` and `len_rquote`, and then examine the values of those variables.

```
(gdb) n
539            len_rquote = strlen(lquote);
(gdb) n
540      }
(gdb) p len_lquote
$3 = 9
(gdb) p len_rquote
$4 = 7
```

That certainly looks wrong, assuming `len_lquote` and `len_rquote` are meant to be the lengths of `lquote` and `rquote` respectively. We can set them to better values using the `p` command, since it can print the value of any expression—and that expression can include subroutine calls and assignments.

```
(gdb) p len_lquote=strlen(lquote)
$5 = 7
(gdb) p len_rquote=strlen(rquote)
$6 = 9
```

Is that enough to fix the problem of using the new quotes with the `m4` built-in `defn`? We can allow `m4` to continue executing with the `c` (`continue`) command, and then try the example that caused trouble initially:

```
(gdb) c
Continuing.

define(baz,defn(<QUOTE>foo<UNQUOTE>))

baz
0000
```

Success! The new quotes now work just as well as the default ones. The problem seems to have been just the two typos defining the wrong lengths. We allow `m4` exit by giving it an EOF as input:

```
C-d
Program exited normally.
```

The message '`Program exited normally.`' is from GDB; it indicates `m4` has finished executing. We can end our GDB session with the GDB `quit` command.

```
(gdb) quit
```

2 Getting In and Out of GDB

This chapter discusses how to start GDB, and how to get out of it. The essentials are:

- type 'gdb' to start GDB.
- type *quit* or *C-d* to exit.

2.1 Invoking GDB

Invoke GDB by running the program **gdb**. Once started, GDB reads commands from the terminal until you tell it to exit.

You can also run **gdb** with a variety of arguments and options, to specify more of your debugging environment at the outset.

The command-line options described here are designed to cover a variety of situations; in some environments, some of these options may effectively be unavailable.

The most usual way to start GDB is with one argument, specifying an executable program:

    gdb *program*

You can also start with both an executable program and a core file specified:

    gdb *program* *core*

You can, instead, specify a process ID as a second argument, if you want to debug a running process:

    gdb *program* 1234

would attach GDB to process **1234** (unless you also have a file named '1234'; GDB does check for a core file first).

Taking advantage of the second command-line argument requires a fairly complete operating system; when you use GDB as a remote debugger attached to a bare board, there may not be any notion of "process", and there is often no way to get a core dump. GDB will warn you if it is unable to attach or to read core dumps.

You can run **gdb** without printing the front material, which describes GDB's non-warranty, by specifying **-silent**:

    gdb -silent

You can further control how GDB starts up by using command-line options. GDB itself can remind you of the options available.

Type

    gdb -help

to display all available options and briefly describe their use ('**gdb -h**' is a shorter equivalent).

All options and command line arguments you give are processed in sequential order. The order makes a difference when the '**-x**' option is used.

2.1.1 Choosing files

When GDB starts, it reads any arguments other than options as specifying an executable file and core file (or process ID). This is the same as if the arguments were specified by the '-se' and '-c' options respectively. (GDB reads the first argument that does not have an associated option flag as equivalent to the '-se' option followed by that argument; and the second argument that does not have an associated option flag, if any, as equivalent to the '-c' option followed by that argument.)

If GDB has not been configured to included core file support, such as for most embedded targets, then it will complain about a second argument and ignore it.

Many options have both long and short forms; both are shown in the following list. GDB also recognizes the long forms if you truncate them, so long as enough of the option is present to be unambiguous. (If you prefer, you can flag option arguments with '--' rather than '-', though we illustrate the more usual convention.)

-symbols *file*
-s *file*   Read symbol table from file *file*.

-exec *file*
-e *file*   Use file *file* as the executable file to execute when appropriate, and for examining pure data in conjunction with a core dump.

-se *file*   Read symbol table from file *file* and use it as the executable file.

-core *file*
-c *file*   Use file *file* as a core dump to examine.

-c *number*

      Connect to process ID *number*, as with the **attach** command (unless there is a file in core-dump format named *number*, in which case '-c' specifies that file as a core dump to read).

-command *file*
-x *file*   Execute GDB commands from file *file*. See Section 17.3 [Command files], page 201.

-directory *directory*
-d *directory*

      Add *directory* to the path to search for source files.

-m
-mapped   *Warning: this option depends on operating system facilities that are not supported on all systems.*

      If memory-mapped files are available on your system through the **mmap** system call, you can use this option to have GDB write the symbols from your program into a reusable file in the current directory. If the program you are debugging is called

'/tmp/fred', the mapped symbol file is '/tmp/fred.syms'. Future GDB debugging sessions notice the presence of this file, and can quickly map in symbol information from it, rather than reading the symbol table from the executable program.

The '.syms' file is specific to the host machine where GDB is run. It holds an exact image of the internal GDB symbol table. It cannot be shared across multiple host platforms.

-r
-readnow   Read each symbol file's entire symbol table immediately, rather than the default, which is to read it incrementally as it is needed. This makes startup slower, but makes future operations faster.

You typically combine the -mapped and -readnow options in order to build a '.syms' file that contains complete symbol information. (See Section 13.1 [Commands to specify files], page 135, for information on '.syms' files.) A simple GDB invocation to do nothing but build a '.syms' file for future use is:

```
gdb -batch -nx -mapped -readnow programname
```

2.1.2 Choosing modes

You can run GDB in various alternative modes—for example, in batch mode or quiet mode.

-nx
-n   Do not execute commands found in any initialization files (normally called '.gdbinit', or 'gdb.ini' on PCs). Normally, GDB executes the commands in these files after all the command options and arguments have been processed. See Section 17.3 [Command files], page 201.

-quiet
-silent
-q   "Quiet". Do not print the introductory and copyright messages. These messages are also suppressed in batch mode.

-batch   Run in batch mode. Exit with status 0 after processing all the command files specified with '-x' (and all commands from initialization files, if not inhibited with '-n'). Exit with nonzero status if an error occurs in executing the GDB commands in the command files.

                Batch mode may be useful for running GDB as a filter, for example to download and run a program on another computer; in order to make this more useful, the message

                ```
                Program exited normally.
                ```

(which is ordinarily issued whenever a program running under GDB control terminates) is not issued when running in batch mode.

`-nowindows`

`-nw` "No windows". If GDB comes with a graphical user interface (GUI) built in, then this option tells GDB to only use the command-line interface. If no GUI is available, this option has no effect.

`-windows`

`-w` If GDB includes a GUI, then this option requires it to be used if possible.

`-cd` *directory*

  Run GDB using *directory* as its working directory, instead of the current directory.

`-fullname`

`-f` GNU Emacs sets this option when it runs GDB as a subprocess. It tells GDB to output the full file name and line number in a standard, recognizable fashion each time a stack frame is displayed (which includes each time your program stops). This recognizable format looks like two '`\032`' characters, followed by the file name, line number and character position separated by colons, and a newline. The Emacs-to-GDB interface program uses the two '`\032`' characters as a signal to display the source code for the frame.

`-epoch` The Epoch Emacs-GDB interface sets this option when it runs GDB as a subprocess. It tells GDB to modify its print routines so as to allow Epoch to display values of expressions in a separate window.

`-annotate` *level*

  This option sets the *annotation level* inside GDB. Its effect is identical to using '`set annotate` *level*' (see Chapter 20 [Annotations], page 213). Annotation level controls how much information does GDB print together with its prompt, values of expressions, source lines, and other types of output. Level 0 is the normal, level 1 is for use when GDB is run as a subprocess of GNU Emacs, level 2 is the maximum annotation suitable for programs that control GDB.

`-async` Use the asynchronous event loop for the command-line interface. GDB processes all events, such as user keyboard input, via a special event loop. This allows GDB to accept and process user commands in parallel with the debugged process being run[1], so

---

[1] GDB built with DJGPP tools for MS-DOS/MS-Windows supports this mode of operation, but the event loop is suspended when the debuggee runs.

you don't need to wait for control to return to GDB before you type the next command. (*Note:* as of version 5.1, the target side of the asynchronous operation is not yet in place, so '-async' does not work fully yet.)

When the standard input is connected to a terminal device, GDB uses the asynchronous event loop by default, unless disabled by the '-noasync' option.

-noasync   Disable the asynchronous event loop for the command-line interface.

-baud *bps*
-b *bps*   Set the line speed (baud rate or bits per second) of any serial interface used by GDB for remote debugging.

-tty *device*
-t *device*   Run using *device* for your program's standard input and output.

-tui   Activate the Terminal User Interface when starting. The Terminal User Interface manages several text windows on the terminal, showing source, assembly, registers and GDB command outputs (see Chapter 18 [GDB Text User Interface], page 205). Do not use this option if you run GDB from Emacs (see Chapter 19 [Using GDB under GNU Emacs], page 209).

-interpreter *interp*
    Use the interpreter *interp* for interface with the controlling program or device. This option is meant to be set by programs which communicate with GDB using it as a back end.

    '--interpreter=mi' (or '--interpreter=mi1') causes GDB to use the *gdb/mi interface* (see Chapter 21 [The GDB/MI Interface], page 223). The older GDB/MI interface, included in GDB version 5.0 can be selected with '--interpreter=mi0'.

-write   Open the executable and core files for both reading and writing. This is equivalent to the 'set write on' command inside GDB (see Section 12.6 [Patching], page 132).

-statistics
    This option causes GDB to print statistics about time and memory usage after it completes each command and returns to the prompt.

-version   This option causes GDB to print its version number and no-warranty blurb, and exit.

2.2 Quitting GDB

quit [*expression*]
q   To exit GDB, use the quit command (abbreviated q), or type an end-of-file character (usually *C-d*). If you do not supply *expres-*

sion, GDB will terminate normally; otherwise it will terminate using the result of *expression* as the error code.

An interrupt (often *C-c*) does not exit from GDB, but rather terminates the action of any GDB command that is in progress and returns to GDB command level. It is safe to type the interrupt character at any time because GDB does not allow it to take effect until a time when it is safe.

If you have been using GDB to control an attached process or device, you can release it with the **detach** command (see Section 4.7 [Debugging an already-running process], page 28).

2.3 Shell commands

If you need to execute occasional shell commands during your debugging session, there is no need to leave or suspend GDB; you can just use the **shell** command.

shell *command string*

> Invoke a standard shell to execute *command string*. If it exists, the environment variable **SHELL** determines which shell to run. Otherwise GDB uses the default shell ('**/bin/sh**' on Unix systems, '**COMMAND.COM**' on MS-DOS, etc.).

The utility **make** is often needed in development environments. You do not have to use the **shell** command for this purpose in GDB:

make *make-args*

> Execute the **make** program with the specified arguments. This is equivalent to '**shell make** *make-args*'.

3 GDB Commands

You can abbreviate a GDB command to the first few letters of the command name, if that abbreviation is unambiguous; and you can repeat certain GDB commands by typing just (RET). You can also use the (TAB) key to get GDB to fill out the rest of a word in a command (or to show you the alternatives available, if there is more than one possibility).

3.1 Command syntax

A GDB command is a single line of input. There is no limit on how long it can be. It starts with a command name, which is followed by arguments whose meaning depends on the command name. For example, the command step accepts an argument which is the number of times to step, as in 'step 5'. You can also use the step command with no arguments. Some commands do not allow any arguments.

GDB command names may always be truncated if that abbreviation is unambiguous. Other possible command abbreviations are listed in the documentation for individual commands. In some cases, even ambiguous abbreviations are allowed; for example, s is specially defined as equivalent to step even though there are other commands whose names start with s. You can test abbreviations by using them as arguments to the help command.

A blank line as input to GDB (typing just (RET)) means to repeat the previous command. Certain commands (for example, run) will not repeat this way; these are commands whose unintentional repetition might cause trouble and which you are unlikely to want to repeat.

The list and x commands, when you repeat them with (RET), construct new arguments rather than repeating exactly as typed. This permits easy scanning of source or memory.

GDB can also use (RET) in another way: to partition lengthy output, in a way similar to the common utility more (see Section 16.4 [Screen size], page 193). Since it is easy to press one (RET) too many in this situation, GDB disables command repetition after any command that generates this sort of display.

Any text from a # to the end of the line is a comment; it does nothing. This is useful mainly in command files (see Section 17.3 [Command files], page 201).

3.2 Command completion

GDB can fill in the rest of a word in a command for you, if there is only one possibility; it can also show you what the valid possibilities are for the next word in a command, at any time. This works for GDB commands, GDB subcommands, and the names of symbols in your program.

Press the (TAB) key whenever you want GDB to fill out the rest of a word. If there is only one possibility, GDB fills in the word, and waits for you to finish the command (or press (RET) to enter it). For example, if you type

    (gdb) info bre (TAB)

GDB fills in the rest of the word 'breakpoints', since that is the only info subcommand beginning with 'bre':

    (gdb) info breakpoints

You can either press (RET) at this point, to run the info breakpoints command, or backspace and enter something else, if 'breakpoints' does not look like the command you expected. (If you were sure you wanted info breakpoints in the first place, you might as well just type (RET) immediately after 'info bre', to exploit command abbreviations rather than command completion).

If there is more than one possibility for the next word when you press (TAB), GDB sounds a bell. You can either supply more characters and try again, or just press (TAB) a second time; GDB displays all the possible completions for that word. For example, you might want to set a breakpoint on a subroutine whose name begins with 'make_', but when you type *b make_*(TAB) GDB just sounds the bell. Typing (TAB) again displays all the function names in your program that begin with those characters, for example:

    (gdb) b make_ (TAB)

GDB sounds bell; press (TAB) again, to see:

    make_a_section_from_file   make_environ
    make_abs_section   make_function_type
    make_blockvector   make_pointer_type
    make_cleanup   make_reference_type
    make_command   make_symbol_completion_list
    (gdb) b make_

After displaying the available possibilities, GDB copies your partial input ('b make_' in the example) so you can finish the command.

If you just want to see the list of alternatives in the first place, you can press *M-?* rather than pressing (TAB) twice. *M-?* means (META) *?*. You can type this either by holding down a key designated as the (META) shift on your keyboard (if there is one) while typing *?*, or as (ESC) followed by *?*.

Sometimes the string you need, while logically a "word", may contain parentheses or other characters that GDB normally excludes from its notion of a word. To permit word completion to work in this situation, you may enclose words in ' (single quote marks) in GDB commands.

The most likely situation where you might need this is in typing the name of a C++ function. This is because C++ allows function overloading (multiple definitions of the same function, distinguished by argument type). For example, when you want to set a breakpoint you may need to distinguish whether you mean the version of name that takes an int parameter, name(int), or the version that takes a float parameter, name(float). To

use the word-completion facilities in this situation, type a single quote ' at
the beginning of the function name. This alerts GDB that it may need to
consider more information than usual when you press (TAB) or *M-?* to request
word completion:

```
(gdb) b 'bubble( M-?
bubble(double,double)      bubble(int,int)
(gdb) b 'bubble(
```

In some cases, GDB can tell that completing a name requires using quotes.
When this happens, GDB inserts the quote for you (while completing as
much as it can) if you do not type the quote in the first place:

```
(gdb) b bub (TAB)
```

GDB alters your input line to the following, and rings a bell:

```
(gdb) b 'bubble(
```

In general, GDB can tell that a quote is needed (and inserts it) if you have
not yet started typing the argument list when you ask for completion on an
overloaded symbol.

For more information about overloaded functions, see Section 10.4.1.3
[C++ expressions], page 107. You can use the command set overload-
resolution off to disable overload resolution; see Section 10.4.1.7 [GDB
features for C++], page 109.

3.3 Getting help

You can always ask GDB itself for information on its commands, using
the command help.

help
h   You can use help (abbreviated h) with no arguments to display
             a short list of named classes of commands:

```
(gdb) help
List of classes of commands:

aliases -- Aliases of other commands
breakpoints -- Making program stop at certain points
data -- Examining data
files -- Specifying and examining files
internals -- Maintenance commands
obscure -- Obscure features
running -- Running the program
stack -- Examining the stack
status -- Status inquiries
support -- Support facilities
tracepoints -- Tracing of program execution without
```

```
                    stopping the program
          user-defined -- User-defined commands


          Type "help" followed by a class name for a list of
          commands in that class.
          Type "help" followed by command name for full
          documentation.
          Command name abbreviations are allowed if unambiguous.
          (gdb)
```

help *class* Using one of the general help classes as an argument, you can get a list of the individual commands in that class. For example, here is the help display for the class **status**:

```
          (gdb) help status
          Status inquiries.

          List of commands:

          info -- Generic command for showing things
           about the program being debugged
          show -- Generic command for showing things
           about the debugger

          Type "help" followed by command name for full
          documentation.
          Command name abbreviations are allowed if unambiguous.
          (gdb)
```

help *command*

> With a command name as **help** argument, GDB displays a short paragraph on how to use that command.

apropos *args*

> The **apropos** *args* command searches through all of the GDB commands, and their documentation, for the regular expression specified in *args*. It prints out all matches found. For example:

```
          apropos reload
```

results in:

```
          set symbol-reloading -- Set dynamic symbol table reloading
                                   multiple times in one run
           show symbol-reloading -- Show dynamic symbol table reloading
                                   multiple times in one run
```

complete *args*

> The **complete** *args* command lists all the possible completions for the beginning of a command. Use *args* to specify the beginning of the command you want completed. For example:

```
complete i
```
results in:
```
if
ignore
info
inspect
```
This is intended for use by GNU Emacs.

In addition to `help`, you can use the GDB commands `info` and `show` to inquire about the state of your program, or the state of GDB itself. Each command supports many topics of inquiry; this manual introduces each of them in the appropriate context. The listings under `info` and under `show` in the Index point to all the sub-commands. See [Index], page 331.

`info`   This command (abbreviated `i`) is for describing the state of your program. For example, you can list the arguments given to your program with `info args`, list the registers currently in use with `info registers`, or list the breakpoints you have set with `info breakpoints`. You can get a complete list of the `info` sub-commands with `help info`.

`set`   You can assign the result of an expression to an environment variable with `set`. For example, you can set the GDB prompt to a $-sign with `set prompt $`.

`show`   In contrast to `info`, `show` is for describing the state of GDB itself. You can change most of the things you can `show`, by using the related command `set`; for example, you can control what number system is used for displays with `set radix`, or simply inquire which is currently in use with `show radix`.

To display all the settable parameters and their current values, you can use `show` with no arguments; you may also use `info set`. Both commands produce the same display.

Here are three miscellaneous `show` subcommands, all of which are exceptional in lacking corresponding `set` commands:

`show version`
Show what version of GDB is running. You should include this information in GDB bug-reports. If multiple versions of GDB are in use at your site, you may need to determine which version of GDB you are running; as GDB evolves, new commands are introduced, and old ones may wither away. Also, many system vendors ship variant versions of GDB, and there are variant versions of GDB in GNU/Linux distributions as well. The version number is the same as the one announced when you start GDB.

`show copying`
Display information about permission for copying GDB.

`show warranty`

> Display the GNU "NO WARRANTY" statement, or a warranty, if your version of GDB comes with one.

4 Running Programs Under GDB

When you run a program under GDB, you must first generate debugging information when you compile it.

You may start GDB with its arguments, if any, in an environment of your choice. If you are doing native debugging, you may redirect your program's input and output, debug an already running process, or kill a child process.

4.1 Compiling for debugging

In order to debug a program effectively, you need to generate debugging information when you compile it. This debugging information is stored in the object file; it describes the data type of each variable or function and the correspondence between source line numbers and addresses in the executable code.

To request debugging information, specify the '-g' option when you run the compiler.

Many C compilers are unable to handle the '-g' and '-O' options together. Using those compilers, you cannot generate optimized executables containing debugging information.

GCC, the GNU C compiler, supports '-g' with or without '-O', making it possible to debug optimized code. We recommend that you *always* use '-g' whenever you compile a program. You may think your program is correct, but there is no sense in pushing your luck.

When you debug a program compiled with '-g -O', remember that the optimizer is rearranging your code; the debugger shows you what is really there. Do not be too surprised when the execution path does not exactly match your source file! An extreme example: if you define a variable, but never use it, GDB never sees that variable—because the compiler optimizes it out of existence.

Some things do not work as well with '-g -O' as with just '-g', particularly on machines with instruction scheduling. If in doubt, recompile with '-g' alone, and if this fixes the problem, please report it to us as a bug (including a test case!).

Older versions of the GNU C compiler permitted a variant option '-gg' for debugging information. GDB no longer supports this format; if your GNU C compiler has this option, do not use it.

4.2 Starting your program

run

r   Use the **run** command to start your program under GDB. You
           must first specify the program name (except on VxWorks) with
           an argument to GDB (see Chapter 2 [Getting In and Out of
           GDB], page 11), or by using the **file** or **exec-file** command
           (see Section 13.1 [Commands to specify files], page 135).

If you are running your program in an execution environment that supports processes, **run** creates an inferior process and makes that process run
your program. (In environments without processes, **run** jumps to the start
of your program.)

The execution of a program is affected by certain information it receives
from its superior. GDB provides ways to specify this information, which
you must do *before* starting your program. (You can change it after starting
your program, but such changes only affect your program the next time you
start it.) This information may be divided into four categories:

The *arguments.*

           Specify the arguments to give your program as the arguments of
           the **run** command. If a shell is available on your target, the shell
           is used to pass the arguments, so that you may use normal con-
           ventions (such as wildcard expansion or variable substitution)
           in describing the arguments. In Unix systems, you can control
           which shell is used with the **SHELL** environment variable. See
           Section 4.3 [Your program's arguments], page 25.

The *environment.*

           Your program normally inherits its environment from GDB, but
           you can use the GDB commands **set environment** and **unset
           environment** to change parts of the environment that affect
           your program. See Section 4.4 [Your program's environment],
           page 25.

The *working directory.*

           Your program inherits its working directory from GDB. You can
           set the GDB working directory with the **cd** command in GDB.
           See Section 4.5 [Your program's working directory], page 27.

The *standard input and output.*

           Your program normally uses the same device for standard in-
           put and standard output as GDB is using. You can redirect
           input and output in the **run** command line, or you can use the
           tty command to set a different device for your program. See
           Section 4.6 [Your program's input and output], page 27.

           Warning: While input and output redirection work, you cannot
           use pipes to pass the output of the program you are debugging

to another program; if you attempt this, GDB is likely to wind up debugging the wrong program.

When you issue the `run` command, your program begins to execute immediately. See Chapter 5 [Stopping and continuing], page 35, for discussion of how to arrange for your program to stop. Once your program has stopped, you may call functions in your program, using the `print` or `call` commands. See Chapter 8 [Examining Data], page 69.

If the modification time of your symbol file has changed since the last time GDB read its symbols, GDB discards its symbol table, and reads it again. When it does this, GDB tries to retain your current breakpoints.

4.3 Your program's arguments

The arguments to your program can be specified by the arguments of the `run` command. They are passed to a shell, which expands wildcard characters and performs redirection of I/O, and thence to your program. Your `SHELL` environment variable (if it exists) specifies what shell GDB uses. If you do not define `SHELL`, GDB uses the default shell ('`/bin/sh`' on Unix).

On non-Unix systems, the program is usually invoked directly by GDB, which emulates I/O redirection via the appropriate system calls, and the wildcard characters are expanded by the startup code of the program, not by the shell.

`run` with no arguments uses the same arguments used by the previous `run`, or those set by the `set args` command.

`set args`   Specify the arguments to be used the next time your program is run. If `set args` has no arguments, `run` executes your program with no arguments. Once you have run your program with arguments, using `set args` before the next `run` is the only way to run it again without arguments.

`show args` Show the arguments to give your program when it is started.

4.4 Your program's environment

The *environment* consists of a set of environment variables and their values. Environment variables conventionally record such things as your user name, your home directory, your terminal type, and your search path for programs to run. Usually you set up environment variables with the shell and they are inherited by all the other programs you run. When debugging, it can be useful to try running your program with a modified environment without having to start GDB over again.

`path` *directory*
        Add *directory* to the front of the `PATH` environment variable (the search path for executables) that will be passed to your

program. The value of **PATH** used by GDB does not change. You may specify several directory names, separated by whitespace or by a system-dependent separator character (':' on Unix, ';' on MS-DOS and MS-Windows). If *directory* is already in the path, it is moved to the front, so it is searched sooner.

You can use the string '**$cwd**' to refer to whatever is the current working directory at the time GDB searches the path. If you use '**.**' instead, it refers to the directory where you executed the **path** command. GDB replaces '**.**' in the *directory* argument (with the current path) before adding *directory* to the search path.

show paths

Display the list of search paths for executables (the **PATH** environment variable).

show environment [*varname*]

Print the value of environment variable *varname* to be given to your program when it starts. If you do not supply *varname*, print the names and values of all environment variables to be given to your program. You can abbreviate **environment** as **env**.

set environment *varname* [=*value*]

Set environment variable *varname* to *value*. The value changes for your program only, not for GDB itself. *value* may be any string; the values of environment variables are just strings, and any interpretation is supplied by your program itself. The *value* parameter is optional; if it is eliminated, the variable is set to a null value.

For example, this command:

```
set env USER = foo
```

tells the debugged program, when subsequently run, that its user is named '**foo**'. (The spaces around '=' are used for clarity here; they are not actually required.)

unset environment *varname*

Remove variable *varname* from the environment to be passed to your program. This is different from '**set env** *varname* ='; **unset environment** removes the variable from the environment, rather than assigning it an empty value.

Warning: On Unix systems, GDB runs your program using the shell indicated by your **SHELL** environment variable if it exists (or **/bin/sh** if not). If your **SHELL** variable names a shell that runs an initialization file— such as '**.cshrc**' for C-shell, or '**.bashrc**' for BASH—any variables you set in that file affect your program. You may wish to move setting of environment variables to files that are only run when you sign on, such as '.login' or '.profile'.

4.5 Your program's working directory

Each time you start your program with run, it inherits its working directory from the current working directory of GDB. The GDB working directory is initially whatever it inherited from its parent process (typically the shell), but you can specify a new working directory in GDB with the cd command.

The GDB working directory also serves as a default for the commands that specify files for GDB to operate on. See Section 13.1 [Commands to specify files], page 135.

cd *directory*
>   Set the GDB working directory to *directory*.

pwd   Print the GDB working directory.

4.6 Your program's input and output

By default, the program you run under GDB does input and output to the same terminal that GDB uses. GDB switches the terminal to its own terminal modes to interact with you, but it records the terminal modes your program was using and switches back to them when you continue running your program.

info terminal
>   Displays information recorded by GDB about the terminal modes your program is using.

You can redirect your program's input and/or output using shell redirection with the run command. For example,

    run > outfile

starts your program, diverting its output to the file 'outfile'.

Another way to specify where your program should do input and output is with the tty command. This command accepts a file name as argument, and causes this file to be the default for future run commands. It also resets the controlling terminal for the child process, for future run commands. For example,

    tty /dev/ttyb

directs that processes started with subsequent run commands default to do input and output on the terminal '/dev/ttyb' and have that as their controlling terminal.

An explicit redirection in run overrides the tty command's effect on the input/output device, but not its effect on the controlling terminal.

When you use the `tty` command or redirect input in the `run` command, only the input *for your program* is affected. The input for GDB still comes from your terminal.

4.7 Debugging an already-running process

`attach` *process-id*

This command attaches to a running process—one that was started outside GDB. (`info files` shows your active targets.) The command takes as argument a process ID. The usual way to find out the process-id of a Unix process is with the `ps` utility, or with the '`jobs -l`' shell command.

`attach` does not repeat if you press (RET) a second time after executing the command.

To use `attach`, your program must be running in an environment which supports processes; for example, `attach` does not work for programs on bareboard targets that lack an operating system. You must also have permission to send the process a signal.

When you use `attach`, the debugger finds the program running in the process first by looking in the current working directory, then (if the program is not found) by using the source file search path (see Section 7.3 [Specifying source directories], page 65). You can also use the `file` command to load the program. See Section 13.1 [Commands to Specify Files], page 135.

The first thing GDB does after arranging to debug the specified process is to stop it. You can examine and modify an attached process with all the GDB commands that are ordinarily available when you start processes with `run`. You can insert breakpoints; you can step and continue; you can modify storage. If you would rather the process continue running, you may use the `continue` command after attaching GDB to the process.

`detach`   When you have finished debugging the attached process, you can use the `detach` command to release it from GDB control. Detaching the process continues its execution. After the `detach` command, that process and GDB become completely independent once more, and you are ready to `attach` another process or start one with `run`. `detach` does not repeat if you press (RET) again after executing the command.

If you exit GDB or use the `run` command while you have an attached process, you kill that process. By default, GDB asks for confirmation if you try to do either of these things; you can control whether or not you need to confirm by using the `set confirm` command (see Section 16.6 [Optional warnings and messages], page 194).

4.8 Killing the child process

kill   Kill the child process in which your program is running under
             GDB.

This command is useful if you wish to debug a core dump instead of a
running process. GDB ignores any core dump file while your program is
running.

On some operating systems, a program cannot be executed outside GDB
while you have breakpoints set on it inside GDB. You can use the kill
command in this situation to permit running your program outside the debugger.

The kill command is also useful if you wish to recompile and relink your
program, since on many systems it is impossible to modify an executable file
while it is running in a process. In this case, when you next type run, GDB
notices that the file has changed, and reads the symbol table again (while
trying to preserve your current breakpoint settings).

4.9 Debugging programs with multiple threads

In some operating systems, such as HP-UX and Solaris, a single program may have more than one *thread* of execution. The precise semantics
of threads differ from one operating system to another, but in general the
threads of a single program are akin to multiple processes—except that they
share one address space (that is, they can all examine and modify the same
variables). On the other hand, each thread has its own registers and execution stack, and perhaps private memory.

GDB provides these facilities for debugging multi-thread programs:

- automatic notification of new threads
- 'thread *threadno*', a command to switch among threads
- 'info threads', a command to inquire about existing threads
- 'thread apply [*threadno*] [*all*] *args*', a command to apply a command
  to a list of threads
- thread-specific breakpoints

  Warning: These facilities are not yet available on every GDB configuration where the operating system supports threads. If your
  GDB does not support threads, these commands have no effect. For
  example, a system without thread support shows no output from
  'info threads', and always rejects the thread command, like this:

  ```
  (gdb) info threads
  (gdb) thread 1
  Thread ID 1 not known.  Use the "info threads" command to
  see the IDs of currently known threads.
  ```

The GDB thread debugging facility allows you to observe all threads while your program runs—but whenever GDB takes control, one thread in particular is always the focus of debugging. This thread is called the *current thread*. Debugging commands show program information from the perspective of the current thread.

Whenever GDB detects a new thread in your program, it displays the target system's identification for the thread with a message in the form '[New *systag*]'. *systag* is a thread identifier whose form varies depending on the particular system. For example, on LynxOS, you might see

    `[New process 35 thread 27]`

when GDB notices a new thread. In contrast, on an SGI system, the *systag* is simply something like '`process 368`', with no further qualifier.

For debugging purposes, GDB associates its own thread number—always a single integer—with each thread in your program.

`info threads`

        Display a summary of all threads currently in your program. GDB displays for each thread (in this order):

        1. the thread number assigned by GDB

        2. the target system's thread identifier (*systag*)

        3. the current stack frame summary for that thread

        An asterisk '`*`' to the left of the GDB thread number indicates the current thread.

        For example,

```
(gdb) info threads
  3 process 35 thread 27  0x34e5 in sigpause ()
  2 process 35 thread 23  0x34e5 in sigpause ()
* 1 process 35 thread 13  main (argc=1, argv=0x7ffffff8)
    at threadtest.c:68
```

On HP-UX systems:

For debugging purposes, GDB associates its own thread number—a small integer assigned in thread-creation order—with each thread in your program.

Whenever GDB detects a new thread in your program, it displays both GDB's thread number and the target system's identification for the thread with a message in the form '[New *systag*]'. *systag* is a thread identifier whose form varies depending on the particular system. For example, on HP-UX, you see

    `[New thread 2 (system thread 26594)]`

when GDB notices a new thread.

`info threads`

        Display a summary of all threads currently in your program. GDB displays for each thread (in this order):

1. the thread number assigned by GDB
2. the target system's thread identifier (*systag*)
3. the current stack frame summary for that thread

An asterisk '*' to the left of the GDB thread number indicates the current thread.

For example,

```
(gdb) info threads
  * 3 system thread 26607   worker (wptr=0x7b09c318 "@") \

                            at quicksort.c:137
    2 system thread 26606   0x7b0030d8 in __ksleep () \

                            from /usr/lib/libc.2
    1 system thread 27905   0x7b003498 in _brk () \

                            from /usr/lib/libc.2
```

thread *threadno*

> Make thread number *threadno* the current thread. The command argument *threadno* is the internal GDB thread number, as shown in the first field of the 'info threads' display. GDB responds by displaying the system identifier of the thread you selected, and its current stack frame summary:
>
> ```
> (gdb) thread 2
> [Switching to process 35 thread 23]
> 0x34e5 in sigpause ()
> ```
>
> As with the '[New ...]' message, the form of the text after 'Switching to' depends on your system's conventions for identifying threads.

thread apply [*threadno*] [*all*] *args*

> The thread apply command allows you to apply a command to one or more threads. Specify the numbers of the threads that you want affected with the command argument *threadno*. *threadno* is the internal GDB thread number, as shown in the first field of the 'info threads' display. To apply a command to all threads, use thread apply all *args*.

Whenever GDB stops your program, due to a breakpoint or a signal, it automatically selects the thread where that breakpoint or signal happened. GDB alerts you to the context switch with a message of the form '[Switching to *systag*]' to identify the thread.

See Section 5.4 [Stopping and starting multi-thread programs], page 55, for more information about how GDB behaves when you stop and start programs with multiple threads.

See Section 5.1.2 [Setting watchpoints], page 40, for information about watchpoints in programs with multiple threads.

4.10 Debugging programs with multiple processes

On most systems, GDB has no special support for debugging programs which create additional processes using the **fork** function. When a program forks, GDB will continue to debug the parent process and the child process will run unimpeded. If you have set a breakpoint in any code which the child then executes, the child will get a **SIGTRAP** signal which (unless it catches the signal) will cause it to terminate.

However, if you want to debug the child process there is a workaround which isn't too painful. Put a call to **sleep** in the code which the child process executes after the fork. It may be useful to sleep only if a certain environment variable is set, or a certain file exists, so that the delay need not occur when you don't want to run GDB on the child. While the child is sleeping, use the **ps** program to get its process ID. Then tell GDB (a new invocation of GDB if you are also debugging the parent process) to attach to the child process (see Section 4.7 [Attach], page 28). From that point on you can debug the child process just like any other process which you attached to.

On HP-UX (11.x and later only?), GDB provides support for debugging programs that create additional processes using the **fork** or **vfork** function.

By default, when a program forks, GDB will continue to debug the parent process and the child process will run unimpeded.

If you want to follow the child process instead of the parent process, use the command **set follow-fork-mode**.

set follow-fork-mode *mode*
> Set the debugger response to a program call of **fork** or **vfork**. A call to **fork** or **vfork** creates a new process. The *mode* can be:
>
> > **parent**   The original process is debugged after a fork. The child process runs unimpeded. This is the default.
> >
> > **child**   The new process is debugged after a fork. The parent process runs unimpeded.
> >
> > **ask**   The debugger will ask for one of the above choices.

show follow-fork-mode
> Display the current debugger response to a **fork** or **vfork** call.

If you ask to debug a child process and a **vfork** is followed by an **exec**, GDB executes the new target up to the first breakpoint in the new target. If you have a breakpoint set on **main** in your original program, the breakpoint will also be set on the child process's **main**.

When a child process is spawned by **vfork**, you cannot debug the child or parent until an **exec** call completes.

If you issue a **run** command to GDB after an **exec** call executes, the new target restarts. To restart the parent process, use the **file** command with the parent executable name as its argument.

You can use the **catch** command to make GDB stop whenever a **fork**, **vfork**, or **exec** call is made. See Section 5.1.3 [Setting catchpoints], page 42.

5 Stopping and Continuing

The principal purposes of using a debugger are so that you can stop your program before it terminates; or so that, if your program runs into trouble, you can investigate and find out why.

Inside GDB, your program may stop for any of several reasons, such as a signal, a breakpoint, or reaching a new line after a GDB command such as `step`. You may then examine and change variables, set new breakpoints or remove old ones, and then continue execution. Usually, the messages shown by GDB provide ample explanation of the status of your program—but you can also explicitly request this information at any time.

`info program`

> Display information about the status of your program: whether it is running or not, what process it is, and why it stopped.

5.1 Breakpoints, watchpoints, and catchpoints

A *breakpoint* makes your program stop whenever a certain point in the program is reached. For each breakpoint, you can add conditions to control in finer detail whether your program stops. You can set breakpoints with the `break` command and its variants (see Section 5.1.1 [Setting breakpoints], page 36), to specify the place where your program should stop by line number, function name or exact address in the program.

In HP-UX, SunOS 4.x, SVR4, and Alpha OSF/1 configurations, you can set breakpoints in shared libraries before the executable is run. There is a minor limitation on HP-UX systems: you must wait until the executable is run in order to set breakpoints in shared library routines that are not called directly by the program (for example, routines that are arguments in a `pthread_create` call).

A *watchpoint* is a special breakpoint that stops your program when the value of an expression changes. You must use a different command to set watchpoints (see Section 5.1.2 [Setting watchpoints], page 40), but aside from that, you can manage a watchpoint like any other breakpoint: you enable, disable, and delete both breakpoints and watchpoints using the same commands.

You can arrange to have values from your program displayed automatically whenever GDB stops at a breakpoint. See Section 8.6 [Automatic display], page 75.

A *catchpoint* is another special breakpoint that stops your program when a certain kind of event occurs, such as the throwing of a C++ exception or the loading of a library. As with watchpoints, you use a different command to set a catchpoint (see Section 5.1.3 [Setting catchpoints], page 42), but aside from that, you can manage a catchpoint like any other breakpoint.

(To stop when your program receives a signal, use the `handle` command; see Section 5.3 [Signals], page 53.)

GDB assigns a number to each breakpoint, watchpoint, or catchpoint when you create it; these numbers are successive integers starting with one. In many of the commands for controlling various features of breakpoints you use the breakpoint number to say which breakpoint you want to change. Each breakpoint may be *enabled* or *disabled*; if disabled, it has no effect on your program until you enable it again.

Some GDB commands accept a range of breakpoints on which to operate. A breakpoint range is either a single breakpoint number, like '5', or two such numbers, in increasing order, separated by a hyphen, like '5-7'. When a breakpoint range is given to a command, all breakpoint in that range are operated on.

5.1.1 Setting breakpoints

Breakpoints are set with the `break` command (abbreviated `b`). The debugger convenience variable '`$bpnum`' records the number of the breakpoint you've set most recently; see Section 8.9 [Convenience variables], page 83, for a discussion of what you can do with convenience variables.

You have several ways to say where the breakpoint should go.

`break` *function*

> Set a breakpoint at entry to function *function*. When using source languages that permit overloading of symbols, such as C++, *function* may refer to more than one possible place to break. See Section 5.1.8 [Breakpoint menus], page 49, for a discussion of that situation.

`break +`*offset*
`break -`*offset*

> Set a breakpoint some number of lines forward or back from the position at which execution stopped in the currently selected *stack frame*. (See Section 6.1 [Frames], page 57, for a description of stack frames.)

`break` *linenum*

> Set a breakpoint at line *linenum* in the current source file. The current source file is the last file whose source text was printed. The breakpoint will stop your program just before it executes any of the code on that line.

`break` *filename*:*linenum*

> Set a breakpoint at line *linenum* in source file *filename*.

`break` *filename*:*function*

> Set a breakpoint at entry to function *function* found in file *filename*. Specifying a file name as well as a function name is super-

fluous except when multiple files contain similarly named functions.

break *address

Set a breakpoint at address *address*. You can use this to set breakpoints in parts of your program which do not have debugging information or source files.

break

When called without any arguments, **break** sets a breakpoint at the next instruction to be executed in the selected stack frame (see Chapter 6 [Examining the Stack], page 57). In any selected frame but the innermost, this makes your program stop as soon as control returns to that frame. This is similar to the effect of a **finish** command in the frame inside the selected frame— except that **finish** does not leave an active breakpoint. If you use **break** without an argument in the innermost frame, GDB stops the next time it reaches the current location; this may be useful inside loops.

GDB normally ignores breakpoints when it resumes execution, until at least one instruction has been executed. If it did not do this, you would be unable to proceed past a breakpoint without first disabling the breakpoint. This rule applies whether or not the breakpoint already existed when your program stopped.

break ... if *cond*

Set a breakpoint with condition *cond*; evaluate the expression *cond* each time the breakpoint is reached, and stop only if the value is nonzero—that is, if *cond* evaluates as true. '. . .' stands for one of the possible arguments described above (or no argument) specifying where to break. See Section 5.1.6 [Break conditions], page 45, for more information on breakpoint conditions.

tbreak *args*

Set a breakpoint enabled only for one stop. *args* are the same as for the **break** command, and the breakpoint is set in the same way, but the breakpoint is automatically deleted after the first time your program stops there. See Section 5.1.5 [Disabling breakpoints], page 44.

hbreak *args*

Set a hardware-assisted breakpoint. *args* are the same as for the **break** command and the breakpoint is set in the same way, but the breakpoint requires hardware support and some target hardware may not have this support. The main purpose of this is EPROM/ROM code debugging, so you can set a breakpoint at an instruction without changing the instruction. This can be used with the new trap-generation provided by SPARClite

DSU and some x86-based targets. These targets will generate traps when a program accesses some data or instruction address that is assigned to the debug registers. However the hardware breakpoint registers can take a limited number of breakpoints. For example, on the DSU, only two data breakpoints can be set at a time, and GDB will reject this command if more than two are used. Delete or disable unused hardware breakpoints before setting new ones (see Section 5.1.5 [Disabling], page 44). See Section 5.1.6 [Break conditions], page 45.

thbreak *args*

Set a hardware-assisted breakpoint enabled only for one stop. *args* are the same as for the **hbreak** command and the breakpoint is set in the same way. However, like the **tbreak** command, the breakpoint is automatically deleted after the first time your program stops there. Also, like the **hbreak** command, the breakpoint requires hardware support and some target hardware may not have this support. See Section 5.1.5 [Disabling breakpoints], page 44. See also Section 5.1.6 [Break conditions], page 45.

rbreak *regex*

Set breakpoints on all functions matching the regular expression *regex*. This command sets an unconditional breakpoint on all matches, printing a list of all breakpoints it set. Once these breakpoints are set, they are treated just like the breakpoints set with the **break** command. You can delete them, disable them, or make them conditional the same way as any other breakpoint.

The syntax of the regular expression is the standard one used with tools like '**grep**'. Note that this is different from the syntax used by shells, so for instance **foo*** matches all functions that include an **fo** followed by zero or more **o**s. There is an implicit **.*** leading and trailing the regular expression you supply, so to match only functions that begin with **foo**, use **^foo**.

When debugging C++ programs, **rbreak** is useful for setting breakpoints on overloaded functions that are not members of any special classes.

info breakpoints [*n*]
info break [*n*]
info watchpoints [*n*]

Print a table of all breakpoints, watchpoints, and catchpoints set and not deleted, with the following columns for each breakpoint:

Breakpoint Numbers
Type   Breakpoint, watchpoint, or catchpoint.

Disposition

Whether the breakpoint is marked to be disabled or deleted when hit.

Enabled or Disabled
> Enabled breakpoints are marked with 'y'. 'n' marks breakpoints that are not enabled.

Address
> Where the breakpoint is in your program, as a memory address.

What
> Where the breakpoint is in the source for your program, as a file and line number.

> If a breakpoint is conditional, `info break` shows the condition on the line following the affected breakpoint; breakpoint commands, if any, are listed after that.

> `info break` with a breakpoint number *n* as argument lists only that breakpoint. The convenience variable `$_` and the default examining-address for the `x` command are set to the address of the last breakpoint listed (see Section 8.5 [Examining memory], page 74).

> `info break` displays a count of the number of times the breakpoint has been hit. This is especially useful in conjunction with the `ignore` command. You can ignore a large number of breakpoint hits, look at the breakpoint info to see how many times the breakpoint was hit, and then run again, ignoring one less than that number. This will get you quickly to the last hit of that breakpoint.

GDB allows you to set any number of breakpoints at the same place in your program. There is nothing silly or meaningless about this. When the breakpoints are conditional, this is even useful (see Section 5.1.6 [Break conditions], page 45).

GDB itself sometimes sets breakpoints in your program for special purposes, such as proper handling of `longjmp` (in C programs). These internal breakpoints are assigned negative numbers, starting with -1; 'info breakpoints' does not display them.

You can see these breakpoints with the GDB maintenance command 'maint info breakpoints'.

`maint info breakpoints`
> Using the same format as 'info breakpoints', display both the breakpoints you've set explicitly, and those GDB is using for internal purposes. Internal breakpoints are shown with negative breakpoint numbers. The type column identifies what kind of breakpoint is shown:

`breakpoint`
> Normal, explicitly set breakpoint.

`watchpoint`
> Normal, explicitly set watchpoint.

longjmp   Internal breakpoint, used to handle correctly step-
                 ping through `longjmp` calls.

`longjmp resume`
                 Internal breakpoint at the target of a `longjmp`.

until   Temporary internal breakpoint used by the GDB
                 `until` command.

finish   Temporary internal breakpoint used by the GDB
                 `finish` command.

`shlib events`
                 Shared library events.

5.1.2 Setting watchpoints

You can use a watchpoint to stop execution whenever the value of an
expression changes, without having to predict a particular place where this
may happen.

Depending on your system, watchpoints may be implemented in software
or hardware. GDB does software watchpointing by single-stepping your
program and testing the variable's value each time, which is hundreds of
times slower than normal execution. (But this may still be worth it, to catch
errors where you have no clue what part of your program is the culprit.)

On some systems, such as HP-UX, Linux and some other x86-based targets, GDB includes support for hardware watchpoints, which do not slow
down the running of your program.

watch *expr*
                 Set a watchpoint for an expression. GDB will break when *expr*
                 is written into by the program and its value changes.

rwatch *expr*
                 Set a watchpoint that will break when watch *expr* is read by the
                 program.

awatch *expr*
                 Set a watchpoint that will break when *expr* is either read or
                 written into by the program.

`info watchpoints`
                 This command prints a list of watchpoints, breakpoints, and
                 catchpoints; it is the same as `info break`.

GDB sets a *hardware watchpoint* if possible. Hardware watchpoints execute very quickly, and the debugger reports a change in value at the exact
instruction where the change occurs. If GDB cannot set a hardware watchpoint, it sets a software watchpoint, which executes more slowly and reports

the change in value at the next statement, not the instruction, after the change occurs.

When you issue the `watch` command, GDB reports

Hardware watchpoint *num*: *expr*

if it was able to set a hardware watchpoint.

Currently, the `awatch` and `rwatch` commands can only set hardware watchpoints, because accesses to data that don't change the value of the watched expression cannot be detected without examining every instruction as it is being executed, and GDB does not do that currently. If GDB finds that it is unable to set a hardware breakpoint with the `awatch` or `rwatch` command, it will print a message like this:

Expression cannot be implemented with read/access watchpoint.

Sometimes, GDB cannot set a hardware watchpoint because the data type of the watched expression is wider than what a hardware watchpoint on the target machine can handle. For example, some systems can only watch regions that are up to 4 bytes wide; on such systems you cannot set hardware watchpoints for an expression that yields a double-precision floating-point number (which is typically 8 bytes wide). As a work-around, it might be possible to break the large region into a series of smaller ones and watch them with separate watchpoints.

If you set too many hardware watchpoints, GDB might be unable to insert all of them when you resume the execution of your program. Since the precise number of active watchpoints is unknown until such time as the program is about to be resumed, GDB might not be able to warn you about this when you set the watchpoints, and the warning will be printed only when the program is resumed:

Hardware watchpoint *num*: Could not insert watchpoint

If this happens, delete or disable some of the watchpoints.

The SPARClite DSU will generate traps when a program accesses some data or instruction address that is assigned to the debug registers. For the data addresses, DSU facilitates the `watch` command. However the hardware breakpoint registers can only take two data watchpoints, and both watchpoints must be the same kind. For example, you can set two watchpoints with `watch` commands, two with `rwatch` commands, **or** two with `awatch` commands, but you cannot set one watchpoint with one command and the other with a different command. GDB will reject the command if you try to mix watchpoints. Delete or disable unused watchpoint commands before setting new ones.

If you call a function interactively using `print` or `call`, any watchpoints you have set will be inactive until GDB reaches another kind of breakpoint or the call completes.

GDB automatically deletes watchpoints that watch local (automatic) variables, or expressions that involve such variables, when they go out of scope, that is, when the execution leaves the block in which these variables were defined. In particular, when the program being debugged terminates, *all* local variables go out of scope, and so only watchpoints that watch global variables remain set. If you rerun the program, you will need to set all such watchpoints again. One way of doing that would be to set a code breakpoint at the entry to the `main` function and when it breaks, set all the watchpoints.

> *Warning:* In multi-thread programs, watchpoints have only limited usefulness. With the current watchpoint implementation, GDB can only watch the value of an expression *in a single thread*. If you are confident that the expression can only change due to the current thread's activity (and if you are also confident that no other thread can become current), then you can use watchpoints as usual. However, GDB may not notice when a non-current thread's activity changes the expression.

> *HP-UX Warning:* In multi-thread programs, software watchpoints have only limited usefulness. If GDB creates a software watchpoint, it can only watch the value of an expression *in a single thread*. If you are confident that the expression can only change due to the current thread's activity (and if you are also confident that no other thread can become current), then you can use software watchpoints as usual. However, GDB may not notice when a non-current thread's activity changes the expression. (Hardware watchpoints, in contrast, watch an expression in all threads.)

5.1.3 Setting catchpoints

You can use *catchpoints* to cause the debugger to stop for certain kinds of program events, such as C++ exceptions or the loading of a shared library. Use the `catch` command to set a catchpoint.

`catch` *event*
> Stop when *event* occurs. *event* can be any of the following:

> | | |
> |---|---|
> | `throw` | The throwing of a C++ exception. |
> | `catch` | The catching of a C++ exception. |
> | `exec` | A call to `exec`. This is currently only available for HP-UX. |
> | `fork` | A call to `fork`. This is currently only available for HP-UX. |
> | `vfork` | A call to `vfork`. This is currently only available for HP-UX. |

load
load *libname*

> The dynamic loading of any shared library, or the loading of the library *libname*. This is currently only available for HP-UX.

unload
unload *libname*

> The unloading of any dynamically loaded shared library, or the unloading of the library *libname*. This is currently only available for HP-UX.

tcatch *event*

> Set a catchpoint that is enabled only for one stop. The catchpoint is automatically deleted after the first time the event is caught.

Use the `info break` command to list the current catchpoints.

There are currently some limitations to C++ exception handling (`catch throw` and `catch catch`) in GDB:

- If you call a function interactively, GDB normally returns control to you when the function has finished executing. If the call raises an exception, however, the call may bypass the mechanism that returns control to you and cause your program either to abort or to simply continue running until it hits a breakpoint, catches a signal that GDB is listening for, or exits. This is the case even if you set a catchpoint for the exception; catchpoints on exceptions are disabled within interactive calls.

- You cannot raise an exception interactively.

- You cannot install an exception handler interactively.

Sometimes `catch` is not the best way to debug exception handling: if you need to know exactly where an exception is raised, it is better to stop *before* the exception handler is called, since that way you can see the stack before any unwinding takes place. If you set a breakpoint in an exception handler instead, it may not be easy to find out where the exception was raised.

To stop just before an exception handler is called, you need some knowledge of the implementation. In the case of GNU C++, exceptions are raised by calling a library function named `__raise_exception` which has the following ANSI C interface:

```
/* addr is where the exception identifier is stored.
   id is the exception identifier. */
void __raise_exception (void **addr, void *id);
```

To make the debugger catch all exceptions before any stack unwinding takes place, set a breakpoint on `__raise_exception` (see Section 5.1 [Breakpoints; watchpoints; and exceptions], page 35).

With a conditional breakpoint (see Section 5.1.6 [Break conditions], page 45) that depends on the value of *id*, you can stop your program when a specific exception is raised. You can use multiple conditional breakpoints to stop your program when any of a number of exceptions are raised.

5.1.4 Deleting breakpoints

It is often necessary to eliminate a breakpoint, watchpoint, or catchpoint once it has done its job and you no longer want your program to stop there. This is called *deleting* the breakpoint. A breakpoint that has been deleted no longer exists; it is forgotten.

With the `clear` command you can delete breakpoints according to where they are in your program. With the `delete` command you can delete individual breakpoints, watchpoints, or catchpoints by specifying their breakpoint numbers.

It is not necessary to delete a breakpoint to proceed past it. GDB automatically ignores breakpoints on the first instruction to be executed when you continue execution without changing the execution address.

clear   Delete any breakpoints at the next instruction to be executed in the selected stack frame (see Section 6.3 [Selecting a frame], page 59). When the innermost frame is selected, this is a good way to delete a breakpoint where your program just stopped.

clear *function*
clear *filename*:*function*
                Delete any breakpoints set at entry to the function *function*.

clear *linenum*
clear *filename*:*linenum*
                Delete any breakpoints set at or within the code of the specified line.

delete [breakpoints] [*range*...]
                Delete the breakpoints, watchpoints, or catchpoints of the breakpoint ranges specified as arguments. If no argument is specified, delete all breakpoints (GDB asks confirmation, unless you have `set confirm off`). You can abbreviate this command as d.

5.1.5 Disabling breakpoints

Rather than deleting a breakpoint, watchpoint, or catchpoint, you might prefer to *disable* it. This makes the breakpoint inoperative as if it had been deleted, but remembers the information on the breakpoint so that you can *enable* it again later.

You disable and enable breakpoints, watchpoints, and catchpoints with the `enable` and `disable` commands, optionally specifying one or more breakpoint numbers as arguments. Use `info break` or `info watch` to print a list of breakpoints, watchpoints, and catchpoints if you do not know which numbers to use.

A breakpoint, watchpoint, or catchpoint can have any of four different states of enablement:

- Enabled. The breakpoint stops your program. A breakpoint set with the **break** command starts out in this state.
- Disabled. The breakpoint has no effect on your program.
- Enabled once. The breakpoint stops your program, but then becomes disabled.
- Enabled for deletion. The breakpoint stops your program, but immediately after it does so it is deleted permanently. A breakpoint set with the **tbreak** command starts out in this state.

You can use the following commands to enable or disable breakpoints, watchpoints, and catchpoints:

disable [breakpoints] [range...]
> Disable the specified breakpoints—or all breakpoints, if none are listed. A disabled breakpoint has no effect but is not forgotten. All options such as ignore-counts, conditions and commands are remembered in case the breakpoint is enabled again later. You may abbreviate **disable** as **dis**.

enable [breakpoints] [range...]
> Enable the specified breakpoints (or all defined breakpoints). They become effective once again in stopping your program.

enable [breakpoints] once range...
> Enable the specified breakpoints temporarily. GDB disables any of these breakpoints immediately after stopping your program.

enable [breakpoints] delete range...
> Enable the specified breakpoints to work once, then die. GDB deletes any of these breakpoints as soon as your program stops there.

Except for a breakpoint set with **tbreak** (see Section 5.1.1 [Setting breakpoints], page 36), breakpoints that you set are initially enabled; subsequently, they become disabled or enabled only when you use one of the commands above. (The command **until** can set and delete a breakpoint of its own, but it does not change the state of your other breakpoints; see Section 5.2 [Continuing and stepping], page 50.)

5.1.6 Break conditions

The simplest sort of breakpoint breaks every time your program reaches a specified place. You can also specify a *condition* for a breakpoint. A condition is just a Boolean expression in your programming language (see Section 8.1 [Expressions], page 69). A breakpoint with a condition evaluates the expression each time your program reaches it, and your program stops only if the condition is *true*.

This is the converse of using assertions for program validation; in that situation, you want to stop when the assertion is violated—that is, when the condition is false. In C, if you want to test an assertion expressed by the condition *assert*, you should set the condition '! *assert*' on the appropriate breakpoint.

Conditions are also accepted for watchpoints; you may not need them, since a watchpoint is inspecting the value of an expression anyhow—but it might be simpler, say, to just set a watchpoint on a variable name, and specify a condition that tests whether the new value is an interesting one.

Break conditions can have side effects, and may even call functions in your program. This can be useful, for example, to activate functions that log program progress, or to use your own print functions to format special data structures. The effects are completely predictable unless there is another enabled breakpoint at the same address. (In that case, GDB might see the other breakpoint first and stop your program without checking the condition of this one.) Note that breakpoint commands are usually more convenient and flexible than break conditions for the purpose of performing side effects when a breakpoint is reached (see Section 5.1.7 [Breakpoint command lists], page 47).

Break conditions can be specified when a breakpoint is set, by using 'if' in the arguments to the **break** command. See Section 5.1.1 [Setting breakpoints], page 36. They can also be changed at any time with the **condition** command.

You can also use the **if** keyword with the **watch** command. The **catch** command does not recognize the **if** keyword; **condition** is the only way to impose a further condition on a catchpoint.

condition *bnum expression*

Specify *expression* as the break condition for breakpoint, watchpoint, or catchpoint number *bnum*. After you set a condition, breakpoint *bnum* stops your program only if the value of *expression* is true (nonzero, in C). When you use **condition**, GDB checks *expression* immediately for syntactic correctness, and to determine whether symbols in it have referents in the context of your breakpoint. If *expression* uses symbols not referenced in the context of the breakpoint, GDB prints an error message:

```
No symbol "foo" in current context.
```

GDB does not actually evaluate *expression* at the time the **condition** command (or a command that sets a breakpoint with a condition, like **break if** ...) is given, however. See Section 8.1 [Expressions], page 69.

condition *bnum*

> Remove the condition from breakpoint number *bnum*. It becomes an ordinary unconditional breakpoint.

A special case of a breakpoint condition is to stop only when the breakpoint has been reached a certain number of times. This is so useful that there is a special way to do it, using the *ignore count* of the breakpoint. Every breakpoint has an ignore count, which is an integer. Most of the time, the ignore count is zero, and therefore has no effect. But if your program reaches a breakpoint whose ignore count is positive, then instead of stopping, it just decrements the ignore count by one and continues. As a result, if the ignore count value is *n*, the breakpoint does not stop the next *n* times your program reaches it.

ignore *bnum count*

> Set the ignore count of breakpoint number *bnum* to *count*. The next *count* times the breakpoint is reached, your program's execution does not stop; other than to decrement the ignore count, GDB takes no action.
>
> To make the breakpoint stop the next time it is reached, specify a count of zero.
>
> When you use **continue** to resume execution of your program from a breakpoint, you can specify an ignore count directly as an argument to **continue**, rather than using **ignore**. See Section 5.2 [Continuing and stepping], page 50.
>
> If a breakpoint has a positive ignore count and a condition, the condition is not checked. Once the ignore count reaches zero, GDB resumes checking the condition.
>
> You could achieve the effect of the ignore count with a condition such as '**$foo-- <= 0**' using a debugger convenience variable that is decremented each time. See Section 8.9 [Convenience variables], page 83.

Ignore counts apply to breakpoints, watchpoints, and catchpoints.

5.1.7 Breakpoint command lists

You can give any breakpoint (or watchpoint or catchpoint) a series of commands to execute when your program stops due to that breakpoint. For example, you might want to print the values of certain expressions, or enable other breakpoints.

commands [*bnum*]
... *command-list* ...
end

> Specify a list of commands for breakpoint number *bnum*. The commands themselves appear on the following lines. Type a line containing just **end** to terminate the commands.

To remove all commands from a breakpoint, type `commands` and follow it immediately with `end`; that is, give no commands.

With no *bnum* argument, `commands` refers to the last breakpoint, watchpoint, or catchpoint set (not to the breakpoint most recently encountered).

Pressing (RET) as a means of repeating the last GDB command is disabled within a *command-list*.

You can use breakpoint commands to start your program up again. Simply use the `continue` command, or `step`, or any other command that resumes execution.

Any other commands in the command list, after a command that resumes execution, are ignored. This is because any time you resume execution (even with a simple `next` or `step`), you may encounter another breakpoint—which could have its own command list, leading to ambiguities about which list to execute.

If the first command you specify in a command list is `silent`, the usual message about stopping at a breakpoint is not printed. This may be desirable for breakpoints that are to print a specific message and then continue. If none of the remaining commands print anything, you see no sign that the breakpoint was reached. `silent` is meaningful only at the beginning of a breakpoint command list.

The commands `echo`, `output`, and `printf` allow you to print precisely controlled output, and are often useful in silent breakpoints. See Section 17.4 [Commands for controlled output], page 202.

For example, here is how you could use breakpoint commands to print the value of `x` at entry to `foo` whenever `x` is positive.

```
break foo if x>0
commands
silent
printf "x is %d\n",x
cont
end
```

One application for breakpoint commands is to compensate for one bug so you can test for another. Put a breakpoint just after the erroneous line of code, give it a condition to detect the case in which something erroneous has been done, and give it commands to assign correct values to any variables that need them. End with the `continue` command so that your program does not stop, and start with the `silent` command so that no output is produced. Here is an example:

```
break 403
commands
silent
set x = y + 4
```

```
cont
end
```

5.1.8 Breakpoint menus

Some programming languages (notably C++) permit a single function name to be defined several times, for application in different contexts. This is called *overloading*. When a function name is overloaded, 'break *function*' is not enough to tell GDB where you want a breakpoint. If you realize this is a problem, you can use something like 'break *function*(*types*)' to specify which particular version of the function you want. Otherwise, GDB offers you a menu of numbered choices for different possible breakpoints, and waits for your selection with the prompt '>'. The first two options are always '[0] cancel' and '[1] all'. Typing *1* sets a breakpoint at each definition of *function*, and typing *0* aborts the break command without setting any new breakpoints.

For example, the following session excerpt shows an attempt to set a breakpoint at the overloaded symbol String::after. We choose three particular definitions of that function name:

```
(gdb) b String::after
[0] cancel
[1] all
[2] file:String.cc; line number:867
[3] file:String.cc; line number:860
[4] file:String.cc; line number:875
[5] file:String.cc; line number:853
[6] file:String.cc; line number:846
[7] file:String.cc; line number:735
> 2 4 6
Breakpoint 1 at 0xb26c: file String.cc, line 867.
Breakpoint 2 at 0xb344: file String.cc, line 875.
Breakpoint 3 at 0xafcc: file String.cc, line 846.
Multiple breakpoints were set.
Use the "delete" command to delete unwanted
 breakpoints.
(gdb)
```

5.1.9 "Cannot insert breakpoints"

Under some operating systems, breakpoints cannot be used in a program if any other process is running that program. In this situation, attempting to run or continue a program with a breakpoint causes GDB to print an error message:

```
Cannot insert breakpoints.
The same program may be running in another process.
```

When this happens, you have three ways to proceed:

1. Remove or disable the breakpoints, then continue.

2. Suspend GDB, and copy the file containing your program to a new name. Resume GDB and use the `exec-file` command to specify that GDB should run your program under that name. Then start your program again.

3. Relink your program so that the text segment is nonsharable, using the linker option '`-N`'. The operating system limitation may not apply to nonsharable executables.

A similar message can be printed if you request too many active hardware-assisted breakpoints and watchpoints:

```
Stopped; cannot insert breakpoints.
You may have requested too many hardware breakpoints and watchpoints.
```

This message is printed when you attempt to resume the program, since only then GDB knows exactly how many hardware breakpoints and watchpoints it needs to insert.

When this message is printed, you need to disable or remove some of the hardware-assisted breakpoints and watchpoints, and then continue.

5.2 Continuing and stepping

Continuing means resuming program execution until your program completes normally. In contrast, *stepping* means executing just one more "step" of your program, where "step" may mean either one line of source code, or one machine instruction (depending on what particular command you use). Either when continuing or when stepping, your program may stop even sooner, due to a breakpoint or a signal. (If it stops due to a signal, you may want to use `handle`, or use '`signal 0`' to resume execution. See Section 5.3 [Signals], page 53.)

continue [*ignore-count*]
c [*ignore-count*]
fg [*ignore-count*]

> Resume program execution, at the address where your program last stopped; any breakpoints set at that address are bypassed. The optional argument *ignore-count* allows you to specify a further number of times to ignore a breakpoint at this location; its effect is like that of `ignore` (see Section 5.1.6 [Break conditions], page 45).
>
> The argument *ignore-count* is meaningful only when your program stopped due to a breakpoint. At other times, the argument to `continue` is ignored.
>
> The synonyms c and fg (for *foreground*, as the debugged program is deemed to be the foreground program) are provided

purely for convenience, and have exactly the same behavior as
`continue`.

To resume execution at a different place, you can use `return` (see Section 12.4 [Returning from a function], page 132) to go back to the calling function; or `jump` (see Section 12.2 [Continuing at a different address], page 130) to go to an arbitrary location in your program.

A typical technique for using stepping is to set a breakpoint (see Section 5.1 [Breakpoints; watchpoints; and catchpoints], page 35) at the beginning of the function or the section of your program where a problem is believed to lie, run your program until it stops at that breakpoint, and then step through the suspect area, examining the variables that are interesting, until you see the problem happen.

step   Continue running your program until control reaches a different source line, then stop it and return control to GDB. This command is abbreviated `s`.

> *Warning:* If you use the `step` command while control is within a function that was compiled without debugging information, execution proceeds until control reaches a function that does have debugging information. Likewise, it will not step into a function which is compiled without debugging information. To step through functions without debugging information, use the `stepi` command, described below.

The `step` command only stops at the first instruction of a source line. This prevents the multiple stops that could otherwise occur in `switch` statements, `for` loops, etc. `step` continues to stop if a function that has debugging information is called within the line. In other words, `step` *steps inside* any functions called within the line.

Also, the `step` command only enters a function if there is line number information for the function. Otherwise it acts like the `next` command. This avoids problems when using `cc -gl` on MIPS machines. Previously, `step` entered subroutines if there was any debugging information about the routine.

step *count*

Continue running as in `step`, but do so *count* times. If a breakpoint is reached, or a signal not related to stepping occurs before *count* steps, stepping stops right away.

next [*count*]

Continue to the next source line in the current (innermost) stack frame. This is similar to `step`, but function calls that appear within the line of code are executed without stopping. Execution stops when control reaches a different line of code at the original stack level that was executing when you gave the **next** command. This command is abbreviated **n**.

An argument *count* is a repeat count, as for **step**.

The **next** command only stops at the first instruction of a source line. This prevents multiple stops that could otherwise occur in **switch** statements, **for** loops, etc.

set step-mode

set step-mode on

The **set step-mode on** command causes the **step** command to stop at the first instruction of a function which contains no debug line information rather than stepping over it.

This is useful in cases where you may be interested in inspecting the machine instructions of a function which has no symbolic info and do not want GDB to automatically skip over this function.

set step-mode off

Causes the **step** command to step over any functions which contains no debug information. This is the default.

finish   Continue running until just after function in the selected stack frame returns. Print the returned value (if any).

Contrast this with the **return** command (see Section 12.4 [Returning from a function], page 132).

until

u   Continue running until a source line past the current line, in the current stack frame, is reached. This command is used to avoid single stepping through a loop more than once. It is like the **next** command, except that when **until** encounters a jump, it automatically continues execution until the program counter is greater than the address of the jump.

This means that when you reach the end of a loop after single stepping though it, **until** makes your program continue execution until it exits the loop. In contrast, a **next** command at the end of a loop simply steps back to the beginning of the loop, which forces you to step through the next iteration.

until always stops your program if it attempts to exit the current stack frame.

until may produce somewhat counterintuitive results if the order of machine code does not match the order of the source lines. For example, in the following excerpt from a debugging session, the **f** (**frame**) command shows that execution is stopped at line 206; yet when we use **until**, we get to line 195:

```
(gdb) f
#0  main (argc=4, argv=0xf7fffae8) at m4.c:206
```

```
206                     expand_input();
(gdb) until
195               for ( ; argc > 0; NEXTARG) {
```

This happened because, for execution efficiency, the compiler had generated code for the loop closure test at the end, rather than the start, of the loop—even though the test in a C for-loop is written before the body of the loop. The until command appeared to step back to the beginning of the loop when it advanced to this expression; however, it has not really gone to an earlier statement—not in terms of the actual machine code.

until with no argument works by means of single instruction stepping, and hence is slower than until with an argument.

until *location*

u *location*   Continue running your program until either the specified location is reached, or the current stack frame returns. *location* is any of the forms of argument acceptable to break (see Section 5.1.1 [Setting breakpoints], page 36). This form of the command uses breakpoints, and hence is quicker than until without an argument.

stepi
stepi *arg*
si   Execute one machine instruction, then stop and return to the debugger.

It is often useful to do 'display/i $pc' when stepping by machine instructions. This makes GDB automatically display the next instruction to be executed, each time your program stops. See Section 8.6 [Automatic display], page 75.

An argument is a repeat count, as in step.

nexti
nexti *arg*
ni   Execute one machine instruction, but if it is a function call, proceed until the function returns.

An argument is a repeat count, as in next.

5.3 Signals

A signal is an asynchronous event that can happen in a program. The operating system defines the possible kinds of signals, and gives each kind a name and a number. For example, in Unix SIGINT is the signal a program gets when you type an interrupt character (often C-c); SIGSEGV is the signal a program gets from referencing a place in memory far away from all the areas in use; SIGALRM occurs when the alarm clock timer goes off (which happens only if your program has requested an alarm).

Some signals, including **SIGALRM**, are a normal part of the functioning of your program. Others, such as **SIGSEGV**, indicate errors; these signals are *fatal* (they kill your program immediately) if the program has not specified in advance some other way to handle the signal. **SIGINT** does not indicate an error in your program, but it is normally fatal so it can carry out the purpose of the interrupt: to kill the program.

GDB has the ability to detect any occurrence of a signal in your program. You can tell GDB in advance what to do for each kind of signal.

Normally, GDB is set up to let the non-erroneous signals like **SIGALRM** be silently passed to your program (so as not to interfere with their role in the program's functioning) but to stop your program immediately whenever an error signal happens. You can change these settings with the **handle** command.

info signals
info handle

> Print a table of all the kinds of signals and how GDB has been told to handle each one. You can use this to see the signal numbers of all the defined types of signals.
>
> **info handle** is an alias for **info signals**.

handle *signal keywords*...

> Change the way GDB handles signal *signal*. *signal* can be the number of a signal or its name (with or without the 'SIG' at the beginning); a list of signal numbers of the form '*low–high*'; or the word '**all**', meaning all the known signals. The *keywords* say what change to make.

The keywords allowed by the **handle** command can be abbreviated. Their full names are:

nostop   GDB should not stop your program when this signal happens. It may still print a message telling you that the signal has come in.

stop   GDB should stop your program when this signal happens. This implies the **print** keyword as well.

print   GDB should print a message when this signal happens.

noprint   GDB should not mention the occurrence of the signal at all. This implies the **nostop** keyword as well.

pass
noignore   GDB should allow your program to see this signal; your program can handle the signal, or else it may terminate if the signal is fatal and not handled. **pass** and **noignore** are synonyms.

nopass
ignore   GDB should not allow your program to see this signal. **nopass** and **ignore** are synonyms.

When a signal stops your program, the signal is not visible to the program until you continue. Your program sees the signal then, if `pass` is in effect for the signal in question *at that time*. In other words, after GDB reports a signal, you can use the `handle` command with `pass` or `nopass` to control whether your program sees that signal when you continue.

The default is set to `nostop`, `noprint`, `pass` for non-erroneous signals such as `SIGALRM`, `SIGWINCH` and `SIGCHLD`, and to `stop`, `print`, `pass` for the erroneous signals.

You can also use the `signal` command to prevent your program from seeing a signal, or cause it to see a signal it normally would not see, or to give it any signal at any time. For example, if your program stopped due to some sort of memory reference error, you might store correct values into the erroneous variables and continue, hoping to see more execution; but your program would probably terminate immediately as a result of the fatal signal once it saw the signal. To prevent this, you can continue with ‘`signal 0`’. See Section 12.3 [Giving your program a signal], page 131.

5.4 Stopping and starting multi-thread programs

When your program has multiple threads (see Section 4.9 [Debugging programs with multiple threads], page 29), you can choose whether to set breakpoints on all threads, or on a particular thread.

`break` *linespec* `thread` *threadno*
`break` *linespec* `thread` *threadno* `if` ...

        linespec specifies source lines; there are several ways of writing them, but the effect is always to specify some source line.

        Use the qualifier ‘`thread` *threadno*’ with a breakpoint command to specify that you only want GDB to stop the program when a particular thread reaches this breakpoint. *threadno* is one of the numeric thread identifiers assigned by GDB, shown in the first column of the ‘`info threads`’ display.

        If you do not specify ‘`thread` *threadno*’ when you set a breakpoint, the breakpoint applies to *all* threads of your program.

        You can use the `thread` qualifier on conditional breakpoints as well; in this case, place ‘`thread` *threadno*’ before the breakpoint condition, like this:

```
(gdb) break frik.c:13 thread 28 if bartab > lim
```

Whenever your program stops under GDB for any reason, *all* threads of execution stop, not just the current thread. This allows you to examine the overall state of the program, including switching between threads, without worrying that things may change underfoot.

Conversely, whenever you restart the program, *all* threads start executing. *This is true even when single-stepping* with commands like `step` or `next`.

In particular, GDB cannot single-step all threads in lockstep. Since thread scheduling is up to your debugging target's operating system (not controlled by GDB), other threads may execute more than one statement while the current thread completes a single step. Moreover, in general other threads stop in the middle of a statement, rather than at a clean statement boundary, when the program stops.

You might even find your program stopped in another thread after continuing or even single-stepping. This happens whenever some other thread runs into a breakpoint, a signal, or an exception before the first thread completes whatever you requested.

On some OSes, you can lock the OS scheduler and thus allow only a single thread to run.

`set scheduler-locking` *mode*

> Set the scheduler locking mode. If it is `off`, then there is no locking and any thread may run at any time. If `on`, then only the current thread may run when the inferior is resumed. The `step` mode optimizes for single-stepping. It stops other threads from "seizing the prompt" by preempting the current thread while you are stepping. Other threads will only rarely (or never) get a chance to run when you step. They are more likely to run when you 'next' over a function call, and they are completely free to run when you use commands like 'continue', 'until', or 'finish'. However, unless another thread hits a breakpoint during its timeslice, they will never steal the GDB prompt away from the thread that you are debugging.

`show scheduler-locking`

> Display the current scheduler locking mode.

6 Examining the Stack

When your program has stopped, the first thing you need to know is where it stopped and how it got there.

Each time your program performs a function call, information about the call is generated. That information includes the location of the call in your program, the arguments of the call, and the local variables of the function being called. The information is saved in a block of data called a *stack frame*. The stack frames are allocated in a region of memory called the *call stack*.

When your program stops, the GDB commands for examining the stack allow you to see all of this information.

One of the stack frames is *selected* by GDB and many GDB commands refer implicitly to the selected frame. In particular, whenever you ask GDB for the value of a variable in your program, the value is found in the selected frame. There are special GDB commands to select whichever frame you are interested in. See Section 6.3 [Selecting a frame], page 59.

When your program stops, GDB automatically selects the currently executing frame and describes it briefly, similar to the **frame** command (see Section 6.4 [Information about a frame], page 60).

6.1 Stack frames

The call stack is divided up into contiguous pieces called *stack frames*, or *frames* for short; each frame is the data associated with one call to one function. The frame contains the arguments given to the function, the function's local variables, and the address at which the function is executing.

When your program is started, the stack has only one frame, that of the function **main**. This is called the *initial* frame or the *outermost* frame. Each time a function is called, a new frame is made. Each time a function returns, the frame for that function invocation is eliminated. If a function is recursive, there can be many frames for the same function. The frame for the function in which execution is actually occurring is called the *innermost* frame. This is the most recently created of all the stack frames that still exist.

Inside your program, stack frames are identified by their addresses. A stack frame consists of many bytes, each of which has its own address; each kind of computer has a convention for choosing one byte whose address serves as the address of the frame. Usually this address is kept in a register called the *frame pointer register* while execution is going on in that frame.

GDB assigns numbers to all existing stack frames, starting with zero for the innermost frame, one for the frame that called it, and so on upward. These numbers do not really exist in your program; they are assigned by GDB to give you a way of designating stack frames in GDB commands.

Some compilers provide a way to compile functions so that they operate without stack frames. (For example, the gcc option

'-fomit-frame-pointer'

generates functions without a frame.) This is occasionally done with heavily used library functions to save the frame setup time. GDB has limited facilities for dealing with these function invocations. If the innermost function invocation has no stack frame, GDB nevertheless regards it as though it had a separate frame, which is numbered zero as usual, allowing correct tracing of the function call chain. However, GDB has no provision for frameless functions elsewhere in the stack.

frame *args*

> The `frame` command allows you to move from one stack frame to another, and to print the stack frame you select. *args* may be either the address of the frame or the stack frame number. Without an argument, `frame` prints the current stack frame.

select-frame

> The `select-frame` command allows you to move from one stack frame to another without printing the frame. This is the silent version of `frame`.

6.2 Backtraces

A backtrace is a summary of how your program got where it is. It shows one line per frame, for many frames, starting with the currently executing frame (frame zero), followed by its caller (frame one), and on up the stack.

backtrace
bt

> Print a backtrace of the entire stack: one line per frame for all frames in the stack.
>
> You can stop the backtrace at any time by typing the system interrupt character, normally *C-c*.

backtrace *n*
bt *n*   Similar, but print only the innermost *n* frames.

backtrace -*n*
bt -*n*   Similar, but print only the outermost *n* frames.

The names `where` and `info stack` (abbreviated `info s`) are additional aliases for `backtrace`.

Each line in the backtrace shows the frame number and the function name. The program counter value is also shown—unless you use `set print address off`. The backtrace also shows the source file name and line number, as well as the arguments to the function. The program counter value is omitted if it is at the beginning of the code for that line number.

Here is an example of a backtrace. It was made with the command 'bt 3', so it shows the innermost three frames.

```
#0  m4_traceon (obs=0x24eb0, argc=1, argv=0x2b8c8)
        at builtin.c:993
#1  0x6e38 in expand_macro (sym=0x2b600) at macro.c:242
#2  0x6840 in expand_token (obs=0x0, t=177664, td=0xf7fffb08)
        at macro.c:71
(More stack frames follow...)
```

The display for frame zero does not begin with a program counter value, indicating that your program has stopped at the beginning of the code for line 993 of builtin.c.

6.3 Selecting a frame

Most commands for examining the stack and other data in your program work on whichever stack frame is selected at the moment. Here are the commands for selecting a stack frame; all of them finish by printing a brief description of the stack frame just selected.

frame *n*

f *n*   Select frame number *n*. Recall that frame zero is the innermost (currently executing) frame, frame one is the frame that called the innermost one, and so on. The highest-numbered frame is the one for main.

frame *addr*

f *addr*   Select the frame at address *addr*. This is useful mainly if the chaining of stack frames has been damaged by a bug, making it impossible for GDB to assign numbers properly to all frames. In addition, this can be useful when your program has multiple stacks and switches between them.

On the SPARC architecture, frame needs two addresses to select an arbitrary frame: a frame pointer and a stack pointer.

On the MIPS and Alpha architecture, it needs two addresses: a stack pointer and a program counter.

On the 29k architecture, it needs three addresses: a register stack pointer, a program counter, and a memory stack pointer.

up *n*   Move *n* frames up the stack. For positive numbers *n*, this advances toward the outermost frame, to higher frame numbers, to frames that have existed longer. *n* defaults to one.

down *n*   Move *n* frames down the stack. For positive numbers *n*, this advances toward the innermost frame, to lower frame numbers, to frames that were created more recently. *n* defaults to one. You may abbreviate down as do.

All of these commands end by printing two lines of output describing the frame. The first line shows the frame number, the function name, the arguments, and the source file and line number of execution in that frame. The second line shows the text of that source line.

For example:

```
(gdb) up
#1  0x22f0 in main (argc=1, argv=0xf7fffbf4, env=0xf7fffbfc)
    at env.c:10
10              read_input_file (argv[i]);
```

After such a printout, the `list` command with no arguments prints ten lines centered on the point of execution in the frame. See Section 7.1 [Printing source lines], page 63.

`up-silently` *n*
`down-silently` *n*

> These two commands are variants of **up** and **down**, respectively; they differ in that they do their work silently, without causing display of the new frame. They are intended primarily for use in GDB command scripts, where the output might be unnecessary and distracting.

6.4 Information about a frame

There are several other commands to print information about the selected stack frame.

`frame`
`f`

> When used without any argument, this command does not change which frame is selected, but prints a brief description of the currently selected stack frame. It can be abbreviated **f**. With an argument, this command is used to select a stack frame. See Section 6.3 [Selecting a frame], page 59.

`info frame`
`info f`

> This command prints a verbose description of the selected stack frame, including:
>
> - the address of the frame
> - the address of the next frame down (called by this frame)
> - the address of the next frame up (caller of this frame)
> - the language in which the source code corresponding to this frame is written
> - the address of the frame's arguments
> - the address of the frame's local variables
> - the program counter saved in it (the address of execution in the caller frame)

- which registers were saved in the frame

The verbose description is useful when something has gone wrong that has made the stack format fail to fit the usual conventions.

`info frame` *addr*
`info f` *addr*

> Print a verbose description of the frame at address *addr*, without selecting that frame. The selected frame remains unchanged by this command. This requires the same kind of address (more than one for some architectures) that you specify in the `frame` command. See Section 6.3 [Selecting a frame], page 59.

`info args` Print the arguments of the selected frame, each on a separate line.

`info locals`

> Print the local variables of the selected frame, each on a separate line. These are all variables (declared either static or automatic) accessible at the point of execution of the selected frame.

`info catch`

> Print a list of all the exception handlers that are active in the current stack frame at the current point of execution. To see other exception handlers, visit the associated frame (using the `up`, `down`, or `frame` commands); then type `info catch`. See Section 5.1.3 [Setting catchpoints], page 42.

7 Examining Source Files

GDB can print parts of your program's source, since the debugging information recorded in the program tells GDB what source files were used to build it. When your program stops, GDB spontaneously prints the line where it stopped. Likewise, when you select a stack frame (see Section 6.3 [Selecting a frame], page 59), GDB prints the line where execution in that frame has stopped. You can print other portions of source files by explicit command.

If you use GDB through its GNU Emacs interface, you may prefer to use Emacs facilities to view source; see Chapter 19 [Using GDB under GNU Emacs], page 209.

7.1 Printing source lines

To print lines from a source file, use the `list` command (abbreviated `l`). By default, ten lines are printed. There are several ways to specify what part of the file you want to print.

Here are the forms of the `list` command most commonly used:

`list` *linenum*
>   Print lines centered around line number *linenum* in the current source file.

`list` *function*
>   Print lines centered around the beginning of function *function*.

`list`
>   Print more lines. If the last lines printed were printed with a `list` command, this prints lines following the last lines printed; however, if the last line printed was a solitary line printed as part of displaying a stack frame (see Chapter 6 [Examining the Stack], page 57), this prints lines centered around that line.

`list -`
>   Print lines just before the lines last printed.

By default, GDB prints ten source lines with any of these forms of the `list` command. You can change this using `set listsize`:

`set listsize` *count*
>   Make the `list` command display *count* source lines (unless the `list` argument explicitly specifies some other number).

`show listsize`
>   Display the number of lines that `list` prints.

Repeating a `list` command with (RET) discards the argument, so it is equivalent to typing just `list`. This is more useful than listing the same lines again. An exception is made for an argument of '-'; that argument is preserved in repetition so that each repetition moves up in the source file.

In general, the `list` command expects you to supply zero, one or two *linespecs*. Linespecs specify source lines; there are several ways of writing them, but the effect is always to specify some source line. Here is a complete description of the possible arguments for `list`:

`list` *linespec*

> Print lines centered around the line specified by *linespec*.

`list` *first*, *last*

> Print lines from *first* to *last*. Both arguments are linespecs.

`list` , *last*   Print lines ending with *last*.

`list` *first*,

> Print lines starting with *first*.

`list +`   Print lines just after the lines last printed.

`list -`   Print lines just before the lines last printed.

`list`   As described in the preceding table.

Here are the ways of specifying a single source line—all the kinds of linespec.

number   Specifies line *number* of the current source file. When a `list` command has two linespecs, this refers to the same source file as the first linespec.

+*offset*   Specifies the line *offset* lines after the last line printed. When used as the second linespec in a `list` command that has two, this specifies the line *offset* lines down from the first linespec.

−*offset*   Specifies the line *offset* lines before the last line printed.

filename: *number*

> Specifies line *number* in the source file *filename*.

function   Specifies the line that begins the body of the function *function*. For example: in C, this is the line with the open brace.

filename: *function*

> Specifies the line of the open-brace that begins the body of the function *function* in the file *filename*. You only need the file name with a function name to avoid ambiguity when there are identically named functions in different source files.

address   Specifies the line containing the program address *address*. *address* may be any expression.

7.2 Searching source files

There are two commands for searching through the current source file for a regular expression.

forward-search *regexp*
search *regexp*
> The command 'forward-search *regexp*' checks each line, starting with the one following the last line listed, for a match for *regexp*. It lists the line that is found. You can use the synonym 'search *regexp*' or abbreviate the command name as fo.

reverse-search *regexp*
> The command 'reverse-search *regexp*' checks each line, starting with the one before the last line listed and going backward, for a match for *regexp*. It lists the line that is found. You can abbreviate this command as rev.

7.3 Specifying source directories

Executable programs sometimes do not record the directories of the source files from which they were compiled, just the names. Even when they do, the directories could be moved between the compilation and your debugging session. GDB has a list of directories to search for source files; this is called the *source path*. Each time GDB wants a source file, it tries all the directories in the list, in the order they are present in the list, until it finds a file with the desired name. Note that the executable search path is *not* used for this purpose. Neither is the current working directory, unless it happens to be in the source path.

If GDB cannot find a source file in the source path, and the object program records a directory, GDB tries that directory too. If the source path is empty, and there is no record of the compilation directory, GDB looks in the current directory as a last resort.

Whenever you reset or rearrange the source path, GDB clears out any information it has cached about where source files are found and where each line is in the file.

When you start GDB, its source path includes only 'cdir' and 'cwd', in that order. To add other directories, use the directory command.

directory *dirname* ...
dir *dirname* ...
> Add directory *dirname* to the front of the source path. Several directory names may be given to this command, separated by ':' (';' on MS-DOS and MS-Windows, where ':' usually appears as part of absolute file names) or whitespace. You may specify a directory that is already in the source path; this moves it forward, so GDB searches it sooner.

You can use the string '`$cdir`' to refer to the compilation directory (if one is recorded), and '`$cwd`' to refer to the current working directory. '`$cwd`' is not the same as '`.`'—the former tracks the current working directory as it changes during your GDB session, while the latter is immediately expanded to the current directory at the time you add an entry to the source path.

`directory`

Reset the source path to empty again. This requires confirmation.

`show directories`

Print the source path: show which directories it contains.

If your source path is cluttered with directories that are no longer of interest, GDB may sometimes cause confusion by finding the wrong versions of source. You can correct the situation as follows:

1. Use `directory` with no argument to reset the source path to empty.

2. Use `directory` with suitable arguments to reinstall the directories you want in the source path. You can add all the directories in one command.

7.4 Source and machine code

You can use the command `info line` to map source lines to program addresses (and vice versa), and the command `disassemble` to display a range of addresses as machine instructions. When run under GNU Emacs mode, the `info line` command causes the arrow to point to the line specified. Also, `info line` prints addresses in symbolic form as well as hex.

`info line` *linespec*

Print the starting and ending addresses of the compiled code for source line *linespec*. You can specify source lines in any of the ways understood by the `list` command (see Section 7.1 [Printing source lines], page 63).

For example, we can use `info line` to discover the location of the object code for the first line of function `m4_changequote`:

```
(gdb) info line m4_changequote
Line 895 of "builtin.c" starts at pc 0x634c and ends at 0x6350.
```

We can also inquire (using *addr* as the form for *linespec*) what source line covers a particular address:

```
(gdb) info line *0x63ff
Line 926 of "builtin.c" starts at pc 0x63e4 and ends at 0x6404.
```

After `info line`, the default address for the `x` command is changed to the starting address of the line, so that '`x/i`' is sufficient to begin examining the machine code (see Section 8.5 [Examining memory], page 74). Also, this address is saved as the value of the convenience variable $_ (see Section 8.9 [Convenience variables], page 83).

disassemble

> This specialized command dumps a range of memory as machine instructions. The default memory range is the function surrounding the program counter of the selected frame. A single argument to this command is a program counter value; GDB dumps the function surrounding this value. Two arguments specify a range of addresses (first inclusive, second exclusive) to dump.

The following example shows the disassembly of a range of addresses of HP PA-RISC 2.0 code:

```
(gdb) disas 0x32c4 0x32e4
Dump of assembler code from 0x32c4 to 0x32e4:
0x32c4 <main+204>:      addil 0,dp
0x32c8 <main+208>:      ldw 0x22c(sr0,r1),r26
0x32cc <main+212>:      ldil 0x3000,r31
0x32d0 <main+216>:      ble 0x3f8(sr4,r31)
0x32d4 <main+220>:      ldo 0(r31),rp
0x32d8 <main+224>:      addil -0x800,dp
0x32dc <main+228>:      ldo 0x588(r1),r26
0x32e0 <main+232>:      ldil 0x3000,r31
End of assembler dump.
```

Some architectures have more than one commonly-used set of instruction mnemonics or other syntax.

set disassembly-flavor *instruction-set*

> Select the instruction set to use when disassembling the program via the disassemble or x/i commands.

> Currently this command is only defined for the Intel x86 family. You can set *instruction-set* to either intel or att. The default is att, the AT&T flavor used by default by Unix assemblers for x86-based targets.

8 Examining Data

The usual way to examine data in your program is with the `print` command (abbreviated `p`), or its synonym `inspect`. It evaluates and prints the value of an expression of the language your program is written in (see Chapter 10 [Using GDB with Different Languages], page 99).

`print` *expr*
`print /f` *expr*

> *expr* is an expression (in the source language). By default the value of *expr* is printed in a format appropriate to its data type; you can choose a different format by specifying '/*f*', where *f* is a letter specifying the format; see Section 8.4 [Output formats], page 73.

`print`
`print /f`   If you omit *expr*, GDB displays the last value again (from the *value history*; see Section 8.8 [Value history], page 82). This allows you to conveniently inspect the same value in an alternative format.

A more low-level way of examining data is with the `x` command. It examines data in memory at a specified address and prints it in a specified format. See Section 8.5 [Examining memory], page 74.

If you are interested in information about types, or about how the fields of a struct or a class are declared, use the `ptype` *exp* command rather than `print`. See Chapter 11 [Examining the Symbol Table], page 123.

8.1 Expressions

`print` and many other GDB commands accept an expression and compute its value. Any kind of constant, variable or operator defined by the programming language you are using is valid in an expression in GDB. This includes conditional expressions, function calls, casts and string constants. It unfortunately does not include symbols defined by preprocessor `#define` commands.

GDB supports array constants in expressions input by the user. The syntax is {*element, element...*}. For example, you can use the command `print {1, 2, 3}` to build up an array in memory that is `malloced` in the target program.

Because C is so widespread, most of the expressions shown in examples in this manual are in C. See Chapter 10 [Using GDB with Different Languages], page 99, for information on how to use expressions in other languages.

In this section, we discuss operators that you can use in GDB expressions regardless of your programming language.

Casts are supported in all languages, not just in C, because it is so useful to cast a number into a pointer in order to examine a structure at that address in memory.

GDB supports these operators, in addition to those common to programming languages:

@   '@' is a binary operator for treating parts of memory as arrays. See Section 8.3 [Artificial arrays], page 72, for more information.

::   '::' allows you to specify a variable in terms of the file or function where it is defined. See Section 8.2 [Program variables], page 70.

{type} addr

            Refers to an object of type *type* stored at address *addr* in memory. *addr* may be any expression whose value is an integer or pointer (but parentheses are required around binary operators, just as in a cast). This construct is allowed regardless of what kind of data is normally supposed to reside at *addr*.

8.2 Program variables

The most common kind of expression to use is the name of a variable in your program.

Variables in expressions are understood in the selected stack frame (see Section 6.3 [Selecting a frame], page 59); they must be either:

- global (or file-static)

or

- visible according to the scope rules of the programming language from the point of execution in that frame

This means that in the function

```
foo (a)
     int a;
{
  bar (a);
  {
    int b = test ();
    bar (b);
  }
}
```

you can examine and use the variable a whenever your program is executing within the function foo, but you can only use or examine the variable b while your program is executing inside the block where b is declared.

There is an exception: you can refer to a variable or function whose scope is a single source file even if the current execution point is not in this file. But it is possible to have more than one such variable or function with the same name (in different source files). If that happens, referring to that name has unpredictable effects. If you wish, you can specify a static variable in a particular function or file, using the colon-colon notation:

> *file*::*variable*
> *function*::*variable*

Here *file* or *function* is the name of the context for the static *variable*. In the case of file names, you can use quotes to make sure GDB parses the file name as a single word—for example, to print a global value of **x** defined in 'f2.c':

```
(gdb) p 'f2.c'::x
```

This use of '::' is very rarely in conflict with the very similar use of the same notation in C++. GDB also supports use of the C++ scope resolution operator in GDB expressions.

> *Warning:* Occasionally, a local variable may appear to have the wrong value at certain points in a function—just after entry to a new scope, and just before exit.

You may see this problem when you are stepping by machine instructions. This is because, on most machines, it takes more than one instruction to set up a stack frame (including local variable definitions); if you are stepping by machine instructions, variables may appear to have the wrong values until the stack frame is completely built. On exit, it usually also takes more than one machine instruction to destroy a stack frame; after you begin stepping through that group of instructions, local variable definitions may be gone.

This may also happen when the compiler does significant optimizations. To be sure of always seeing accurate values, turn off all optimization when compiling.

Another possible effect of compiler optimizations is to optimize unused variables out of existence, or assign variables to registers (as opposed to memory addresses). Depending on the support for such cases offered by the debug info format used by the compiler, GDB might not be able to display values for such local variables. If that happens, GDB will print a message like this:

```
No symbol "foo" in current context.
```

To solve such problems, either recompile without optimizations, or use a different debug info format, if the compiler supports several such formats. For example, GCC, the GNU C/C++ compiler usually supports the '-gstabs' option. '-gstabs' produces debug info in a format that is superior to formats such as COFF. You may be able to use DWARF2 ('-gdwarf-2'), which is also an effective form for debug info. See section "Options for Debugging Your Program or GNU CC" in *Using GNU CC*, for more information.

8.3 Artificial arrays

It is often useful to print out several successive objects of the same type in memory; a section of an array, or an array of dynamically determined size for which only a pointer exists in the program.

You can do this by referring to a contiguous span of memory as an artificial array, using the binary operator '@'. The left operand of '@' should be the first element of the desired array and be an individual object. The right operand should be the desired length of the array. The result is an array value whose elements are all of the type of the left argument. The first element is actually the left argument; the second element comes from bytes of memory immediately following those that hold the first element, and so on. Here is an example. If a program says

```
int *array = (int *) malloc (len * sizeof (int));
```

you can print the contents of array with

```
p *array@len
```

The left operand of '@' must reside in memory. Array values made with '@' in this way behave just like other arrays in terms of subscripting, and are coerced to pointers when used in expressions. Artificial arrays most often appear in expressions via the value history (see Section 8.8 [Value history], page 82), after printing one out.

Another way to create an artificial array is to use a cast. This re-interprets a value as if it were an array. The value need not be in memory:

```
(gdb) p/x (short[2])0x12345678
$1 = {0x1234, 0x5678}
```

As a convenience, if you leave the array length out (as in '(type[]) value') GDB calculates the size to fill the value (as 'sizeof(value)/sizeof(type)':

```
(gdb) p/x (short[])0x12345678
$2 = {0x1234, 0x5678}
```

Sometimes the artificial array mechanism is not quite enough; in moderately complex data structures, the elements of interest may not actually be adjacent—for example, if you are interested in the values of pointers in an array. One useful work-around in this situation is to use a convenience variable (see Section 8.9 [Convenience variables], page 83) as a counter in an expression that prints the first interesting value, and then repeat that expression via ⟨RET⟩. For instance, suppose you have an array dtab of pointers to structures, and you are interested in the values of a field fv in each structure. Here is an example of what you might type:

```
set $i = 0
p dtab[$i++]->fv
⟨RET⟩
⟨RET⟩
...
```

8.4 Output formats

By default, GDB prints a value according to its data type. Sometimes this is not what you want. For example, you might want to print a number in hex, or a pointer in decimal. Or you might want to view data in memory at a certain address as a character string or as an instruction. To do these things, specify an *output format* when you print a value.

The simplest use of output formats is to say how to print a value already computed. This is done by starting the arguments of the **print** command with a slash and a format letter. The format letters supported are:

x   Regard the bits of the value as an integer, and print the integer in hexadecimal.

d   Print as integer in signed decimal.

u   Print as integer in unsigned decimal.

o   Print as integer in octal.

t   Print as integer in binary. The letter 't' stands for "two".[1]

a   Print as an address, both absolute in hexadecimal and as an offset from the nearest preceding symbol. You can use this format used to discover where (in what function) an unknown address is located:

            (gdb) p/a 0x54320
            $3 = 0x54320 <_initialize_vx+396>

            The command **info symbol 0x54320** yields similar results. See Chapter 11 [Symbols], page 123.

c   Regard as an integer and print it as a character constant.

f   Regard the bits of the value as a floating point number and print using typical floating point syntax.

For example, to print the program counter in hex (see Section 8.10 [Registers], page 85), type

    p/x $pc

Note that no space is required before the slash; this is because command names in GDB cannot contain a slash.

To reprint the last value in the value history with a different format, you can use the **print** command with just a format and no expression. For example, 'p/x' reprints the last value in hex.

---

[1] 'b' cannot be used because these format letters are also used with the x command, where 'b' stands for "byte"; see Section 8.5 [Examining memory], page 74.

8.5 Examining memory

You can use the command x (for "examine") to examine memory in any of several formats, independently of your program's data types.

x/*nfu addr*
x *addr*
x   Use the **x** command to examine memory.

    n, *f*, and *u* are all optional parameters that specify how much memory to display and how to format it; *addr* is an expression giving the address where you want to start displaying memory. If you use defaults for *nfu*, you need not type the slash '/'. Several commands set convenient defaults for *addr*.

n, the repeat count
> The repeat count is a decimal integer; the default is 1. It specifies how much memory (counting by units *u*) to display.

f, the display format
> The display format is one of the formats used by **print**, 's' (null-terminated string), or 'i' (machine instruction). The default is 'x' (hexadecimal) initially. The default changes each time you use either **x** or **print**.

u, the unit size
> The unit size is any of

> b   Bytes.

> h   Halfwords (two bytes).

> w   Words (four bytes). This is the initial default.

> g   Giant words (eight bytes).

> Each time you specify a unit size with **x**, that size becomes the default unit the next time you use **x**. (For the 's' and 'i' formats, the unit size is ignored and is normally not written.)

addr, starting display address
> *addr* is the address where you want GDB to begin displaying memory. The expression need not have a pointer value (though it may); it is always interpreted as an integer address of a byte of memory. See Section 8.1 [Expressions], page 69, for more information on expressions. The default for *addr* is usually just after the last address examined—but several other commands also set the default address: **info breakpoints** (to the address of the last breakpoint listed), **info line** (to the starting address of a line), and **print** (if you use it to display a value from memory).

    For example, 'x/3uh 0x54320' is a request to display three halfwords (h) of memory, formatted as unsigned decimal integers ('u'), starting at address

0x54320. 'x/4xw $sp' prints the four words ('w') of memory above the stack pointer (here, '$sp'; see Section 8.10 [Registers], page 85) in hexadecimal ('x').

Since the letters indicating unit sizes are all distinct from the letters specifying output formats, you do not have to remember whether unit size or format comes first; either order works. The output specifications '4xw' and '4wx' mean exactly the same thing. (However, the count n must come first; 'wx4' does not work.)

Even though the unit size u is ignored for the formats 's' and 'i', you might still want to use a count n; for example, '3i' specifies that you want to see three machine instructions, including any operands. The command disassemble gives an alternative way of inspecting machine instructions; see Section 7.4 [Source and machine code], page 66.

All the defaults for the arguments to x are designed to make it easy to continue scanning memory with minimal specifications each time you use x. For example, after you have inspected three machine instructions with 'x/3i addr', you can inspect the next seven with just 'x/7'. If you use (RET) to repeat the x command, the repeat count n is used again; the other arguments default as for successive uses of x.

The addresses and contents printed by the x command are not saved in the value history because there is often too much of them and they would get in the way. Instead, GDB makes these values available for subsequent use in expressions as values of the convenience variables $_ and $__. After an x command, the last address examined is available for use in expressions in the convenience variable $_. The contents of that address, as examined, are available in the convenience variable $__.

If the x command has a repeat count, the address and contents saved are from the last memory unit printed; this is not the same as the last address printed if several units were printed on the last line of output.

8.6 Automatic display

If you find that you want to print the value of an expression frequently (to see how it changes), you might want to add it to the *automatic display list* so that GDB prints its value each time your program stops. Each expression added to the list is given a number to identify it; to remove an expression from the list, you specify that number. The automatic display looks like this:

```
2: foo = 38
3: bar[5] = (struct hack *) 0x3804
```

This display shows item numbers, expressions and their current values. As with displays you request manually using x or print, you can specify the output format you prefer; in fact, display decides whether to use print or x depending on how elaborate your format specification is—it uses x if you specify a unit size, or one of the two formats ('i' and 's') that are only supported by x; otherwise it uses print.

display *expr*

> Add the expression *expr* to the list of expressions to display each time your program stops. See Section 8.1 [Expressions], page 69.
>
> display does not repeat if you press (RET) again after using it.

display/*fmt* *expr*

> For *fmt* specifying only a display format and not a size or count, add the expression *expr* to the auto-display list but arrange to display it each time in the specified format *fmt*. See Section 8.4 [Output formats], page 73.

display/*fmt* *addr*

> For *fmt* 'i' or 's', or including a unit-size or a number of units, add the expression *addr* as a memory address to be examined each time your program stops. Examining means in effect doing 'x/*fmt* *addr*'. See Section 8.5 [Examining memory], page 74.

For example, 'display/i $pc' can be helpful, to see the machine instruction about to be executed each time execution stops ('$pc' is a common name for the program counter; see Section 8.10 [Registers], page 85).

undisplay *dnums*...
delete display *dnums*...

> Remove item numbers *dnums* from the list of expressions to display.
>
> undisplay does not repeat if you press (RET) after using it. (Otherwise you would just get the error 'No display number ...'.)

disable display *dnums*...

> Disable the display of item numbers *dnums*. A disabled display item is not printed automatically, but is not forgotten. It may be enabled again later.

enable display *dnums*...

> Enable display of item numbers *dnums*. It becomes effective once again in auto display of its expression, until you specify otherwise.

display   Display the current values of the expressions on the list, just as is done when your program stops.

info display

> Print the list of expressions previously set up to display automatically, each one with its item number, but without showing the values. This includes disabled expressions, which are marked as such. It also includes expressions which would not be displayed

right now because they refer to automatic variables not currently available.

If a display expression refers to local variables, then it does not make sense outside the lexical context for which it was set up. Such an expression is disabled when execution enters a context where one of its variables is not defined. For example, if you give the command display last_char while inside a function with an argument last_char, GDB displays this argument while your program continues to stop inside that function. When it stops elsewhere—where there is no variable last_char—the display is disabled automatically. The next time your program stops where last_char is meaningful, you can enable the display expression once again.

8.7 Print settings

GDB provides the following ways to control how arrays, structures, and symbols are printed.

These settings are useful for debugging programs in any language:

set print address
set print address on
> GDB prints memory addresses showing the location of stack traces, structure values, pointer values, breakpoints, and so forth, even when it also displays the contents of those addresses. The default is **on**. For example, this is what a stack frame display looks like with **set print address on**:
>
> ```
> (gdb) f
> #0  set_quotes (lq=0x34c78 "<<", rq=0x34c88 ">>")
>         at input.c:530
> 530             if (lquote != def_lquote)
> ```

set print address off
> Do not print addresses when displaying their contents. For example, this is the same stack frame displayed with **set print address off**:
>
> ```
> (gdb) set print addr off
> (gdb) f
> #0  set_quotes (lq="<<", rq=">>") at input.c:530
> 530             if (lquote != def_lquote)
> ```
>
> You can use 'set print address off' to eliminate all machine dependent displays from the GDB interface. For example, with print address off, you should get the same text for backtraces on all machines—whether or not they involve pointer arguments.

show print address
> Show whether or not addresses are to be printed.

When GDB prints a symbolic address, it normally prints the closest earlier symbol plus an offset. If that symbol does not uniquely identify the address (for example, it is a name whose scope is a single source file), you may need to clarify. One way to do this is with `info line`, for example 'info line *0x4537'. Alternately, you can set GDB to print the source file and line number when it prints a symbolic address:

set print symbol-filename on
>Tell GDB to print the source file name and line number of a symbol in the symbolic form of an address.

set print symbol-filename off
>Do not print source file name and line number of a symbol. This is the default.

show print symbol-filename
>Show whether or not GDB will print the source file name and line number of a symbol in the symbolic form of an address.

Another situation where it is helpful to show symbol filenames and line numbers is when disassembling code; GDB shows you the line number and source file that corresponds to each instruction.

Also, you may wish to see the symbolic form only if the address being printed is reasonably close to the closest earlier symbol:

set print max-symbolic-offset *max-offset*
>Tell GDB to only display the symbolic form of an address if the offset between the closest earlier symbol and the address is less than *max-offset*. The default is 0, which tells GDB to always print the symbolic form of an address if any symbol precedes it.

show print max-symbolic-offset
>Ask how large the maximum offset is that GDB prints in a symbolic address.

If you have a pointer and you are not sure where it points, try 'set print symbol-filename on'. Then you can determine the name and source file location of the variable where it points, using 'p/a *pointer*'. This interprets the address in symbolic form. For example, here GDB shows that a variable ptt points at another variable t, defined in 'hi2.c':

```
(gdb) set print symbol-filename on
(gdb) p/a ptt
$4 = 0xe008 <t in hi2.c>
```

Warning: For pointers that point to a local variable, 'p/a' does not show the symbol name and filename of the referent, even with the appropriate `set print` options turned on.

Other settings control how different kinds of objects are printed:

`set print array`
`set print array on`

> Pretty print arrays. This format is more convenient to read, but uses more space. The default is off.

`set print array off`

> Return to compressed format for arrays.

`show print array`

> Show whether compressed or pretty format is selected for displaying arrays.

`set print elements` *number-of-elements*

> Set a limit on how many elements of an array GDB will print. If GDB is printing a large array, it stops printing after it has printed the number of elements set by the `set print elements` command. This limit also applies to the display of strings. When GDB starts, this limit is set to 200. Setting *number-of-elements* to zero means that the printing is unlimited.

`show print elements`

> Display the number of elements of a large array that GDB will print. If the number is 0, then the printing is unlimited.

`set print null-stop`

> Cause GDB to stop printing the characters of an array when the first NULL is encountered. This is useful when large arrays actually contain only short strings. The default is off.

`set print pretty on`

> Cause GDB to print structures in an indented format with one member per line, like this:

```
$1 = {
  next = 0x0,
  flags = {
    sweet = 1,
    sour = 1
  },
  meat = 0x54 "Pork"
}
```

`set print pretty off`

> Cause GDB to print structures in a compact format, like this:

```
$1 = {next = 0x0, flags = {sweet = 1, sour = 1}, \
meat = 0x54 "Pork"}
```

> This is the default format.

`show print pretty`

> Show which format GDB is using to print structures.

set print sevenbit-strings on

> Print using only seven-bit characters; if this option is set, GDB displays any eight-bit characters (in strings or character values) using the notation \nnn. This setting is best if you are working in English (ASCII) and you use the high-order bit of characters as a marker or "meta" bit.

set print sevenbit-strings off

> Print full eight-bit characters. This allows the use of more international character sets, and is the default.

show print sevenbit-strings

> Show whether or not GDB is printing only seven-bit characters.

set print union on

> Tell GDB to print unions which are contained in structures. This is the default setting.

set print union off

> Tell GDB not to print unions which are contained in structures.

show print union

> Ask GDB whether or not it will print unions which are contained in structures.
>
> For example, given the declarations

```
typedef enum {Tree, Bug} Species;
typedef enum {Big_tree, Acorn, Seedling} Tree_forms;
typedef enum {Caterpillar, Cocoon, Butterfly}
            Bug_forms;

struct thing {
  Species it;
  union {
    Tree_forms tree;
    Bug_forms bug;
  } form;
};

struct thing foo = {Tree, {Acorn}};
```

with **set print union on** in effect 'p foo' would print

```
$1 = {it = Tree, form = {tree = Acorn, bug = Cocoon}}
```

and with **set print union off** in effect it would print

```
$1 = {it = Tree, form = {...}}
```

These settings are of interest when debugging C++ programs:

`set print demangle`
`set print demangle on`
> Print C++ names in their source form rather than in the encoded ("mangled") form passed to the assembler and linker for type-safe linkage. The default is on.

`show print demangle`
> Show whether C++ names are printed in mangled or demangled form.

`set print asm-demangle`
`set print asm-demangle on`
> Print C++ names in their source form rather than their mangled form, even in assembler code printouts such as instruction disassemblies. The default is off.

`show print asm-demangle`
> Show whether C++ names in assembly listings are printed in mangled or demangled form.

`set demangle-style` *style*
> Choose among several encoding schemes used by different compilers to represent C++ names. The choices for *style* are currently:
>
> auto
> > Allow GDB to choose a decoding style by inspecting your program.
>
> gnu
> > Decode based on the GNU C++ compiler (g++) encoding algorithm. This is the default.
>
> hp
> > Decode based on the HP ANSI C++ (aCC) encoding algorithm.
>
> lucid
> > Decode based on the Lucid C++ compiler (lcc) encoding algorithm.
>
> arm
> > Decode using the algorithm in the *C++ Annotated Reference Manual*. **Warning:** this setting alone is not sufficient to allow debugging cfront-generated executables. GDB would require further enhancement to permit that.
>
> If you omit *style*, you will see a list of possible formats.

`show demangle-style`
> Display the encoding style currently in use for decoding C++ symbols.

`set print object`
`set print object on`

> When displaying a pointer to an object, identify the *actual* (derived) type of the object rather than the *declared* type, using the virtual function table.

`set print object off`

> Display only the declared type of objects, without reference to the virtual function table. This is the default setting.

`show print object`

> Show whether actual, or declared, object types are displayed.

`set print static-members`
`set print static-members on`

> Print static members when displaying a C++ object. The default is on.

`set print static-members off`

> Do not print static members when displaying a C++ object.

`show print static-members`

> Show whether C++ static members are printed, or not.

`set print vtbl`
`set print vtbl on`

> Pretty print C++ virtual function tables. The default is off. (The `vtbl` commands do not work on programs compiled with the HP ANSI C++ compiler (`aCC`).)

`set print vtbl off`

> Do not pretty print C++ virtual function tables.

`show print vtbl`

> Show whether C++ virtual function tables are pretty printed, or not.

8.8 Value history

Values printed by the `print` command are saved in the GDB *value history*. This allows you to refer to them in other expressions. Values are kept until the symbol table is re-read or discarded (for example with the `file` or `symbol-file` commands). When the symbol table changes, the value history is discarded, since the values may contain pointers back to the types defined in the symbol table.

The values printed are given *history numbers* by which you can refer to them. These are successive integers starting with one. `print` shows you the history number assigned to a value by printing '$*num* = ' before the value; here *num* is the history number.

To refer to any previous value, use '$' followed by the value's history number. The way `print` labels its output is designed to remind you of this. Just $ refers to the most recent value in the history, and $$ refers to the value before that. $$*n* refers to the *n*th value from the end; $$2 is the value just prior to $$, $$1 is equivalent to $$, and $$0 is equivalent to $.

For example, suppose you have just printed a pointer to a structure and want to see the contents of the structure. It suffices to type

```
p *$
```

If you have a chain of structures where the component `next` points to the next one, you can print the contents of the next one with this:

```
p *$.next
```

You can print successive links in the chain by repeating this command— which you can do by just typing (RET).

Note that the history records values, not expressions. If the value of x is 4 and you type these commands:

```
print x
set x=5
```

then the value recorded in the value history by the `print` command remains 4 even though the value of x has changed.

show values

> Print the last ten values in the value history, with their item numbers. This is like 'p $$9' repeated ten times, except that `show values` does not change the history.

show values *n*

> Print ten history values centered on history item number *n*.

show values +

> Print ten history values just after the values last printed. If no more values are available, `show values +` produces no display.

Pressing (RET) to repeat `show values n` has exactly the same effect as 'show values +'.

8.9 Convenience variables

GDB provides *convenience variables* that you can use within GDB to hold on to a value and refer to it later. These variables exist entirely within GDB; they are not part of your program, and setting a convenience variable has no direct effect on further execution of your program. That is why you can use them freely.

Convenience variables are prefixed with '$'. Any name preceded by '$' can be used for a convenience variable, unless it is one of the predefined machine-specific register names (see Section 8.10 [Registers], page 85). (Value history references, in contrast, are *numbers* preceded by '$'. See Section 8.8 [Value history], page 82.)

You can save a value in a convenience variable with an assignment expression, just as you would set a variable in your program. For example:

```
set $foo = *object_ptr
```

would save in `$foo` the value contained in the object pointed to by `object_ptr`.

Using a convenience variable for the first time creates it, but its value is `void` until you assign a new value. You can alter the value with another assignment at any time.

Convenience variables have no fixed types. You can assign a convenience variable any type of value, including structures and arrays, even if that variable already has a value of a different type. The convenience variable, when used as an expression, has the type of its current value.

`show convenience`

> Print a list of convenience variables used so far, and their values. Abbreviated `show conv`.

One of the ways to use a convenience variable is as a counter to be incremented or a pointer to be advanced. For example, to print a field from successive elements of an array of structures:

```
set $i = 0
print bar[$i++]->contents
```

Repeat that command by typing (RET).

Some convenience variables are created automatically by GDB and given values likely to be useful.

`$_`

> The variable `$_` is automatically set by the `x` command to the last address examined (see Section 8.5 [Examining memory], page 74). Other commands which provide a default address for `x` to examine also set `$_` to that address; these commands include `info line` and `info breakpoint`. The type of `$_` is `void *` except when set by the `x` command, in which case it is a pointer to the type of `$__`.

`$__`

> The variable `$__` is automatically set by the `x` command to the value found in the last address examined. Its type is chosen to match the format in which the data was printed.

`$_exitcode`

> The variable `$_exitcode` is automatically set to the exit code when the program being debugged terminates.

On HP-UX systems, if you refer to a function or variable name that begins with a dollar sign, GDB searches for a user or system name first, before it searches for a convenience variable.

8.10 Registers

You can refer to machine register contents, in expressions, as variables with names starting with '$'. The names of registers are different for each machine; use `info registers` to see the names used on your machine.

`info registers`
> Print the names and values of all registers except floating-point registers (in the selected stack frame).

`info all-registers`
> Print the names and values of all registers, including floating-point registers.

`info registers` *regname* ...
> Print the *relativized* value of each specified register *regname*. As discussed in detail below, register values are normally relative to the selected stack frame. *regname* may be any register name valid on the machine you are using, with or without the initial '$'.

GDB has four "standard" register names that are available (in expressions) on most machines—whenever they do not conflict with an architecture's canonical mnemonics for registers. The register names `$pc` and `$sp` are used for the program counter register and the stack pointer. `$fp` is used for a register that contains a pointer to the current stack frame, and `$ps` is used for a register that contains the processor status. For example, you could print the program counter in hex with

    p/x $pc

or print the instruction to be executed next with

    x/i $pc

or add four to the stack pointer[2] with

    set $sp += 4

Whenever possible, these four standard register names are available on your machine even though the machine has different canonical mnemonics, so long as there is no conflict. The `info registers` command shows the canonical names. For example, on the SPARC, `info registers` displays the processor status register as `$psr` but you can also refer to it as `$ps`; and on x86-based machines `$ps` is an alias for the EFLAGS register.

GDB always considers the contents of an ordinary register as an integer when the register is examined in this way. Some machines have special registers which can hold nothing but floating point; these registers are considered

---

[2] This is a way of removing one word from the stack, on machines where stacks grow downward in memory (most machines, nowadays). This assumes that the innermost stack frame is selected; setting `$sp` is not allowed when other stack frames are selected. To pop entire frames off the stack, regardless of machine architecture, use `return`; see Section 12.4 [Returning from a function], page 132.

to have floating point values. There is no way to refer to the contents of
an ordinary register as floating point value (although you can *print* it as a
floating point value with 'print/f $*regname*').

Some registers have distinct "raw" and "virtual" data formats. This
means that the data format in which the register contents are saved by the
operating system is not the same one that your program normally sees. For
example, the registers of the 68881 floating point coprocessor are always
saved in "extended" (raw) format, but all C programs expect to work with
"double" (virtual) format. In such cases, GDB normally works with the
virtual format only (the format that makes sense for your program), but the
`info registers` command prints the data in both formats.

Normally, register values are relative to the selected stack frame (see
Section 6.3 [Selecting a frame], page 59). This means that you get the value
that the register would contain if all stack frames farther in were exited and
their saved registers restored. In order to see the true contents of hardware
registers, you must select the innermost frame (with 'frame 0').

However, GDB must deduce where registers are saved, from the machine
code generated by your compiler. If some registers are not saved, or if GDB
is unable to locate the saved registers, the selected stack frame makes no
difference.

8.11 Floating point hardware

Depending on the configuration, GDB may be able to give you more
information about the status of the floating point hardware.

info float

> Display hardware-dependent information about the floating
> point unit. The exact contents and layout vary depending on
> the floating point chip. Currently, 'info float' is supported
> on the ARM and x86 machines.

8.12 Memory Region Attributes

Memory region attributes allow you to describe special handling required
by regions of your target's memory. GDB uses attributes to determine
whether to allow certain types of memory accesses; whether to use specific
width accesses; and whether to cache target memory.

Defined memory regions can be individually enabled and disabled. When
a memory region is disabled, GDB uses the default attributes when accessing
memory in that region. Similarly, if no memory regions have been defined,
GDB uses the default attributes when accessing all memory.

When a memory region is defined, it is given a number to identify it; to
enable, disable, or remove a memory region, you specify that number.

`mem` *address1 address1 attributes*...

  Define memory region bounded by *address1* and *address2* with
  attributes *attributes*....

`delete mem` *nums*...

  Remove memory region numbers *nums*.

`disable mem` *nums*...

  Disable memory region numbers *nums*. A disabled memory region is not forgotten. It may be enabled again later.

`enable mem` *nums*...

  Enable memory region numbers *nums*.

`info mem` Print a table of all defined memory regions, with the following
  columns for each region.

  Memory Region Number
  Enabled or Disabled.
    Enabled memory regions are marked with 'y'. Dis-
    abled memory regions are marked with 'n'.

  Lo Address

    The address defining the inclusive lower bound of
    the memory region.

  Hi Address

    The address defining the exclusive upper bound of
    the memory region.

  Attributes The list of attributes set for this memory region.

8.12.1 Attributes

8.12.1.1 Memory Access Mode

The access mode attributes set whether GDB may make read or write
accesses to a memory region.

While these attributes prevent GDB from performing invalid memory
accesses, they do nothing to prevent the target system, I/O DMA, etc. from
accessing memory.

`ro`   Memory is read only.

`wo`   Memory is write only.

`rw`   Memory is read/write (default).

8.12.1.2 Memory Access Size

The acccess size attributes tells GDB to use specific sized accesses in the memory region. Often memory mapped device registers require specific sized accesses. If no access size attribute is specified, GDB may use accesses of any size.

8   Use 8 bit memory accesses.

16   Use 16 bit memory accesses.

32   Use 32 bit memory accesses.

64   Use 64 bit memory accesses.

8.12.1.3 Data Cache

The data cache attributes set whether GDB will cache target memory. While this generally improves performance by reducing debug protocol overhead, it can lead to incorrect results because GDB does not know about volatile variables or memory mapped device registers.

cache   Enable GDB to cache target memory.

nocache (default)
             Disable GDB from caching target memory.

9 Tracepoints

In some applications, it is not feasible for the debugger to interrupt the program's execution long enough for the developer to learn anything helpful about its behavior. If the program's correctness depends on its real-time behavior, delays introduced by a debugger might cause the program to change its behavior drastically, or perhaps fail, even when the code itself is correct. It is useful to be able to observe the program's behavior without interrupting it.

Using GDB's `trace` and `collect` commands, you can specify locations in the program, called *tracepoints*, and arbitrary expressions to evaluate when those tracepoints are reached. Later, using the `tfind` command, you can examine the values those expressions had when the program hit the tracepoints. The expressions may also denote objects in memory—structures or arrays, for example—whose values GDB should record; while visiting a particular tracepoint, you may inspect those objects as if they were in memory at that moment. However, because GDB records these values without interacting with you, it can do so quickly and unobtrusively, hopefully not disturbing the program's behavior.

The tracepoint facility is currently available only for remote targets. See Chapter 14 [Targets], page 143. In addition, your remote target must know how to collect trace data. This functionality is implemented in the remote stub; however, none of the stubs distributed with GDB support tracepoints as of this writing.

This chapter describes the tracepoint commands and features.

9.1 Commands to Set Tracepoints

Before running such a *trace experiment*, an arbitrary number of tracepoints can be set. Like a breakpoint (see Section 5.1.1 [Set Breaks], page 36), a tracepoint has a number assigned to it by GDB. Like with breakpoints, tracepoint numbers are successive integers starting from one. Many of the commands associated with tracepoints take the tracepoint number as their argument, to identify which tracepoint to work on.

For each tracepoint, you can specify, in advance, some arbitrary set of data that you want the target to collect in the trace buffer when it hits that tracepoint. The collected data can include registers, local variables, or global data. Later, you can use GDB commands to examine the values these data had at the time the tracepoint was hit.

This section describes commands to set tracepoints and associated conditions and actions.

9.1.1 Create and Delete Tracepoints

trace   The trace command is very similar to the break command. Its
                 argument can be a source line, a function name, or an address
                 in the target program. See Section 5.1.1 [Set Breaks], page 36.
                 The trace command defines a tracepoint, which is a point in
                 the target program where the debugger will briefly stop, collect
                 some data, and then allow the program to continue. Setting a
                 tracepoint or changing its commands doesn't take effect until the
                 next tstart command; thus, you cannot change the tracepoint
                 attributes once a trace experiment is running.

                 Here are some examples of using the trace command:

                      (gdb) trace foo.c:121   // a source file and line number

                      (gdb) trace +2   // 2 lines forward

                      (gdb) trace my_function   // first source line of function

                      (gdb) trace *my_function // EXACT start address of function

                      (gdb) trace *0x2117c4   // an address

                 You can abbreviate trace as tr.

                 The convenience variable $tpnum records the tracepoint number
                 of the most recently set tracepoint.

delete tracepoint [num]
                 Permanently delete one or more tracepoints. With no argument,
                 the default is to delete all tracepoints.

                 Examples:

                      (gdb) delete trace 1 2 3 // remove three tracepoints

                      (gdb) delete trace   // remove all tracepoints

                 You can abbreviate this command as del tr.

9.1.2 Enable and Disable Tracepoints

disable tracepoint [num]
                 Disable tracepoint num, or all tracepoints if no argument num is
                 given. A disabled tracepoint will have no effect during the next
                 trace experiment, but it is not forgotten. You can re-enable a
                 disabled tracepoint using the enable tracepoint command.

enable tracepoint [num]
                 Enable tracepoint num, or all tracepoints. The enabled trace-
                 points will become effective the next time a trace experiment is
                 run.

9.1.3 Tracepoint Passcounts

passcount [n [num]]

Set the *passcount* of a tracepoint. The passcount is a way to automatically stop a trace experiment. If a tracepoint's passcount is n, then the trace experiment will be automatically stopped on the n'th time that tracepoint is hit. If the tracepoint number *num* is not specified, the `passcount` command sets the passcount of the most recently defined tracepoint. If no passcount is given, the trace experiment will run until stopped explicitly by the user.

Examples:

```
(gdb) passcount 5 2 // Stop on the 5th execution of
                    // tracepoint 2

(gdb) passcount 12  // Stop on the 12th execution of the
                    // most recently defined tracepoint.
(gdb) trace foo
(gdb) pass 3
(gdb) trace bar
(gdb) pass 2
(gdb) trace baz
(gdb) pass 1        // Stop tracing when foo has been
                    // executed 3 times OR when bar has
                    // been executed 2 times
                    // OR when baz has been executed 1 time.
```

9.1.4 Tracepoint Action Lists

actions [num]

This command will prompt for a list of actions to be taken when the tracepoint is hit. If the tracepoint number *num* is not specified, this command sets the actions for the one that was most recently defined (so that you can define a tracepoint and then say `actions` without bothering about its number). You specify the actions themselves on the following lines, one action at a time, and terminate the actions list with a line containing just `end`. So far, the only defined actions are `collect` and `while-stepping`.

To remove all actions from a tracepoint, type 'actions *num*' and follow it immediately with 'end'.

```
(gdb) collect data // collect some data

(gdb) while-stepping 5 // single-step 5 times, collect data
```

```
(gdb) end              // signals the end of actions.
```

In the following example, the action list begins with `collect` commands indicating the things to be collected when the tracepoint is hit. Then, in order to single-step and collect additional data following the tracepoint, a `while-stepping` command is used, followed by the list of things to be collected while stepping. The `while-stepping` command is terminated by its own separate `end` command. Lastly, the action list is terminated by an `end` command.

```
(gdb) trace foo
(gdb) actions
Enter actions for tracepoint 1, one per line:
> collect bar,baz
> collect $regs
> while-stepping 12
  > collect $fp, $sp
  > end
end
```

`collect` *expr1*, *expr2*, ...

Collect values of the given expressions when the tracepoint is hit. This command accepts a comma-separated list of any valid expressions. In addition to global, static, or local variables, the following special arguments are supported:

`$regs`   collect all registers

`$args`   collect all function arguments

`$locals`   collect all local variables.

You can give several consecutive `collect` commands, each one with a single argument, or one `collect` command with several arguments separated by commas: the effect is the same.

The command `info scope` (see Chapter 11 [Symbols], page 123) is particularly useful for figuring out what data to collect.

`while-stepping` *n*

Perform *n* single-step traces after the tracepoint, collecting new data at each step. The `while-stepping` command is followed by the list of what to collect while stepping (followed by its own `end` command):

```
> while-stepping 12
  > collect $regs, myglobal
  > end
>
```

You may abbreviate `while-stepping` as `ws` or `stepping`.

9.1.5 Listing Tracepoints

info tracepoints [*num*]

Display information about the tracepoint *num*. If you don't specify a tracepoint number, displays information about all the tracepoints defined so far. For each tracepoint, the following information is shown:

- its number
- whether it is enabled or disabled
- its address
- its passcount as given by the **passcount** *n* command
- its step count as given by the **while-stepping** *n* command
- where in the source files is the tracepoint set
- its action list as given by the **actions** command

```
(gdb) info trace
Num Enb Address     PassC StepC What
1   y   0x002117c4 0     0     <gdb_asm>
2   y   0x0020dc64 0     0     in g_test at g_test.c:1375
3   y   0x0020b1f4 0     0     in get_data at ../foo.c:41
(gdb)
```

This command can be abbreviated **info tp**.

9.1.6 Starting and Stopping Trace Experiment

tstart   This command takes no arguments. It starts the trace experiment, and begins collecting data. This has the side effect of discarding all the data collected in the trace buffer during the previous trace experiment.

tstop   This command takes no arguments. It ends the trace experiment, and stops collecting data.

Note: a trace experiment and data collection may stop automatically if any tracepoint's passcount is reached (see Section 9.1.3 [Tracepoint Passcounts], page 91), or if the trace buffer becomes full.

tstatus   This command displays the status of the current trace data collection.

Here is an example of the commands we described so far:

```
(gdb) trace gdb_c_test
(gdb) actions
Enter actions for tracepoint #1, one per line.
> collect $regs,$locals,$args
> while-stepping 11
```

```
  > collect $regs
  > end
> end
(gdb) tstart
[time passes ...]
(gdb) tstop
```

9.2 Using the collected data

After the tracepoint experiment ends, you use GDB commands for examining the trace data. The basic idea is that each tracepoint collects a trace *snapshot* every time it is hit and another snapshot every time it single-steps. All these snapshots are consecutively numbered from zero and go into a buffer, and you can examine them later. The way you examine them is to *focus* on a specific trace snapshot. When the remote stub is focused on a trace snapshot, it will respond to all GDB requests for memory and registers by reading from the buffer which belongs to that snapshot, rather than from *real* memory or registers of the program being debugged. This means that **all** GDB commands (`print`, `info registers`, `backtrace`, etc.) will behave as if we were currently debugging the program state as it was when the tracepoint occurred. Any requests for data that are not in the buffer will fail.

9.2.1 tfind *n*

The basic command for selecting a trace snapshot from the buffer is `tfind` *n*, which finds trace snapshot number *n*, counting from zero. If no argument *n* is given, the next snapshot is selected.

Here are the various forms of using the `tfind` command.

tfind start
> Find the first snapshot in the buffer. This is a synonym for `tfind 0` (since 0 is the number of the first snapshot).

tfind none
> Stop debugging trace snapshots, resume *live* debugging.

tfind end   Same as 'tfind none'.

tfind   No argument means find the next trace snapshot.

tfind -   Find the previous trace snapshot before the current one. This permits retracing earlier steps.

tfind tracepoint *num*
> Find the next snapshot associated with tracepoint *num*. Search proceeds forward from the last examined trace snapshot. If no argument *num* is given, it means find the next snapshot collected for the same tracepoint as the current snapshot.

tfind pc *addr*
> Find the next snapshot associated with the value *addr* of the program counter. Search proceeds forward from the last examined trace snapshot. If no argument *addr* is given, it means find the next snapshot with the same value of PC as the current snapshot.

tfind outside *addr1*, *addr2*
> Find the next snapshot whose PC is outside the given range of addresses.

tfind range *addr1*, *addr2*
> Find the next snapshot whose PC is between *addr1* and *addr2*.

tfind line [*file*:]*n*
> Find the next snapshot associated with the source line *n*. If the optional argument *file* is given, refer to line *n* in that source file. Search proceeds forward from the last examined trace snapshot. If no argument *n* is given, it means find the next line other than the one currently being examined; thus saying tfind line repeatedly can appear to have the same effect as stepping from line to line in a *live* debugging session.

The default arguments for the tfind commands are specifically designed to make it easy to scan through the trace buffer. For instance, tfind with no argument selects the next trace snapshot, and tfind - with no argument selects the previous trace snapshot. So, by giving one tfind command, and then simply hitting (RET) repeatedly you can examine all the trace snapshots in order. Or, by saying tfind - and then hitting (RET) repeatedly you can examine the snapshots in reverse order. The tfind line command with no argument selects the snapshot for the next source line executed. The tfind pc command with no argument selects the next snapshot with the same program counter (PC) as the current frame. The tfind tracepoint command with no argument selects the next trace snapshot collected by the same tracepoint as the current one.

In addition to letting you scan through the trace buffer manually, these commands make it easy to construct GDB scripts that scan through the trace buffer and print out whatever collected data you are interested in. Thus, if we want to examine the PC, FP, and SP registers from each trace frame in the buffer, we can say this:

```
(gdb) tfind start
(gdb) while ($trace_frame != -1)
> printf "Frame %d, PC = %08X, SP = %08X, FP = %08X\n", \
        $trace_frame, $pc, $sp, $fp
> tfind
> end

Frame 0, PC = 0020DC64, SP = 0030BF3C, FP = 0030BF44
```

```
Frame 1, PC = 0020DC6C, SP = 0030BF38, FP = 0030BF44
Frame 2, PC = 0020DC70, SP = 0030BF34, FP = 0030BF44
Frame 3, PC = 0020DC74, SP = 0030BF30, FP = 0030BF44
Frame 4, PC = 0020DC78, SP = 0030BF2C, FP = 0030BF44
Frame 5, PC = 0020DC7C, SP = 0030BF28, FP = 0030BF44
Frame 6, PC = 0020DC80, SP = 0030BF24, FP = 0030BF44
Frame 7, PC = 0020DC84, SP = 0030BF20, FP = 0030BF44
Frame 8, PC = 0020DC88, SP = 0030BF1C, FP = 0030BF44
Frame 9, PC = 0020DC8E, SP = 0030BF18, FP = 0030BF44
Frame 10, PC = 00203F6C, SP = 0030BE3C, FP = 0030BF14
```

Or, if we want to examine the variable X at each source line in the buffer:

```
(gdb) tfind start
(gdb) while ($trace_frame != -1)
> printf "Frame %d, X == %d\n", $trace_frame, X
> tfind line
> end

Frame 0, X = 1
Frame 7, X = 2
Frame 13, X = 255
```

9.2.2 tdump

This command takes no arguments. It prints all the data collected at the current trace snapshot.

```
(gdb) trace 444
(gdb) actions
Enter actions for tracepoint #2, one per line:
> collect $regs, $locals, $args, gdb_long_test
> end

(gdb) tstart

(gdb) tfind line 444
#0  gdb_test (p1=0x11, p2=0x22, p3=0x33, p4=0x44, p5=0x55, p6=0x66)
at gdb_test.c:444
444          printp( "%s: arguments = 0x%X 0x%X 0x%X 0x%X 0x%X 0x%X\n", )

(gdb) tdump
Data collected at tracepoint 2, trace frame 1:
d0            0xc4aa0085      -995491707
d1            0x18            24
d2            0x80            128
d3            0x33            51
```

```
      d4              0x71aea3d        119204413
      d5              0x22      34
      d6              0xe0      224
      d7              0x380035 3670069
      a0              0x19e24a 1696330
      a1              0x3000668        50333288
      a2              0x100     256
      a3              0x322000 3284992
      a4              0x3000698        50333336
      a5              0x1ad3cc 1758156
      fp              0x30bf3c 0x30bf3c
      sp              0x30bf34 0x30bf34
      ps              0x0       0
      pc              0x20b2c8 0x20b2c8
      fpcontrol       0x0       0
      fpstatus        0x0       0
      fpiaddr         0x0       0
      p = 0x20e5b4 "gdb-test"
      p1 = (void *) 0x11
      p2 = (void *) 0x22
      p3 = (void *) 0x33
      p4 = (void *) 0x44
      p5 = (void *) 0x55
      p6 = (void *) 0x66
      gdb_long_test = 17 '\021'

      (gdb)
```

9.2.3 `save-tracepoints` *filename*

This command saves all current tracepoint definitions together with their
actions and passcounts, into a file 'filename' suitable for use in a later debugging session. To read the saved tracepoint definitions, use the `source`
command (see Section 17.3 [Command Files], page 201).

9.3 Convenience Variables for Tracepoints

`(int) $trace_frame`

> The current trace snapshot (a.k.a. *frame*) number, or -1 if no
> snapshot is selected.

`(int) $tracepoint`

> The tracepoint for the current trace snapshot.

`(int) $trace_line`

> The line number for the current trace snapshot.

`(char [])` `$trace_file`
> The source file for the current trace snapshot.

`(char [])` `$trace_func`
> The name of the function containing `$tracepoint`.

Note: `$trace_file` is not suitable for use in `printf`, use output instead.

Here's a simple example of using these convenience variables for stepping through all the trace snapshots and printing some of their data.

```
(gdb) tfind start

(gdb) while $trace_frame != -1
> output $trace_file
> printf ", line %d (tracepoint #%d)\n", $trace_line, $tracepoint
> tfind
> end
```

10 Using GDB with Different Languages

Although programming languages generally have common aspects, they are rarely expressed in the same manner. For instance, in ANSI C, dereferencing a pointer p is accomplished by *p, but in Modula-2, it is accomplished by p^. Values can also be represented (and displayed) differently. Hex numbers in C appear as '0x1ae', while in Modula-2 they appear as '1AEH'.

Language-specific information is built into GDB for some languages, allowing you to express operations like the above in your program's native language, and allowing GDB to output values in a manner consistent with the syntax of your program's native language. The language you use to build expressions is called the *working language*.

10.1 Switching between source languages

There are two ways to control the working language—either have GDB set it automatically, or select it manually yourself. You can use the **set language** command for either purpose. On startup, GDB defaults to setting the language automatically. The working language is used to determine how expressions you type are interpreted, how values are printed, etc.

In addition to the working language, every source file that GDB knows about has its own working language. For some object file formats, the compiler might indicate which language a particular source file is in. However, most of the time GDB infers the language from the name of the file. The language of a source file controls whether C++ names are demangled—this way **backtrace** can show each frame appropriately for its own language. There is no way to set the language of a source file from within GDB, but you can set the language associated with a filename extension. See Section 10.2 [Displaying the language], page 101.

This is most commonly a problem when you use a program, such as **cfront** or **f2c**, that generates C but is written in another language. In that case, make the program use **#line** directives in its C output; that way GDB will know the correct language of the source code of the original program, and will display that source code, not the generated C code.

10.1.1 List of filename extensions and languages

If a source file name ends in one of the following extensions, then GDB infers that its language is the one indicated.

'.c'   C source file

'.c'
'.cc'
'.cp'
'.cpp'
'.cxx'
'.c++'   C++ source file

'.f'
'.F'   Fortran source file

'.ch'
'.c186'
'.c286'   CHILL source file

'.mod'   Modula-2 source file

'.s'
'.S'   Assembler source file. This actually behaves almost like C, but
                  GDB does not skip over function prologues when stepping.

In addition, you may set the language associated with a filename extension. See Section 10.2 [Displaying the language], page 101.

10.1.2 Setting the working language

If you allow GDB to set the language automatically, expressions are interpreted the same way in your debugging session and your program.

If you wish, you may set the language manually. To do this, issue the
command 'set language *lang*', where *lang* is the name of a language, such
as c or modula-2. For a list of the supported languages, type 'set language'.

Setting the language manually prevents GDB from updating the working
language automatically. This can lead to confusion if you try to debug a
program when the working language is not the same as the source language,
when an expression is acceptable to both languages—but means different
things. For instance, if the current source file were written in C, and GDB
was parsing Modula-2, a command such as:

    print a = b + c

might not have the effect you intended. In C, this means to add b and c
and place the result in a. The result printed would be the value of a. In
Modula-2, this means to compare a to the result of b+c, yielding a BOOLEAN
value.

10.1.3 Having GDB infer the source language

To have GDB set the working language automatically, use 'set language
local' or 'set language auto'. GDB then infers the working language.
That is, when your program stops in a frame (usually by encountering a
breakpoint), GDB sets the working language to the language recorded for

the function in that frame. If the language for a frame is unknown (that is, if the function or block corresponding to the frame was defined in a source file that does not have a recognized extension), the current working language is not changed, and GDB issues a warning.

This may not seem necessary for most programs, which are written entirely in one source language. However, program modules and libraries written in one source language can be used by a main program written in a different source language. Using 'set language auto' in this case frees you from having to set the working language manually.

10.2 Displaying the language

The following commands help you find out which language is the working language, and also what language source files were written in.

show language

> Display the current working language. This is the language you can use with commands such as print to build and compute expressions that may involve variables in your program.

info frame

> Display the source language for this frame. This language becomes the working language if you use an identifier from this frame. See Section 6.4 [Information about a frame], page 60, to identify the other information listed here.

info source

> Display the source language of this source file. See Chapter 11 [Examining the Symbol Table], page 123, to identify the other information listed here.

In unusual circumstances, you may have source files with extensions not in the standard list. You can then set the extension associated with a language explicitly:

set extension-language .ext *language*

> Set source files with extension .*ext* to be assumed to be in the source language *language*.

info extensions

> List all the filename extensions and the associated languages.

10.3 Type and range checking

> *Warning:* In this release, the GDB commands for type and range checking are included, but they do not yet have any effect. This section documents the intended facilities.

Some languages are designed to guard you against making seemingly common errors through a series of compile- and run-time checks. These include checking the type of arguments to functions and operators, and making sure mathematical overflows are caught at run time. Checks such as these help to ensure a program's correctness once it has been compiled by eliminating type mismatches, and providing active checks for range errors when your program is running.

GDB can check for conditions like the above if you wish. Although GDB does not check the statements in your program, it can check expressions entered directly into GDB for evaluation via the `print` command, for example. As with the working language, GDB can also decide whether or not to check automatically based on your program's source language. See Section 10.4 [Supported languages], page 104, for the default settings of supported languages.

10.3.1 An overview of type checking

Some languages, such as Modula-2, are strongly typed, meaning that the arguments to operators and functions have to be of the correct type, otherwise an error occurs. These checks prevent type mismatch errors from ever causing any run-time problems. For example,

1 + 2 $\Rightarrow$ 3

but

error   1 + 2.3

The second example fails because the `CARDINAL` 1 is not type-compatible with the `REAL` 2.3.

For the expressions you use in GDB commands, you can tell the GDB type checker to skip checking; to treat any mismatches as errors and abandon the expression; or to only issue warnings when type mismatches occur, but evaluate the expression anyway. When you choose the last of these, GDB evaluates expressions like the second example above, but also issues a warning.

Even if you turn type checking off, there may be other reasons related to type that prevent GDB from evaluating an expression. For instance, GDB does not know how to add an `int` and a `struct foo`. These particular type errors have nothing to do with the language in use, and usually arise from expressions, such as the one described above, which make little sense to evaluate anyway.

Each language defines to what degree it is strict about type. For instance, both Modula-2 and C require the arguments to arithmetical operators to be numbers. In C, enumerated types and pointers can be represented as numbers, so that they are valid arguments to mathematical operators. See Section 10.4 [Supported languages], page 104, for further details on specific languages.

GDB provides some additional commands for controlling the type checker:

set check type auto
> Set type checking on or off based on the current working language. See Section 10.4 [Supported languages], page 104, for the default settings for each language.

set check type on
set check type off
> Set type checking on or off, overriding the default setting for the current working language. Issue a warning if the setting does not match the language default. If any type mismatches occur in evaluating an expression while type checking is on, GDB prints a message and aborts evaluation of the expression.

set check type warn
> Cause the type checker to issue warnings, but to always attempt to evaluate the expression. Evaluating the expression may still be impossible for other reasons. For example, GDB cannot add numbers and structures.

show type Show the current setting of the type checker, and whether or not GDB is setting it automatically.

10.3.2 An overview of range checking

In some languages (such as Modula-2), it is an error to exceed the bounds of a type; this is enforced with run-time checks. Such range checking is meant to ensure program correctness by making sure computations do not overflow, or indices on an array element access do not exceed the bounds of the array.

For expressions you use in GDB commands, you can tell GDB to treat range errors in one of three ways: ignore them, always treat them as errors and abandon the expression, or issue warnings but evaluate the expression anyway.

A range error can result from numerical overflow, from exceeding an array index bound, or when you type a constant that is not a member of any type. Some languages, however, do not treat overflows as an error. In many implementations of C, mathematical overflow causes the result to "wrap around" to lower values—for example, if m is the largest integer value, and s is the smallest, then

$$m + 1 \Rightarrow s$$

This, too, is specific to individual languages, and in some cases specific to individual compilers or machines. See Section 10.4 [Supported languages], page 104, for further details on specific languages.

GDB provides some additional commands for controlling the range checker:

set check range auto

> Set range checking on or off based on the current working language. See Section 10.4 [Supported languages], page 104, for the default settings for each language.

set check range on
set check range off

> Set range checking on or off, overriding the default setting for the current working language. A warning is issued if the setting does not match the language default. If a range error occurs and range checking is on, then a message is printed and evaluation of the expression is aborted.

set check range warn

> Output messages when the GDB range checker detects a range error, but attempt to evaluate the expression anyway. Evaluating the expression may still be impossible for other reasons, such as accessing memory that the process does not own (a typical example from many Unix systems).

show range

> Show the current setting of the range checker, and whether or not it is being set automatically by GDB.

10.4 Supported languages

GDB supports C, C++, Fortran, Java, Chill, assembly, and Modula-2. Some GDB features may be used in expressions regardless of the language you use: the GDB @ and :: operators, and the '{type}addr' construct (see Section 8.1 [Expressions], page 69) can be used with the constructs of any supported language.

The following sections detail to what degree each source language is supported by GDB. These sections are not meant to be language tutorials or references, but serve only as a reference guide to what the GDB expression parser accepts, and what input and output formats should look like for different languages. There are many good books written on each of these languages; please look to these for a language reference or tutorial.

10.4.1 C and C++

Since C and C++ are so closely related, many features of GDB apply to both languages. Whenever this is the case, we discuss those languages together.

The C++ debugging facilities are jointly implemented by the C++ compiler and GDB. Therefore, to debug your C++ code effectively, you must compile your C++ programs with a supported C++ compiler, such as GNU g++, or the HP ANSI C++ compiler (aCC).

For best results when using GNU C++, use the stabs debugging format. You can select that format explicitly with the g++ command-line options '-gstabs' or '-gstabs+'. See section "Options for Debugging Your Program or GNU CC" in *Using GNU CC*, for more information.

10.4.1.1 C and C++ operators

Operators must be defined on values of specific types. For instance, + is defined on numbers, but not on structures. Operators are often defined on groups of types.

For the purposes of C and C++, the following definitions hold:

- *Integral types* include int with any of its storage-class specifiers; char; enum; and, for C++, bool.
- *Floating-point types* include float, double, and long double (if supported by the target platform).
- *Pointer types* include all types defined as (*type* *).
- *Scalar types* include all of the above.

The following operators are supported. They are listed here in order of increasing precedence:

,   The comma or sequencing operator. Expressions in a comma-separated list are evaluated from left to right, with the result of the entire expression being the last expression evaluated.

=   Assignment. The value of an assignment expression is the value assigned. Defined on scalar types.

op=   Used in an expression of the form *a op*= *b*, and translated to *a* = *a op b*. *op*= and = have the same precedence. *op* is any one of the operators |, ^, &, <<, >>, +, -, *, /, %.

?:   The ternary operator. *a* ? *b* : *c* can be thought of as: if *a* then *b* else *c*. *a* should be of an integral type.

|| Logical OR. Defined on integral types.

&&   Logical AND. Defined on integral types.

| Bitwise OR. Defined on integral types.

^   Bitwise exclusive-OR. Defined on integral types.

&   Bitwise AND. Defined on integral types.

==, !=   Equality and inequality. Defined on scalar types. The value of these expressions is 0 for false and non-zero for true.

<, >, <=, >=
      Less than, greater than, less than or equal, greater than or equal. Defined on scalar types. The value of these expressions is 0 for false and non-zero for true.

`<<, >>`   left shift, and right shift. Defined on integral types.

`@`   The GDB "artificial array" operator (see Section 8.1 [Expressions], page 69).

`+, -`   Addition and subtraction. Defined on integral types, floating-point types and pointer types.

`*, /, %`   Multiplication, division, and modulus. Multiplication and division are defined on integral and floating-point types. Modulus is defined on integral types.

`++, --`   Increment and decrement. When appearing before a variable, the operation is performed before the variable is used in an expression; when appearing after it, the variable's value is used before the operation takes place.

`*`   Pointer dereferencing. Defined on pointer types. Same precedence as `++`.

`&`   Address operator. Defined on variables. Same precedence as `++`.

   For debugging C++, GDB implements a use of '`&`' beyond what is allowed in the C++ language itself: you can use '`&(&ref)`' (or, if you prefer, simply '`&&ref`') to examine the address where a C++ reference variable (declared with '`&ref`') is stored.

`-`   Negative. Defined on integral and floating-point types. Same precedence as `++`.

`!`   Logical negation. Defined on integral types. Same precedence as `++`.

`~`   Bitwise complement operator. Defined on integral types. Same precedence as `++`.

`., ->`   Structure member, and pointer-to-structure member. For convenience, GDB regards the two as equivalent, choosing whether to dereference a pointer based on the stored type information. Defined on **struct** and **union** data.

`.*, ->*`   Dereferences of pointers to members.

`[]`   Array indexing. `a[i]` is defined as `*(a+i)`. Same precedence as `->`.

`()`   Function parameter list. Same precedence as `->`.

`::`   C++ scope resolution operator. Defined on **struct**, **union**, and **class** types.

`::`   Doubled colons also represent the GDB scope operator (see Section 8.1 [Expressions], page 69). Same precedence as `::`, above.

   If an operator is redefined in the user code, GDB usually attempts to invoke the redefined version instead of using the operator's predefined meaning.

10.4.1.2 C and C++ constants

GDB allows you to express the constants of C and C++ in the following ways:

- Integer constants are a sequence of digits. Octal constants are specified by a leading '0' (i.e. zero), and hexadecimal constants by a leading '0x' or '0X'. Constants may also end with a letter 'l', specifying that the constant should be treated as a **long** value.

- Floating point constants are a sequence of digits, followed by a decimal point, followed by a sequence of digits, and optionally followed by an exponent. An exponent is of the form: 'e[[+]|-]nnn', where nnn is another sequence of digits. The '+' is optional for positive exponents. A floating-point constant may also end with a letter 'f' or 'F', specifying that the constant should be treated as being of the **float** (as opposed to the default **double**) type; or with a letter 'l' or 'L', which specifies a **long double** constant.

- Enumerated constants consist of enumerated identifiers, or their integral equivalents.

- Character constants are a single character surrounded by single quotes ('), or a number—the ordinal value of the corresponding character (usually its ASCII value). Within quotes, the single character may be represented by a letter or by *escape sequences*, which are of the form '\nnn', where nnn is the octal representation of the character's ordinal value; or of the form '\x', where 'x' is a predefined special character—for example, '\n' for newline.

- String constants are a sequence of character constants surrounded by double quotes ("). Any valid character constant (as described above) may appear. Double quotes within the string must be preceded by a backslash, so for instance '"a\"b'c"' is a string of five characters.

- Pointer constants are an integral value. You can also write pointers to constants using the C operator '&'.

- Array constants are comma-separated lists surrounded by braces '{' and '}'; for example, '{1,2,3}' is a three-element array of integers, '{{1,2}, {3,4}, {5,6}}' is a three-by-two array, and '{&"hi", &"there", &"fred"}' is a three-element array of pointers.

10.4.1.3 C++ expressions

GDB expression handling can interpret most C++ expressions.

Warning: GDB can only debug C++ code if you use the proper compiler. Typically, C++ debugging depends on the use of additional debugging information in the symbol table, and thus requires special support. In particular, if your compiler generates a.out, MIPS ECOFF, RS/6000 XCOFF, or ELF with stabs extensions to the symbol table, these facilities are all available. (With GNU CC, you can use the '-gstabs' option to request stabs debugging extensions explicitly.) Where the object code format is standard COFF or DWARF in ELF, on the other hand, most of the C++ support in GDB does *not* work.

1. Member function calls are allowed; you can use expressions like

   ```
   count = aml->GetOriginal(x, y)
   ```

2. While a member function is active (in the selected stack frame), your expressions have the same namespace available as the member function; that is, GDB allows implicit references to the class instance pointer `this` following the same rules as C++.

3. You can call overloaded functions; GDB resolves the function call to the right definition, with some restrictions. GDB does not perform overload resolution involving user-defined type conversions, calls to constructors, or instantiations of templates that do not exist in the program. It also cannot handle ellipsis argument lists or default arguments.

   It does perform integral conversions and promotions, floating-point promotions, arithmetic conversions, pointer conversions, conversions of class objects to base classes, and standard conversions such as those of functions or arrays to pointers; it requires an exact match on the number of function arguments.

   Overload resolution is always performed, unless you have specified `set overload-resolution off`. See Section 10.4.1.7 [GDB features for C++], page 109.

   You must specify `set overload-resolution off` in order to use an explicit function signature to call an overloaded function, as in

   ```
   p 'foo(char,int)'('x', 13)
   ```

   The GDB command-completion facility can simplify this; see Section 3.2 [Command completion], page 17.

4. GDB understands variables declared as C++ references; you can use them in expressions just as you do in C++ source—they are automatically dereferenced.

   In the parameter list shown when GDB displays a frame, the values of reference variables are not displayed (unlike other variables); this avoids clutter, since references are often used for large structures. The *address* of a reference variable is always shown, unless you have specified 'set print address off'.

5. GDB supports the C++ name resolution operator ::—your expressions can use it just as expressions in your program do. Since one scope may be defined in another, you can use :: repeatedly if necessary, for example in an expression like '*scope1*::*scope2*::*name*'. GDB also allows resolving name scope by reference to source files, in both C and C++ debugging (see Section 8.2 [Program variables], page 70).

In addition, when used with HP's C++ compiler, GDB supports calling virtual functions correctly, printing out virtual bases of objects, calling functions in a base subobject, casting objects, and invoking user-defined operators.

10.4.1.4 C and C++ defaults

If you allow GDB to set type and range checking automatically, they both default to `off` whenever the working language changes to C or C++. This happens regardless of whether you or GDB selects the working language.

If you allow GDB to set the language automatically, it recognizes source files whose names end with '.c', '.C', or '.cc', etc, and when GDB enters code compiled from one of these files, it sets the working language to C or C++. See Section 10.1.3 [Having GDB infer the source language], page 100, for further details.

10.4.1.5 C and C++ type and range checks

By default, when GDB parses C or C++ expressions, type checking is not used. However, if you turn type checking on, GDB considers two variables type equivalent if:

- The two variables are structured and have the same structure, union, or enumerated tag.

- The two variables have the same type name, or types that have been declared equivalent through `typedef`.

Range checking, if turned on, is done on mathematical operations. Array indices are not checked, since they are often used to index a pointer that is not itself an array.

10.4.1.6 GDB and C

The `set print union` and `show print union` commands apply to the `union` type. When set to 'on', any `union` that is inside a `struct` or `class` is also printed. Otherwise, it appears as '{...}'.

The `@` operator aids in the debugging of dynamic arrays, formed with pointers and a memory allocation function. See Section 8.1 [Expressions], page 69.

10.4.1.7 GDB features for C++

Some GDB commands are particularly useful with C++, and some are designed specifically for use with C++. Here is a summary:

breakpoint menus

> When you want a breakpoint in a function whose name is overloaded, GDB breakpoint menus help you specify which function definition you want. See Section 5.1.8 [Breakpoint menus], page 49.

rbreak *regex*

> Setting breakpoints using regular expressions is helpful for setting breakpoints on overloaded functions that are not members of any special classes. See Section 5.1.1 [Setting breakpoints], page 36.

catch throw
catch catch

> Debug C++ exception handling using these commands. See Section 5.1.3 [Setting catchpoints], page 42.

ptype *typename*

> Print inheritance relationships as well as other information for type *typename*. See Chapter 11 [Examining the Symbol Table], page 123.

set print demangle
show print demangle
set print asm-demangle
show print asm-demangle

> Control whether C++ symbols display in their source form, both when displaying code as C++ source and when displaying disassemblies. See Section 8.7 [Print settings], page 77.

set print object
show print object

> Choose whether to print derived (actual) or declared types of objects. See Section 8.7 [Print settings], page 77.

set print vtbl
show print vtbl

> Control the format for printing virtual function tables. See Section 8.7 [Print settings], page 77. (The vtbl commands do not work on programs compiled with the HP ANSI C++ compiler (aCC).)

set overload-resolution on

> Enable overload resolution for C++ expression evaluation. The default is on. For overloaded functions, GDB evaluates the arguments and searches for a function whose signature matches the argument types, using the standard C++ conversion rules (see Section 10.4.1.3 [C++ expressions], page 107, for details). If it cannot find a match, it emits a message.

`set overload-resolution off`

> Disable overload resolution for C++ expression evaluation. For overloaded functions that are not class member functions, GDB chooses the first function of the specified name that it finds in the symbol table, whether or not its arguments are of the correct type. For overloaded functions that are class member functions, GDB searches for a function whose signature *exactly* matches the argument types.

Overloaded symbol names

> You can specify a particular definition of an overloaded symbol, using the same notation that is used to declare such symbols in C++: type *symbol*(*types*) rather than just *symbol*. You can also use the GDB command-line word completion facilities to list the available choices, or to finish the type list for you. See Section 3.2 [Command completion], page 17, for details on how to do this.

10.4.2 Modula-2

The extensions made to GDB to support Modula-2 only support output from the GNU Modula-2 compiler (which is currently being developed). Other Modula-2 compilers are not currently supported, and attempting to debug executables produced by them is most likely to give an error as GDB reads in the executable's symbol table.

10.4.2.1 Operators

Operators must be defined on values of specific types. For instance, `+` is defined on numbers, but not on structures. Operators are often defined on groups of types. For the purposes of Modula-2, the following definitions hold:

- *Integral types* consist of `INTEGER`, `CARDINAL`, and their subranges.
- *Character types* consist of `CHAR` and its subranges.
- *Floating-point types* consist of `REAL`.
- *Pointer types* consist of anything declared as `POINTER TO` *type*.
- *Scalar types* consist of all of the above.
- *Set types* consist of `SET` and `BITSET` types.
- *Boolean types* consist of `BOOLEAN`.

The following operators are supported, and appear in order of increasing precedence:

`,` Function argument or array index separator.

`:=` Assignment. The value of *var* `:=` *value* is *value*.

<, >	Less than, greater than on integral, floating-point, or enumerated types.
<=, >=	Less than or equal to, greater than or equal to on integral, floating-point and enumerated types, or set inclusion on set types. Same precedence as **<**.
=, <>, #	Equality and two ways of expressing inequality, valid on scalar types. Same precedence as **<**. In GDB scripts, only **<>** is available for inequality, since **#** conflicts with the script comment character.
IN	Set membership. Defined on set types and the types of their members. Same precedence as **<**.
OR	Boolean disjunction. Defined on boolean types.
AND, &	Boolean conjunction. Defined on boolean types.
@	The GDB "artificial array" operator (see Section 8.1 [Expressions], page 69).
+, -	Addition and subtraction on integral and floating-point types, or union and difference on set types.
*	Multiplication on integral and floating-point types, or set intersection on set types.
/	Division on floating-point types, or symmetric set difference on set types. Same precedence as *****.
DIV, MOD	Integer division and remainder. Defined on integral types. Same precedence as *****.
-	Negative. Defined on **INTEGER** and **REAL** data.
^	Pointer dereferencing. Defined on pointer types.
NOT	Boolean negation. Defined on boolean types. Same precedence as **^**.
.	**RECORD** field selector. Defined on **RECORD** data. Same precedence as **^**.
[]	Array indexing. Defined on **ARRAY** data. Same precedence as **^**.
()	Procedure argument list. Defined on **PROCEDURE** objects. Same precedence as **^**.
::, .	GDB and Modula-2 scope operators.

Warning: Sets and their operations are not yet supported, so GDB treats the use of the operator **IN**, or the use of operators **+, -, *, /, =, , <>, #, <=**, and **>=** on sets as an error.

10.4.2.2 Built-in functions and procedures

Modula-2 also makes available several built-in procedures and functions. In describing these, the following metavariables are used:

a	represents an **ARRAY** variable.
c	represents a **CHAR** constant or variable.
i	represents a variable or constant of integral type.
m	represents an identifier that belongs to a set. Generally used in the same function with the metavariable s. The type of s should be **SET OF** mtype (where mtype is the type of m).
n	represents a variable or constant of integral or floating-point type.
r	represents a variable or constant of floating-point type.
t	represents a type.
v	represents a variable.
x	represents a variable or constant of one of many types. See the explanation of the function for details.

All Modula-2 built-in procedures also return a result, described below.

ABS(n)	Returns the absolute value of n.
CAP(c)	If c is a lower case letter, it returns its upper case equivalent, otherwise it returns its argument.
CHR(i)	Returns the character whose ordinal value is i.
DEC(v)	Decrements the value in the variable v by one. Returns the new value.
DEC(v,i)	Decrements the value in the variable v by i. Returns the new value.
EXCL(m,s)	Removes the element m from the set s. Returns the new set.
FLOAT(i)	Returns the floating point equivalent of the integer i.
HIGH(a)	Returns the index of the last member of a.
INC(v)	Increments the value in the variable v by one. Returns the new value.
INC(v,i)	Increments the value in the variable v by i. Returns the new value.
INCL(m,s)	Adds the element m to the set s if it is not already there. Returns the new set.

MAX(*t*)   Returns the maximum value of the type *t*.

MIN(*t*)   Returns the minimum value of the type *t*.

ODD(*i*)   Returns boolean TRUE if *i* is an odd number.

ORD(*x*)   Returns the ordinal value of its argument. For example, the ordinal value of a character is its ASCII value (on machines supporting the ASCII character set). *x* must be of an ordered type, which include integral, character and enumerated types.

SIZE(*x*)   Returns the size of its argument. *x* can be a variable or a type.

TRUNC(*r*) Returns the integral part of *r*.

VAL(*t*,*i*) Returns the member of the type *t* whose ordinal value is *i*.

Warning: Sets and their operations are not yet supported, so GDB treats the use of procedures INCL and EXCL as an error.

10.4.2.3 Constants

GDB allows you to express the constants of Modula-2 in the following ways:

- Integer constants are simply a sequence of digits. When used in an expression, a constant is interpreted to be type-compatible with the rest of the expression. Hexadecimal integers are specified by a trailing 'H', and octal integers by a trailing 'B'.

- Floating point constants appear as a sequence of digits, followed by a decimal point and another sequence of digits. An optional exponent can then be specified, in the form 'E[+|-]*nnn*', where '[+|-]*nnn*' is the desired exponent. All of the digits of the floating point constant must be valid decimal (base 10) digits.

- Character constants consist of a single character enclosed by a pair of like quotes, either single (') or double ("). They may also be expressed by their ordinal value (their ASCII value, usually) followed by a 'C'.

- String constants consist of a sequence of characters enclosed by a pair of like quotes, either single (') or double ("). Escape sequences in the style of C are also allowed. See Section 10.4.1.2 [C and C++ constants], page 107, for a brief explanation of escape sequences.

- Enumerated constants consist of an enumerated identifier.

- Boolean constants consist of the identifiers TRUE and FALSE.

- Pointer constants consist of integral values only.

- Set constants are not yet supported.

10.4.2.4 Modula-2 defaults

If type and range checking are set automatically by GDB, they both default to **on** whenever the working language changes to Modula-2. This happens regardless of whether you or GDB selected the working language.

If you allow GDB to set the language automatically, then entering code compiled from a file whose name ends with '.mod' sets the working language to Modula-2. See Section 10.1.3 [Having GDB set the language automatically], page 100, for further details.

10.4.2.5 Deviations from standard Modula-2

A few changes have been made to make Modula-2 programs easier to debug. This is done primarily via loosening its type strictness:

- Unlike in standard Modula-2, pointer constants can be formed by integers. This allows you to modify pointer variables during debugging. (In standard Modula-2, the actual address contained in a pointer variable is hidden from you; it can only be modified through direct assignment to another pointer variable or expression that returned a pointer.)

- C escape sequences can be used in strings and characters to represent non-printable characters. GDB prints out strings with these escape sequences embedded. Single non-printable characters are printed using the 'CHR(*nnn*)' format.

- The assignment operator (:=) returns the value of its right-hand argument.

- All built-in procedures both modify *and* return their argument.

10.4.2.6 Modula-2 type and range checks

Warning: in this release, GDB does not yet perform type or range checking.

GDB considers two Modula-2 variables type equivalent if:

- They are of types that have been declared equivalent via a **TYPE** *t1* = *t2* statement

- They have been declared on the same line. (Note: This is true of the GNU Modula-2 compiler, but it may not be true of other compilers.)

As long as type checking is enabled, any attempt to combine variables whose types are not equivalent is an error.

Range checking is done on all mathematical operations, assignment, array index bounds, and all built-in functions and procedures.

10.4.2.7 The scope operators :: and .

There are a few subtle differences between the Modula-2 scope operator
(.) and the GDB scope operator (::). The two have similar syntax:

>   *module* . *id*
>   *scope* :: *id*

where *scope* is the name of a module or a procedure, *module* the name
of a module, and *id* is any declared identifier within your program, except
another module.

Using the :: operator makes GDB search the scope specified by *scope* for
the identifier *id*. If it is not found in the specified scope, then GDB searches
all scopes enclosing the one specified by *scope*.

Using the . operator makes GDB search the current scope for the identifier specified by *id* that was imported from the definition module specified
by *module*. With this operator, it is an error if the identifier *id* was not imported from definition module *module*, or if *id* is not an identifier in *module*.

10.4.2.8 GDB and Modula-2

Some GDB commands have little use when debugging Modula-2 programs. Five subcommands of set print and show print apply specifically
to C and C++: 'vtbl', 'demangle', 'asm-demangle', 'object', and 'union'.
The first four apply to C++, and the last to the C union type, which has no
direct analogue in Modula-2.

The @ operator (see Section 8.1 [Expressions], page 69), while available
with any language, is not useful with Modula-2. Its intent is to aid the
debugging of *dynamic arrays*, which cannot be created in Modula-2 as they
can in C or C++. However, because an address can be specified by an integral
constant, the construct '{*type*}*adrexp*' is still useful.

In GDB scripts, the Modula-2 inequality operator # is interpreted as the
beginning of a comment. Use <> instead.

10.4.3 Chill

The extensions made to GDB to support Chill only support output from
the GNU Chill compiler. Other Chill compilers are not currently supported,
and attempting to debug executables produced by them is most likely to
give an error as GDB reads in the executable's symbol table.

This section covers the Chill related topics and the features of GDB which
support these topics.

10.4.3.1 How modes are displayed

The Chill Datatype- (Mode) support of GDB is directly related with the functionality of the GNU Chill compiler, and therefore deviates slightly from the standard specification of the Chill language. The provided modes are:

Discrete modes:
- *Integer Modes* which are predefined by BYTE, UBYTE, INT, UINT, LONG, ULONG,
- *Boolean Mode* which is predefined by BOOL,
- *Character Mode* which is predefined by CHAR,
- *Set Mode* which is displayed by the keyword SET.

      (gdb) ptype x
      type = SET (karli = 10, susi = 20, fritzi = 100)

  If the type is an unnumbered set the set element values are omitted.
- *Range Mode* which is displayed by

      type = <basemode>(<lower bound> : <upper bound>)

  where <lower bound>, <upper bound> can be of any discrete literal expression (e.g. set element names).

Powerset Mode:
A Powerset Mode is displayed by the keyword POWERSET followed by the member mode of the powerset. The member mode can be any discrete mode.

      (gdb) ptype x
      type = POWERSET SET (egon, hugo, otto)

Reference Modes:
- *Bound Reference Mode* which is displayed by the keyword REF followed by the mode name to which the reference is bound.
- *Free Reference Mode* which is displayed by the keyword PTR.

Procedure mode
The procedure mode is displayed by type = PROC(<parameter list>) <return mode> EXCEPTIONS (<exception list>). The <parameter list> is a list of the parameter modes. <return mode> indicates the mode of the result of the procedure if any. The exceptionlist lists all possible exceptions which can be raised by the procedure.

Synchronization Modes:
- *Event Mode* which is displayed by

      EVENT (<event length>)

  where (<event length>) is optional.
- *Buffer Mode* which is displayed by

```
BUFFER (<buffer length>)<buffer element mode>
```
where (**<buffer length>**) is optional.

Timing Modes:

- *Duration Mode* which is predefined by **DURATION**
- *Absolute Time Mode* which is predefined by **TIME**

Real Modes:

Real Modes are predefined with **REAL** and **LONG_REAL**.

String Modes:

- *Character String Mode* which is displayed by

  ```
  CHARS(<string length>)
  ```

  followed by the keyword **VARYING** if the String Mode is a varying mode
- *Bit String Mode* which is displayed by

  ```
  BOOLS(<string
  length>)
  ```

Array Mode:

The Array Mode is displayed by the keyword **ARRAY(<range>)** followed by the element mode (which may in turn be an array mode).

```
(gdb) ptype x
type = ARRAY (1:42)
          ARRAY (1:20)
              SET (karli = 10, susi = 20, fritzi = 100)
```

Structure Mode

The Structure mode is displayed by the keyword **STRUCT(<field list>)**. The **<field list>** consists of names and modes of fields of the structure. Variant structures have the keyword **CASE <field> OF <variant fields> ESAC** in their field list. Since the current version of the GNU Chill compiler doesn't implement tag processing (no runtime checks of variant fields, and therefore no debugging info), the output always displays all variant fields.

```
(gdb) ptype str
type = STRUCT (
    as x,
    bs x,
    CASE bs OF
    (karli):
        cs a
    (ott):
        ds x
    ESAC
)
```

10.4.3.2 Locations and their accesses

A location in Chill is an object which can contain values.

A value of a location is generally accessed by the (declared) name of the location. The output conforms to the specification of values in Chill programs. How values are specified is the topic of the next section, Section 10.4.3.3 [Values and their Operations], page 119.

The pseudo-location RESULT (or result) can be used to display or change the result of a currently-active procedure:

```
set result := EXPR
```

This does the same as the Chill action RESULT EXPR (which is not available in GDB).

Values of reference mode locations are printed by PTR(<hex value>) in case of a free reference mode, and by (REF <reference mode>) (<hexvalue>) in case of a bound reference. <hex value> represents the address where the reference points to. To access the value of the location referenced by the pointer, use the dereference operator '->'.

Values of procedure mode locations are displayed by

```
{ PROC
(<argument modes> ) <return mode> } <address> <name of procedure
location>
```

<argument modes> is a list of modes according to the parameter specification of the procedure and <address> shows the address of the entry point.

Substructures of string mode-, array mode- or structure mode-values (e.g. array slices, fields of structure locations) are accessed using certain operations which are described in the next section, Section 10.4.3.3 [Values and their Operations], page 119.

A location value may be interpreted as having a different mode using the location conversion. This mode conversion is written as <mode name>(<location>). The user has to consider that the sizes of the modes have to be equal otherwise an error occurs. Furthermore, no range checking of the location against the destination mode is performed, and therefore the result can be quite confusing.

```
(gdb) print int (s(3 up 4)) XXX TO be filled in !! XXX
```

10.4.3.3 Values and their Operations

Values are used to alter locations, to investigate complex structures in more detail or to filter relevant information out of a large amount of data. There are several (mode dependent) operations defined which enable such investigations. These operations are not only applicable to constant values but also to locations, which can become quite useful when debugging complex structures. During parsing the command line (e.g. evaluating an expression) GDB treats location names as the values behind these locations.

This section describes how values have to be specified and which operations are legal to be used with such values.

Literal Values

Literal values are specified in the same manner as in GNU Chill programs. For detailed specification refer to the GNU Chill implementation Manual chapter 1.5.

Tuple Values

A tuple is specified by `<mode name>[<tuple>]`, where `<mode name>` can be omitted if the mode of the tuple is unambiguous. This unambiguity is derived from the context of a evaluated expression. `<tuple>` can be one of the following:

- *Powerset Tuple*
- *Array Tuple*
- *Structure Tuple* Powerset tuples, array tuples and structure tuples are specified in the same manner as in Chill programs refer to z200/88 chpt 5.2.5.

String Element Value

A string element value is specified by

`<string value>(<index>)`

where `<index>` is a integer expression. It delivers a character value which is equivalent to the character indexed by `<index>` in the string.

String Slice Value

A string slice value is specified by `<string value>(<slice spec>)`, where `<slice spec>` can be either a range of integer expressions or specified by `<start expr> up <size>`. `<size>` denotes the number of elements which the slice contains. The delivered value is a string value, which is part of the specified string.

Array Element Values

An array element value is specified by `<array value>(<expr>)` and delivers a array element value of the mode of the specified array.

Array Slice Values

An array slice is specified by `<array value>(<slice spec>)`, where `<slice spec>` can be either a range specified by expressions or by `<start expr> up <size>`. `<size>` denotes the number of arrayelements the slice contains. The delivered value is an array value which is part of the specified array.

Structure Field Values

A structure field value is derived by `<structure value>.<field name>`, where `<field name>` indicates the name of a field specified in the mode definition of the structure. The mode of the delivered value corresponds to this mode definition in the structure definition.

Procedure Call Value

The procedure call value is derived from the return value of the procedure[1].

Values of duration mode locations are represented by `ULONG` literals.

Values of time mode locations appear as

```
TIME(<secs>:<nsecs>)
```

Zero-adic Operator Value

The zero-adic operator value is derived from the instance value for the current active process.

Expression Values

The value delivered by an expression is the result of the evaluation of the specified expression. If there are error conditions (mode incompatibility, etc.) the evaluation of expressions is aborted with a corresponding error message. Expressions may be parenthesised which causes the evaluation of this expression before any other expression which uses the result of the parenthesised expression. The following operators are supported by GDB:

`OR, ORIF, XOR`
`AND, ANDIF`
`NOT`   Logical operators defined over operands of boolean mode.

`=, /=`   Equality and inequality operators defined over all modes.

`>, >=`
`<, <=`   Relational operators defined over predefined modes.

`+, -`
`*, /, MOD, REM`
       Arithmetic operators defined over predefined modes.

`-`   Change sign operator.

`//`   String concatenation operator.

---

[1] If a procedure call is used for instance in an expression, then this procedure is called with all its side effects. This can lead to confusing results if used carelessly.

()	String repetition operator.
->	Referenced location operator which can be used either to take the address of a location (->loc), or to dereference a reference location (loc->).
OR, XOR AND NOT	Powerset and bitstring operators.
>, >= <, <=	Powerset inclusion operators.
IN	Membership operator.

10.4.3.4 Chill type and range checks

GDB considers two Chill variables mode equivalent if the sizes of the two modes are equal. This rule applies recursively to more complex datatypes which means that complex modes are treated equivalent if all element modes (which also can be complex modes like structures, arrays, etc.) have the same size.

Range checking is done on all mathematical operations, assignment, array index bounds and all built in procedures.

Strong type checks are forced using the GDB command set check strong. This enforces strong type and range checks on all operations where Chill constructs are used (expressions, built in functions, etc.) in respect to the semantics as defined in the z.200 language specification.

All checks can be disabled by the GDB command set check off.

10.4.3.5 Chill defaults

If type and range checking are set automatically by GDB, they both default to on whenever the working language changes to Chill. This happens regardless of whether you or GDB selected the working language.

If you allow GDB to set the language automatically, then entering code compiled from a file whose name ends with '.ch' sets the working language to Chill. See Section 10.1.3 [Having GDB set the language automatically], page 100, for further details.

11 Examining the Symbol Table

The commands described in this chapter allow you to inquire about the symbols (names of variables, functions and types) defined in your program. This information is inherent in the text of your program and does not change as your program executes. GDB finds it in your program's symbol table, in the file indicated when you started GDB (see Section 2.1.1 [Choosing files], page 12), or by one of the file-management commands (see Section 13.1 [Commands to specify files], page 135).

Occasionally, you may need to refer to symbols that contain unusual characters, which GDB ordinarily treats as word delimiters. The most frequent case is in referring to static variables in other source files (see Section 8.2 [Program variables], page 70). File names are recorded in object files as debugging symbols, but GDB would ordinarily parse a typical file name, like 'foo.c', as the three words 'foo' '.' 'c'. To allow GDB to recognize 'foo.c' as a single symbol, enclose it in single quotes; for example,

```
p 'foo.c'::x
```

looks up the value of x in the scope of the file 'foo.c'.

info address *symbol*

> Describe where the data for *symbol* is stored. For a register variable, this says which register it is kept in. For a non-register local variable, this prints the stack-frame offset at which the variable is always stored.

> Note the contrast with 'print &*symbol*', which does not work at all for a register variable, and for a stack local variable prints the exact address of the current instantiation of the variable.

info symbol *addr*

> Print the name of a symbol which is stored at the address *addr*. If no symbol is stored exactly at *addr*, GDB prints the nearest symbol and an offset from it:

> ```
> (gdb) info symbol 0x54320
> _initialize_vx + 396 in section .text
> ```

> This is the opposite of the info address command. You can use it to find out the name of a variable or a function given its address.

whatis *expr*

> Print the data type of expression *expr*. *expr* is not actually evaluated, and any side-effecting operations (such as assignments or function calls) inside it do not take place. See Section 8.1 [Expressions], page 69.

whatis   Print the data type of $, the last value in the value history.

ptype *typename*

>Print a description of data type *typename*. *typename* may be the
>name of a type, or for C code it may have the form 'class *class-name*', 'struct *struct-tag*', 'union *union-tag*' or 'enum *enum-tag*'.

ptype *expr*

ptype

>Print a description of the type of expression *expr*. ptype differs
>from whatis by printing a detailed description, instead of just
>the name of the type.
>
>For example, for this variable declaration:
>
>>   struct complex {double real; double imag;} v;
>
>the two commands give this output:
>
>```
>(gdb) whatis v
>type = struct complex
>(gdb) ptype v
>type = struct complex {
>    double real;
>    double imag;
>}
>```
>
>As with whatis, using ptype without an argument refers to the
>type of $, the last value in the value history.

info types *regexp*

info types

>Print a brief description of all types whose names match *reg-exp* (or all types in your program, if you supply no argument).
>Each complete typename is matched as though it were a com-plete line; thus, 'i type value' gives information on all types
>in your program whose names include the string value, but 'i
>type ^value$' gives information only on types whose complete
>name is value.
>
>This command differs from ptype in two ways: first, like whatis,
>it does not print a detailed description; second, it lists all source
>files where a type is defined.

info scope *addr*

>List all the variables local to a particular scope. This command
>accepts a location—a function name, a source line, or an address
>preceded by a '*', and prints all the variables local to the scope
>defined by that location. For example:
>
>```
>(gdb) info scope command_line_handler
>Scope for command_line_handler:
>Symbol rl is an argument at stack/frame offset 8, length 4.
>Symbol linebuffer is in static storage at address 0x150a18, length 4.
>```

```
Symbol linelength is in static storage at address 0x150a1c, length 4.
Symbol p is a local variable in register $esi, length 4.
Symbol p1 is a local variable in register $ebx, length 4.
Symbol nline is a local variable in register $edx, length 4.
Symbol repeat is a local variable at frame offset -8, length 4.
```

This command is especially useful for determining what data to collect during a *trace experiment*, see Section 9.1.4 [Tracepoint Actions], page 91.

info source

> Show the name of the current source file—that is, the source file for the function containing the current point of execution—and the language it was written in.

info sources

> Print the names of all source files in your program for which there is debugging information, organized into two lists: files whose symbols have already been read, and files whose symbols will be read when needed.

info functions

> Print the names and data types of all defined functions.

info functions *regexp*

> Print the names and data types of all defined functions whose names contain a match for regular expression *regexp*. Thus, 'info fun step' finds all functions whose names include step; 'info fun ^step' finds those whose names start with step.

info variables

> Print the names and data types of all variables that are declared outside of functions (i.e., excluding local variables).

info variables *regexp*

> Print the names and data types of all variables (except for local variables) whose names contain a match for regular expression *regexp*.
>
> Some systems allow individual object files that make up your program to be replaced without stopping and restarting your program. For example, in VxWorks you can simply recompile a defective object file and keep on running. If you are running on one of these systems, you can allow GDB to reload the symbols for automatically relinked modules:

set symbol-reloading on

> > Replace symbol definitions for the corresponding source file when an object file with a particular name is seen again.

`set symbol-reloading off`

> Do not replace symbol definitions when encountering object files of the same name more than once. This is the default state; if you are not running on a system that permits automatic relinking of modules, you should leave `symbol-reloading` off, since otherwise GDB may discard symbols when linking large programs, that may contain several modules (from different directories or libraries) with the same name.

`show symbol-reloading`

> Show the current `on` or `off` setting.

`set opaque-type-resolution on`

> Tell GDB to resolve opaque types. An opaque type is a type declared as a pointer to a `struct`, `class`, or `union`—for example, `struct MyType *`—that is used in one source file although the full declaration of `struct MyType` is in another source file. The default is on.

> A change in the setting of this subcommand will not take effect until the next time symbols for a file are loaded.

`set opaque-type-resolution off`

> Tell GDB not to resolve opaque types. In this case, the type is printed as follows:

> `{<no data fields>}`

`show opaque-type-resolution`

> Show whether opaque types are resolved or not.

`maint print symbols` *filename*
`maint print psymbols` *filename*
`maint print msymbols` *filename*

> Write a dump of debugging symbol data into the file *filename*. These commands are used to debug the GDB symbol-reading code. Only symbols with debugging data are included. If you use 'maint print symbols', GDB includes all the symbols for which it has already collected full details: that is, *filename* reflects symbols for only those files whose symbols GDB has read. You can use the command `info sources` to find out which files these are. If you use 'maint print psymbols' instead, the dump shows information about symbols that GDB only knows partially—that is, symbols defined in files that GDB has skimmed, but not yet read completely. Finally, 'maint print msymbols' dumps just the minimal symbol information required for each object file from which GDB has read some symbols. See Section 13.1

[Commands to specify files], page 135, for a discussion of how GDB reads symbols (in the description of `symbol-file`).

12 Altering Execution

Once you think you have found an error in your program, you might want to find out for certain whether correcting the apparent error would lead to correct results in the rest of the run. You can find the answer by experiment, using the GDB features for altering execution of the program.

For example, you can store new values into variables or memory locations, give your program a signal, restart it at a different address, or even return prematurely from a function.

12.1 Assignment to variables

To alter the value of a variable, evaluate an assignment expression. See Section 8.1 [Expressions], page 69. For example,

    print x=4

stores the value 4 into the variable x, and then prints the value of the assignment expression (which is 4). See Chapter 10 [Using GDB with Different Languages], page 99, for more information on operators in supported languages.

If you are not interested in seeing the value of the assignment, use the set command instead of the print command. set is really the same as print except that the expression's value is not printed and is not put in the value history (see Section 8.8 [Value history], page 82). The expression is evaluated only for its effects.

If the beginning of the argument string of the set command appears identical to a set subcommand, use the set variable command instead of just set. This command is identical to set except for its lack of subcommands. For example, if your program has a variable width, you get an error if you try to set a new value with just 'set width=13', because GDB has the command set width:

    (gdb) whatis width
    type = double
    (gdb) p width
    $4 = 13
    (gdb) set width=47
    Invalid syntax in expression.

The invalid expression, of course, is '=47'. In order to actually set the program's variable width, use

    (gdb) set var width=47

Because the set command has many subcommands that can conflict with the names of program variables, it is a good idea to use the set variable command instead of just set. For example, if your program has a variable g, you run into problems if you try to set a new value with just 'set g=4', because GDB has the command set gnutarget, abbreviated set g:

```
(gdb) whatis g
type = double
(gdb) p g
$1 = 1
(gdb) set g=4
(gdb) p g
$2 = 1
(gdb) r
The program being debugged has been started already.
Start it from the beginning? (y or n) y
Starting program: /home/smith/cc_progs/a.out
"/home/smith/cc_progs/a.out": can't open to read symbols:
                              Invalid bfd target.
(gdb) show g
The current BFD target is "=4".
```

The program variable g did not change, and you silently set the gnutarget to an invalid value. In order to set the variable g, use

```
(gdb) set var g=4
```

GDB allows more implicit conversions in assignments than C; you can freely store an integer value into a pointer variable or vice versa, and you can convert any structure to any other structure that is the same length or shorter.

To store values into arbitrary places in memory, use the '{...}' construct to generate a value of specified type at a specified address (see Section 8.1 [Expressions], page 69). For example, {int}0x83040 refers to memory location 0x83040 as an integer (which implies a certain size and representation in memory), and

```
set {int}0x83040 = 4
```

stores the value 4 into that memory location.

12.2 Continuing at a different address

Ordinarily, when you continue your program, you do so at the place where it stopped, with the continue command. You can instead continue at an address of your own choosing, with the following commands:

jump *linespec*

Resume execution at line *linespec*. Execution stops again immediately if there is a breakpoint there. See Section 7.1 [Printing source lines], page 63, for a description of the different forms of *linespec*. It is common practice to use the tbreak command in conjunction with jump. See Section 5.1.1 [Setting breakpoints], page 36.

The `jump` command does not change the current stack frame, or the stack pointer, or the contents of any memory location or any register other than the program counter. If line *linespec* is in a different function from the one currently executing, the results may be bizarre if the two functions expect different patterns of arguments or of local variables. For this reason, the `jump` command requests confirmation if the specified line is not in the function currently executing. However, even bizarre results are predictable if you are well acquainted with the machine-language code of your program.

`jump *address`

>   Resume execution at the instruction at address *address*.

On many systems, you can get much the same effect as the `jump` command by storing a new value into the register `$pc`. The difference is that this does not start your program running; it only changes the address of where it *will* run when you continue. For example,

    set $pc = 0x485

makes the next `continue` command or stepping command execute at address `0x485`, rather than at the address where your program stopped. See Section 5.2 [Continuing and stepping], page 50.

The most common occasion to use the `jump` command is to back up—perhaps with more breakpoints set—over a portion of a program that has already executed, in order to examine its execution in more detail.

12.3 Giving your program a signal

`signal` *signal*

>   Resume execution where your program stopped, but immediately give it the signal *signal*. *signal* can be the name or the number of a signal. For example, on many systems `signal 2` and `signal SIGINT` are both ways of sending an interrupt signal.
>
>   Alternatively, if *signal* is zero, continue execution without giving a signal. This is useful when your program stopped on account of a signal and would ordinary see the signal when resumed with the `continue` command; '`signal 0`' causes it to resume without a signal.
>
>   `signal` does not repeat when you press (RET) a second time after executing the command.

Invoking the `signal` command is not the same as invoking the `kill` utility from the shell. Sending a signal with `kill` causes GDB to decide what to do with the signal depending on the signal handling tables (see Section 5.3 [Signals], page 53). The `signal` command passes the signal directly to your program.

12.4 Returning from a function

return
return *expression*

> You can cancel execution of a function call with the return command. If you give an *expression* argument, its value is used as the function's return value.

When you use return, GDB discards the selected stack frame (and all frames within it). You can think of this as making the discarded frame return prematurely. If you wish to specify a value to be returned, give that value as the argument to return.

This pops the selected stack frame (see Section 6.3 [Selecting a frame], page 59), and any other frames inside of it, leaving its caller as the innermost remaining frame. That frame becomes selected. The specified value is stored in the registers used for returning values of functions.

The return command does not resume execution; it leaves the program stopped in the state that would exist if the function had just returned. In contrast, the finish command (see Section 5.2 [Continuing and stepping], page 50) resumes execution until the selected stack frame returns naturally.

12.5 Calling program functions

call *expr*   Evaluate the expression *expr* without displaying void returned values.

You can use this variant of the print command if you want to execute a function from your program, but without cluttering the output with void returned values. If the result is not void, it is printed and saved in the value history.

For the A29K, a user-controlled variable call_scratch_address, specifies the location of a scratch area to be used when GDB calls a function in the target. This is necessary because the usual method of putting the scratch area on the stack does not work in systems that have separate instruction and data spaces.

12.6 Patching programs

By default, GDB opens the file containing your program's executable code (or the corefile) read-only. This prevents accidental alterations to machine code; but it also prevents you from intentionally patching your program's binary.

If you'd like to be able to patch the binary, you can specify that explicitly with the set write command. For example, you might want to turn on internal debugging flags, or even to make emergency repairs.

`set write on`
`set write off`

> If you specify 'set write on', GDB opens executable and core files for both reading and writing; if you specify 'set write off' (the default), GDB opens them read-only.
>
> If you have already loaded a file, you must load it again (using the `exec-file` or `core-file` command) after changing `set write`, for your new setting to take effect.

`show write`

> Display whether executable files and core files are opened for writing as well as reading.

13 GDB Files

GDB needs to know the file name of the program to be debugged, both in order to read its symbol table and in order to start your program. To debug a core dump of a previous run, you must also tell GDB the name of the core dump file.

13.1 Commands to specify files

You may want to specify executable and core dump file names. The usual way to do this is at start-up time, using the arguments to GDB's start-up commands (see Chapter 2 [Getting In and Out of GDB], page 11).

Occasionally it is necessary to change to a different file during a GDB session. Or you may run GDB and forget to specify a file you want to use. In these situations the GDB commands to specify new files are useful.

`file` *filename*

> Use *filename* as the program to be debugged. It is read for its symbols and for the contents of pure memory. It is also the program executed when you use the `run` command. If you do not specify a directory and the file is not found in the GDB working directory, GDB uses the environment variable `PATH` as a list of directories to search, just as the shell does when looking for a program to run. You can change the value of this variable, for both GDB and your program, using the `path` command.
>
> On systems with memory-mapped files, an auxiliary file named '*filename*.`syms`' may hold symbol table information for *filename*. If so, GDB maps in the symbol table from '*filename*.`syms`', starting up more quickly. See the descriptions of the file options '-`mapped`' and '-`readnow`' (available on the command line, and with the commands `file`, `symbol-file`, or `add-symbol-file`, described below), for more information.

`file`

> `file` with no argument makes GDB discard any information it has on both executable file and the symbol table.

`exec-file` [*filename*]

> Specify that the program to be run (but not the symbol table) is found in *filename*. GDB searches the environment variable `PATH` if necessary to locate your program. Omitting *filename* means to discard information on the executable file.

`symbol-file` [*filename*]

> Read symbol table information from file *filename*. `PATH` is searched when necessary. Use the `file` command to get both symbol table and program to run from the same file.

`symbol-file` with no argument clears out GDB information on your program's symbol table.

The `symbol-file` command causes GDB to forget the contents of its convenience variables, the value history, and all breakpoints and auto-display expressions. This is because they may contain pointers to the internal data recording symbols and data types, which are part of the old symbol table data being discarded inside GDB.

`symbol-file` does not repeat if you press (RET) again after executing it once.

When GDB is configured for a particular environment, it understands debugging information in whatever format is the standard generated for that environment; you may use either a GNU compiler, or other compilers that adhere to the local conventions. Best results are usually obtained from GNU compilers; for example, using `gcc` you can generate debugging information for optimized code.

For most kinds of object files, with the exception of old SVR3 systems using COFF, the `symbol-file` command does not normally read the symbol table in full right away. Instead, it scans the symbol table quickly to find which source files and which symbols are present. The details are read later, one source file at a time, as they are needed.

The purpose of this two-stage reading strategy is to make GDB start up faster. For the most part, it is invisible except for occasional pauses while the symbol table details for a particular source file are being read. (The `set verbose` command can turn these pauses into messages if desired. See Section 16.6 [Optional warnings and messages], page 194.)

We have not implemented the two-stage strategy for COFF yet. When the symbol table is stored in COFF format, `symbol-file` reads the symbol table data in full right away. Note that "stabs-in-COFF" still does the two-stage strategy, since the debug info is actually in stabs format.

`symbol-file` *filename* [`-readnow`] [`-mapped`]
`file` *filename* [`-readnow`] [`-mapped`]

You can override the GDB two-stage strategy for reading symbol tables by using the '`-readnow`' option with any of the commands that load symbol table information, if you want to be sure GDB has the entire symbol table available.

If memory-mapped files are available on your system through the `mmap` system call, you can use another option, '`-mapped`', to cause GDB to write the symbols for your program into a reusable file. Future GDB debugging sessions map in symbol information from this auxiliary symbol file (if the program has not changed), rather than spending time reading the symbol table from the executable program. Using the '-mapped' option has the same effect as starting GDB with the '-mapped' command-line option.

You can use both options together, to make sure the auxiliary symbol file has all the symbol information for your program.

The auxiliary symbol file for a program called *myprog* is called '*myprog*.syms'. Once this file exists (so long as it is newer than the corresponding executable), GDB always attempts to use it when you debug *myprog*; no special options or commands are needed.

The '.syms' file is specific to the host machine where you run GDB. It holds an exact image of the internal GDB symbol table. It cannot be shared across multiple host platforms.

core-file [*filename*]
> Specify the whereabouts of a core dump file to be used as the "contents of memory". Traditionally, core files contain only some parts of the address space of the process that generated them; GDB can access the executable file itself for other parts.
>
> core-file with no argument specifies that no core file is to be used.
>
> Note that the core file is ignored when your program is actually running under GDB. So, if you have been running your program and you wish to debug a core file instead, you must kill the subprocess in which the program is running. To do this, use the kill command (see Section 4.8 [Killing the child process], page 29).

add-symbol-file *filename address*
add-symbol-file *filename address* [-readnow] [-mapped]
add-symbol-file *filename* -s*section address*
> The add-symbol-file command reads additional symbol table information from the file *filename*. You would use this command when *filename* has been dynamically loaded (by some other means) into the program that is running. *address* should be the memory address at which the file has been loaded; GDB cannot figure this out for itself. You can additionally specify an arbitrary number of '-s*section address*' pairs, to give an explicit section name and base address for that section. You can specify any *address* as an expression.
>
> The symbol table of the file *filename* is added to the symbol table originally read with the symbol-file command. You can use the add-symbol-file command any number of times; the new symbol data thus read keeps adding to the old. To discard all old

symbol data instead, use the `symbol-file` command without any arguments.

`add-symbol-file` does not repeat if you press (RET) after using it.

You can use the '`-mapped`' and '`-readnow`' options just as with the `symbol-file` command, to change how GDB manages the symbol table information for *filename*.

add-shared-symbol-file
> The `add-shared-symbol-file` command can be used only under Harris' CXUX operating system for the Motorola 88k. GDB automatically looks for shared libraries, however if GDB does not find yours, you can run `add-shared-symbol-file`. It takes no arguments.

section
> The `section` command changes the base address of section SECTION of the exec file to ADDR. This can be used if the exec file does not contain section addresses, (such as in the a.out format), or when the addresses specified in the file itself are wrong. Each section must be changed separately. The `info files` command, described below, lists all the sections and their addresses.

info files
info target
> `info files` and `info target` are synonymous; both print the current target (see Chapter 14 [Specifying a Debugging Target], page 143), including the names of the executable and core dump files currently in use by GDB, and the files from which symbols were loaded. The command `help target` lists all possible targets rather than current ones.

All file-specifying commands allow both absolute and relative file names as arguments. GDB always converts the file name to an absolute file name and remembers it that way.

GDB supports HP-UX, SunOS, SVr4, Irix 5, and IBM RS/6000 shared libraries.

GDB automatically loads symbol definitions from shared libraries when you use the `run` command, or when you examine a core file. (Before you issue the `run` command, GDB does not understand references to a function in a shared library, however—unless you are debugging a core file).

On HP-UX, if the program loads a library explicitly, GDB automatically loads the symbols at the time of the `shl_load` call.

info share
info sharedlibrary
> Print the names of the shared libraries which are currently loaded.

sharedlibrary *regex*
share *regex*

> Load shared object library symbols for files matching a Unix regular expression. As with files loaded automatically, it only loads shared libraries required by your program for a core file or after typing **run**. If *regex* is omitted all shared libraries required by your program are loaded.

On HP-UX systems, GDB detects the loading of a shared library and automatically reads in symbols from the newly loaded library, up to a threshold that is initially set but that you can modify if you wish.

Beyond that threshold, symbols from shared libraries must be explicitly loaded. To load these symbols, use the command **sharedlibrary** *filename*. The base address of the shared library is determined automatically by GDB and need not be specified.

To display or set the threshold, use the commands:

set auto-solib-add *threshold*

> Set the autoloading size threshold, in megabytes. If *threshold* is nonzero, symbols from all shared object libraries will be loaded automatically when the inferior begins execution or when the dynamic linker informs GDB that a new library has been loaded, until the symbol table of the program and libraries exceeds this threshold. Otherwise, symbols must be loaded manually, using the **sharedlibrary** command. The default threshold is 100 megabytes.

show auto-solib-add

> Display the current autoloading size threshold, in megabytes.

13.2 Errors reading symbol files

While reading a symbol file, GDB occasionally encounters problems, such as symbol types it does not recognize, or known bugs in compiler output. By default, GDB does not notify you of such problems, since they are relatively common and primarily of interest to people debugging compilers. If you are interested in seeing information about ill-constructed symbol tables, you can either ask GDB to print only one message about each such type of problem, no matter how many times the problem occurs; or you can ask GDB to print more messages, to see how many times the problems occur, with the **set complaints** command (see Section 16.6 [Optional warnings and messages], page 194).

The messages currently printed, and their meanings, include:

inner block not inside outer block in *symbol*

> The symbol information shows where symbol scopes begin and end (such as at the start of a function or a block of statements).

This error indicates that an inner scope block is not fully contained in its outer scope blocks.

GDB circumvents the problem by treating the inner block as if it had the same scope as the outer block. In the error message, *symbol* may be shown as "(don't know)" if the outer block is not a function.

block at *address* out of order

The symbol information for symbol scope blocks should occur in order of increasing addresses. This error indicates that it does not do so.

GDB does not circumvent this problem, and has trouble locating symbols in the source file whose symbols it is reading. (You can often determine what source file is affected by specifying set verbose on. See Section 16.6 [Optional warnings and messages], page 194.)

bad block start address patched

The symbol information for a symbol scope block has a start address smaller than the address of the preceding source line. This is known to occur in the SunOS 4.1.1 (and earlier) C compiler.

GDB circumvents the problem by treating the symbol scope block as starting on the previous source line.

bad string table offset in symbol *n*

Symbol number *n* contains a pointer into the string table which is larger than the size of the string table.

GDB circumvents the problem by considering the symbol to have the name foo, which may cause other problems if many symbols end up with this name.

unknown symbol type 0x*nn*

The symbol information contains new data types that GDB does not yet know how to read. 0x*nn* is the symbol type of the uncomprehended information, in hexadecimal.

GDB circumvents the error by ignoring this symbol information. This usually allows you to debug your program, though certain symbols are not accessible. If you encounter such a problem and feel like debugging it, you can debug gdb with itself, breakpoint on complain, then go up to the function read_dbx_symtab and examine *bufp to see the symbol.

stub type has NULL name

GDB could not find the full definition for a struct or class.

const/volatile indicator missing (ok if using g++ v1.x), got...

The symbol information for a C++ member function is missing some information that recent versions of the compiler should have output for it.

`info mismatch between compiler and debugger`
>   GDB could not parse a type specification output by the compiler.

14 Specifying a Debugging Target

A *target* is the execution environment occupied by your program.

Often, GDB runs in the same host environment as your program; in that case, the debugging target is specified as a side effect when you use the `file` or `core` commands. When you need more flexibility—for example, running GDB on a physically separate host, or controlling a standalone system over a serial port or a realtime system over a TCP/IP connection—you can use the `target` command to specify one of the target types configured for GDB (see Section 14.2 [Commands for managing targets], page 143).

14.1 Active targets

There are three classes of targets: processes, core files, and executable files. GDB can work concurrently on up to three active targets, one in each class. This allows you to (for example) start a process and inspect its activity without abandoning your work on a core file.

For example, if you execute 'gdb a.out', then the executable file `a.out` is the only active target. If you designate a core file as well—presumably from a prior run that crashed and coredumped—then GDB has two active targets and uses them in tandem, looking first in the corefile target, then in the executable file, to satisfy requests for memory addresses. (Typically, these two classes of target are complementary, since core files contain only a program's read-write memory—variables and so on—plus machine status, while executable files contain only the program text and initialized data.)

When you type `run`, your executable file becomes an active process target as well. When a process target is active, all GDB commands requesting memory addresses refer to that target; addresses in an active core file or executable file target are obscured while the process target is active.

Use the `core-file` and `exec-file` commands to select a new core file or executable target (see Section 13.1 [Commands to specify files], page 135). To specify as a target a process that is already running, use the `attach` command (see Section 4.7 [Debugging an already-running process], page 28).

14.2 Commands for managing targets

`target` *type parameters*

Connects the GDB host environment to a target machine or process. A target is typically a protocol for talking to debugging facilities. You use the argument *type* to specify the type or protocol of the target machine.

Further *parameters* are interpreted by the target protocol, but typically include things like device names or host names to connect with, process numbers, and baud rates.

The `target` command does not repeat if you press (RET) again after executing the command.

`help target`

> Displays the names of all targets available. To display targets currently selected, use either `info target` or `info files` (see Section 13.1 [Commands to specify files], page 135).

`help target` *name*

> Describe a particular target, including any parameters necessary to select it.

`set gnutarget` *args*

> GDB uses its own library BFD to read your files. GDB knows whether it is reading an *executable*, a *core*, or a *.o* file; however, you can specify the file format with the `set gnutarget` command. Unlike most `target` commands, with `gnutarget` the `target` refers to a program, not a machine.
>
> > *Warning:* To specify a file format with `set gnutarget`, you must know the actual BFD name.
>
> See Section 13.1 [Commands to specify files], page 135.

`show gnutarget`

> Use the `show gnutarget` command to display what file format `gnutarget` is set to read. If you have not set `gnutarget`, GDB will determine the file format for each file automatically, and `show gnutarget` displays 'The current BDF target is "auto"'.

Here are some common targets (available, or not, depending on the GDB configuration):

`target exec` *program*

> An executable file. 'target exec *program*' is the same as 'exec-file *program*'.

`target core` *filename*

> A core dump file. 'target core *filename*' is the same as 'core-file *filename*'.

`target remote` *dev*

> Remote serial target in GDB-specific protocol. The argument *dev* specifies what serial device to use for the connection (e.g. '/dev/ttya'). See Section 14.4 [Remote debugging], page 146. `target remote` supports the `load` command. This is only useful if you have some other way of getting the stub to the target system, and you can put it somewhere in memory where it won't get clobbered by the download.

`target sim`

Builtin CPU simulator. GDB includes simulators for most architectures. In general,

```
target sim
load
run
```

works; however, you cannot assume that a specific memory map, device drivers, or even basic I/O is available, although some simulators do provide these. For info about any processor-specific simulator details, see the appropriate section in Section 15.3 [Embedded Processors], page 174.

Some configurations may include these targets as well:

`target nrom` *dev*

NetROM ROM emulator. This target only supports downloading.

Different targets are available on different configurations of GDB; your configuration may have more or fewer targets.

Many remote targets require you to download the executable's code once you've successfully established a connection.

`load` *filename*

Depending on what remote debugging facilities are configured into GDB, the `load` command may be available. Where it exists, it is meant to make *filename* (an executable) available for debugging on the remote system—by downloading, or dynamic linking, for example. `load` also records the *filename* symbol table in GDB, like the `add-symbol-file` command.

If your GDB does not have a `load` command, attempting to execute it gets the error message "`You can't do that when your target is ...`"

The file is loaded at whatever address is specified in the executable. For some object file formats, you can specify the load address when you link the program; for other formats, like a.out, the object file format specifies a fixed address.

`load` does not repeat if you press (RET) again after using it.

14.3 Choosing target byte order

Some types of processors, such as the MIPS, PowerPC, and Hitachi SH, offer the ability to run either big-endian or little-endian byte orders. Usually the executable or symbol will include a bit to designate the endian-ness, and you will not need to worry about which to use. However, you may still find it useful to adjust GDB's idea of processor endian-ness manually.

`set endian big`
> Instruct GDB to assume the target is big-endian.

`set endian little`
> Instruct GDB to assume the target is little-endian.

`set endian auto`
> Instruct GDB to use the byte order associated with the executable.

`show endian`
> Display GDB's current idea of the target byte order.

Note that these commands merely adjust interpretation of symbolic data on the host, and that they have absolutely no effect on the target system.

14.4 Remote debugging

If you are trying to debug a program running on a machine that cannot run GDB in the usual way, it is often useful to use remote debugging. For example, you might use remote debugging on an operating system kernel, or on a small system which does not have a general purpose operating system powerful enough to run a full-featured debugger.

Some configurations of GDB have special serial or TCP/IP interfaces to make this work with particular debugging targets. In addition, GDB comes with a generic serial protocol (specific to GDB, but not specific to any particular target system) which you can use if you write the remote stubs—the code that runs on the remote system to communicate with GDB.

Other remote targets may be available in your configuration of GDB; use `help target` to list them.

14.4.1 The GDB remote serial protocol

To debug a program running on another machine (the debugging *target* machine), you must first arrange for all the usual prerequisites for the program to run by itself. For example, for a C program, you need:

1. A startup routine to set up the C runtime environment; these usually have a name like 'crt0'. The startup routine may be supplied by your hardware supplier, or you may have to write your own.

2. A C subroutine library to support your program's subroutine calls, notably managing input and output.

3. A way of getting your program to the other machine—for example, a download program. These are often supplied by the hardware manufacturer, but you may have to write your own from hardware documentation.

The next step is to arrange for your program to use a serial port to communicate with the machine where GDB is running (the *host* machine). In general terms, the scheme looks like this:

On the host,
> GDB already understands how to use this protocol; when everything else is set up, you can simply use the 'target remote' command (see Chapter 14 [Specifying a Debugging Target], page 143).

On the target,
> you must link with your program a few special-purpose subroutines that implement the GDB remote serial protocol. The file containing these subroutines is called a *debugging stub*.

> On certain remote targets, you can use an auxiliary program gdbserver instead of linking a stub into your program. See Section 14.4.1.5 [Using the gdbserver program], page 164, for details.

The debugging stub is specific to the architecture of the remote machine; for example, use 'sparc-stub.c' to debug programs on SPARC boards.

These working remote stubs are distributed with GDB:

i386-stub.c
> For Intel 386 and compatible architectures.

m68k-stub.c
> For Motorola 680x0 architectures.

sh-stub.c
> For Hitachi SH architectures.

sparc-stub.c
> For SPARC architectures.

sparcl-stub.c
> For Fujitsu SPARCLITE architectures.

The 'README' file in the GDB distribution may list other recently added stubs.

14.4.1.1 What the stub can do for you

The debugging stub for your architecture supplies these three subroutines:

set_debug_traps
> This routine arranges for handle_exception to run when your program stops. You must call this subroutine explicitly near the beginning of your program.

handle_exception

> This is the central workhorse, but your program never calls it explicitly—the setup code arranges for `handle_exception` to run when a trap is triggered.
>
> `handle_exception` takes control when your program stops during execution (for example, on a breakpoint), and mediates communications with GDB on the host machine. This is where the communications protocol is implemented; `handle_exception` acts as the GDB representative on the target machine. It begins by sending summary information on the state of your program, then continues to execute, retrieving and transmitting any information GDB needs, until you execute a GDB command that makes your program resume; at that point, `handle_exception` returns control to your own code on the target machine.

breakpoint

> Use this auxiliary subroutine to make your program contain a breakpoint. Depending on the particular situation, this may be the only way for GDB to get control. For instance, if your target machine has some sort of interrupt button, you won't need to call this; pressing the interrupt button transfers control to `handle_exception`—in effect, to GDB. On some machines, simply receiving characters on the serial port may also trigger a trap; again, in that situation, you don't need to call breakpoint from your own program—simply running 'target remote' from the host GDB session gets control.
>
> Call breakpoint if none of these is true, or if you simply want to make certain your program stops at a predetermined point for the start of your debugging session.

14.4.1.2 What you must do for the stub

The debugging stubs that come with GDB are set up for a particular chip architecture, but they have no information about the rest of your debugging target machine.

First of all you need to tell the stub how to communicate with the serial port.

int getDebugChar()

> Write this subroutine to read a single character from the serial port. It may be identical to `getchar` for your target system; a different name is used to allow you to distinguish the two if you wish.

void putDebugChar(int)

> Write this subroutine to write a single character to the serial port. It may be identical to `putchar` for your target system; a

different name is used to allow you to distinguish the two if you wish.

If you want GDB to be able to stop your program while it is running, you need to use an interrupt-driven serial driver, and arrange for it to stop when it receives a ^C ('\003', the control-C character). That is the character which GDB uses to tell the remote system to stop.

Getting the debugging target to return the proper status to GDB probably requires changes to the standard stub; one quick and dirty way is to just execute a breakpoint instruction (the "dirty" part is that GDB reports a SIGTRAP instead of a SIGINT).

Other routines you need to supply are:

void exceptionHandler (int *exception_number*, void *exception_address*)

> Write this function to install *exception_address* in the exception handling tables. You need to do this because the stub does not have any way of knowing what the exception handling tables on your target system are like (for example, the processor's table might be in ROM, containing entries which point to a table in RAM). *exception_number* is the exception number which should be changed; its meaning is architecture-dependent (for example, different numbers might represent divide by zero, misaligned access, etc). When this exception occurs, control should be transferred directly to *exception_address*, and the processor state (stack, registers, and so on) should be just as it is when a processor exception occurs. So if you want to use a jump instruction to reach *exception_address*, it should be a simple jump, not a jump to subroutine.

> For the 386, *exception_address* should be installed as an interrupt gate so that interrupts are masked while the handler runs. The gate should be at privilege level 0 (the most privileged level). The SPARC and 68k stubs are able to mask interrupts themselves without help from exceptionHandler.

void flush_i_cache ()

> On SPARC and SPARCLITE only, write this subroutine to flush the instruction cache, if any, on your target machine. If there is no instruction cache, this subroutine may be a no-op.

> On target machines that have instruction caches, GDB requires this function to make certain that the state of your program is stable.

You must also make sure this library routine is available:

void *memset (void *, int, int)

> This is the standard library function memset that sets an area of memory to a known value. If you have one of the free versions of

`libc.a`, `memset` can be found there; otherwise, you must either obtain it from your hardware manufacturer, or write your own.

If you do not use the GNU C compiler, you may need other standard library subroutines as well; this varies from one stub to another, but in general the stubs are likely to use any of the common library subroutines which `gcc` generates as inline code.

14.4.1.3 Putting it all together

In summary, when your program is ready to debug, you must follow these steps.

1. Make sure you have defined the supporting low-level routines (see Section 14.4.1.2 [What you must do for the stub], page 148):

   `getDebugChar`, `putDebugChar`,
   `flush_i_cache`, `memset`, `exceptionHandler`.

2. Insert these lines near the top of your program:

   ```
   set_debug_traps();
   breakpoint();
   ```

3. For the 680x0 stub only, you need to provide a variable called `exceptionHook`. Normally you just use:

   ```
   void (*exceptionHook)() = 0;
   ```

   but if before calling `set_debug_traps`, you set it to point to a function in your program, that function is called when GDB continues after stopping on a trap (for example, bus error). The function indicated by `exceptionHook` is called with one parameter: an `int` which is the exception number.

4. Compile and link together: your program, the GDB debugging stub for your target architecture, and the supporting subroutines.

5. Make sure you have a serial connection between your target machine and the GDB host, and identify the serial port on the host.

6. Download your program to your target machine (or get it there by whatever means the manufacturer provides), and start it.

7. To start remote debugging, run GDB on the host machine, and specify as an executable file the program that is running in the remote machine. This tells GDB how to find your program's symbols and the contents of its pure text.

8. Establish communication using the `target remote` command. Its argument specifies how to communicate with the target machine—either via a devicename attached to a direct serial line, or a TCP port (usually to a terminal server which in turn has a serial line to the target). For example, to use a serial line connected to the device named '`/dev/ttyb`':

   ```
   target remote /dev/ttyb
   ```

To use a TCP connection, use an argument of the form *host*:`port`. For example, to connect to port 2828 on a terminal server named `manyfarms`:

```
target remote manyfarms:2828
```

Now you can use all the usual commands to examine and change data and to step and continue the remote program.

To resume the remote program and stop debugging it, use the `detach` command.

Whenever GDB is waiting for the remote program, if you type the interrupt character (often $\overline{\text{C-C}}$), GDB attempts to stop the program. This may or may not succeed, depending in part on the hardware and the serial drivers the remote system uses. If you type the interrupt character once again, GDB displays this prompt:

```
Interrupted while waiting for the program.
Give up (and stop debugging it)?  (y or n)
```

If you type *y*, GDB abandons the remote debugging session. (If you decide you want to try again later, you can use '`target remote`' again to connect once more.) If you type *n*, GDB goes back to waiting.

14.4.1.4 Communication protocol

The stub files provided with GDB implement the target side of the communication protocol, and the GDB side is implemented in the GDB source file '`remote.c`'. Normally, you can simply allow these subroutines to communicate, and ignore the details. (If you're implementing your own stub file, you can still ignore the details: start with one of the existing stub files. '`sparc-stub.c`' is the best organized, and therefore the easiest to read.)

However, there may be occasions when you need to know something about the protocol—for example, if there is only one serial port to your target machine, you might want your program to do something special if it recognizes a packet meant for GDB.

In the examples below, '<-' and '->' are used to indicate transmitted and received data respectfully.

All GDB commands and responses (other than acknowledgments) are sent as a *packet*. A *packet* is introduced with the character '`$`', the actual *packet-data*, and the terminating character '`#`' followed by a two-digit *checksum*:

$*packet-data*#*checksum*

The two-digit *checksum* is computed as the modulo 256 sum of all characters between the leading '`$`' and the trailing '`#`' (an eight bit unsigned checksum).

Implementors should note that prior to GDB 5.0 the protocol specification also included an optional two-digit *sequence-id*:

$*sequence-id*:*packet-data*#*checksum*

That *sequence-id* was appended to the acknowledgment. GDB has never output *sequence-ids*. Stubs that handle packets added since GDB 5.0 must not accept *sequence-id*.

When either the host or the target machine receives a packet, the first response expected is an acknowledgment: either '+' (to indicate the package was received correctly) or '-' (to request retransmission):

```
<- $packet-data#checksum
-> +
```

The host (GDB) sends *commands*, and the target (the debugging stub incorporated in your program) sends a *response*. In the case of step and continue *commands*, the response is only sent when the operation has completed (the target has again stopped).

packet-data consists of a sequence of characters with the exception of '#' and '$' (see 'X' packet for additional exceptions).

Fields within the packet should be separated using ',' ';' or ':'. Except where otherwise noted all numbers are represented in HEX with leading zeros suppressed.

Implementors should note that prior to GDB 5.0, the character ':' could not appear as the third character in a packet (as it would potentially conflict with the *sequence-id*).

Response *data* can be run-length encoded to save space. A '*' means that the next character is an ASCII encoding giving a repeat count which stands for that many repetitions of the character preceding the '*'. The encoding is n+29, yielding a printable character where n >=3 (which is where rle starts to win). The printable characters '$', '#', '+' and '-' or with a numeric value greater than 126 should not be used.

Some remote systems have used a different run-length encoding mechanism loosely refered to as the cisco encoding. Following the '*' character are two hex digits that indicate the size of the packet.

So:

```
"0* "
```

means the same as "0000".

The error response returned for some packets includes a two character error number. That number is not well defined.

For any *command* not supported by the stub, an empty response ('$#00') should be returned. That way it is possible to extend the protocol. A newer GDB can tell if a packet is supported based on that response.

A stub is required to support the 'g', 'G', 'm', 'M', 'c', and 's' *commands*. All other *commands* are optional.

Below is a complete list of all currently defined *commands* and their corresponding response *data*:

Packet	Request	Description
extended mode	!	Enable extended mode. In extended mode, the remote server is made persistent. The 'R' packet is used to restart the program being debugged.
	reply 'OK'	The remote target both supports and has enabled extended mode.
last signal	?	Indicate the reason the target halted. The reply is the same as for step and continue.
	reply	see below
reserved	a	Reserved for future use
set program arguments **(reserved)**	A$arglen$,$argnum$,arg,...	
		Initialized 'argv[]' array passed into program. $arglen$ specifies the number of bytes in the hex encoded byte stream arg. See 'gdbserver' for more details.
	reply OK	
	reply ENN	

set baud (deprecated)	b*baud*	Change the serial line speed to *baud*. JTC: *When does the transport layer state change? When it's received, or after the ACK is transmitted. In either case, there are problems if the command or the acknowledgment packet is dropped.* Stan: *If people really wanted to add something like this, and get it working for the first time, they ought to modify ser-unix.c to send some kind of out-of-band message to a specially-setup stub and have the switch happen "in between" packets, so that from remote protocol's point of view, nothing actually happened.*
set breakpoint (deprecated)	B*addr,mode*	Set (*mode* is 'S') or clear (*mode* is 'C') a breakpoint at addr. *This has been replaced by the 'Z' and 'z' packets.*
continue	c*addr*	*addr* is address to resume. If *addr* is omitted, resume at current address.
	reply	see below
continue with signal	C*sig*;*addr*	Continue with signal *sig* (hex signal number). If ;*addr* is omitted, resume at same address.
	reply	see below
toggle debug (deprecated)	d	toggle debug flag.
detach	D	Detach GDB from the remote system. Sent to the remote target before GDB disconnects.

	reply *no response*	GDB does not check for any response after sending this packet.
reserved	e	Reserved for future use
reserved	E	Reserved for future use
reserved	f	Reserved for future use
reserved	F	Reserved for future use
read registers	g reply *XX*...	Read general registers. Each byte of register data is described by two hex digits. The bytes with the register are transmitted in target byte order. The size of each register and their position within the 'g' *packet* are determined by the GDB internal macros *REGISTER_RAW_SIZE* and *REGISTER_NAME* macros. The specification of several standard g packets is specified below.
	E*NN*	for an error.
write regs	G*XX*... reply OK reply E*NN*	See 'g' for a description of the *XX*... data. for success for an error
reserved	h	Reserved for future use
set thread	H*ct*... reply OK reply E*NN*	Set thread for subsequent operations ('m', 'M', 'g', 'G', et.al.). *c* = 'c' for thread used in step and continue; *t*... can be -1 for all threads. *c* = 'g' for thread used in other operations. If zero, pick a thread, any thread. for success for an error

cycle step **(draft)**	i*addr*,*nnn*	Step the remote target by a single clock cycle. If ,*nnn* is present, cycle step *nnn* cycles. If *addr* is present, cycle step starting at that address.
signal then cycle step **(reserved)**	I	See 'i' and 'S' for likely syntax and semantics.
reserved	j	Reserved for future use
reserved	J	Reserved for future use
kill request	k	FIXME: *There is no description of how operate when a specific thread context has been selected (ie. does 'k' kill only that thread?).*
reserved	l	Reserved for future use
reserved	L	Reserved for future use
read memory	m*addr*,*length*	Read *length* bytes of memory starting at address *addr*. Neither GDB nor the stub assume that sized memory transfers are assumed using word alligned accesses. FIXME: *A word aligned memory transfer mechanism is needed.*
	reply *XX...*	*XX...* is mem contents. Can be fewer bytes than requested if able to read only part of the data. Neither GDB nor the stub assume that sized memory transfers are assumed using word aligned accesses. FIXME: *A word aligned memory transfer mechanism is needed.*
	reply E*NN*	*NN* is errno
write mem	M*addr*,*length*:*XX...*	Write *length* bytes of memory starting at address *addr*. *XX...* is the data.

	reply OK	for success
	reply E*NN*	for an error (this includes the case where only part of the data was written).
reserved	n	Reserved for future use
reserved	N	Reserved for future use
reserved	o	Reserved for future use
reserved	O	Reserved for future use
read reg **(reserved)**	p*n*...	See write register.
	return *r*....	The hex encoded value of the register in target byte order.
write reg	P*n*...=*r*...	Write register *n*... with value *r*..., which contains two hex digits for each byte in the register (target byte order).
	reply OK	for success
	reply E*NN*	for an error
general query	q*query*	Request info about *query*. In general GDB queries have a leading upper case letter. Custom vendor queries should use a company prefix (in lower case) ex: 'qfsf.var'. *query* may optionally be followed by a ',' or ';' separated list. Stubs must ensure that they match the full *query* name.
	reply XX...	Hex encoded data from query. The reply can not be empty.
	reply E*NN*	error reply
	reply ''	Indicating an unrecognized *query*.
general set	Q*var*=*val*	Set value of *var* to *val*. See 'q' for a discussing of naming conventions.
reset **(deprecated)**	r	Reset the entire system.

remote restart	R*XX*	Restart the program being debugged. *XX*, while needed, is ignored. This packet is only available in extended mode.
	no reply	The 'R' packet has no reply.
step	s*addr*	*addr* is address to resume. If *addr* is omitted, resume at same address.
	reply	see below
step with signal	S*sig*;*addr*	Like 'C' but step not continue.
	reply	see below
search	t*addr*:*PP*,*MM*	Search backwards starting at address *addr* for a match with pattern *PP* and mask *MM*. *PP* and *MM* are 4 bytes. *addr* must be at least 3 digits.
thread alive	T*XX*	Find out if the thread XX is alive.
	reply OK	thread is still alive
	reply E*NN*	thread is dead
reserved	u	Reserved for future use
reserved	U	Reserved for future use
reserved	v	Reserved for future use
reserved	V	Reserved for future use
reserved	w	Reserved for future use
reserved	W	Reserved for future use
reserved	x	Reserved for future use
write mem (binary)	X*addr*,*length*:*XX*...	*addr* is address, *length* is number of bytes, *XX*... is binary data. The characters $, #, and 0x7d are escaped using 0x7d.
	reply OK	for success
	reply E*NN*	for an error
reserved	y	Reserved for future use
reserved	Y	Reserved for future use

remove break or watchpoint (**draft**)	**z**t,addr,length	See 'Z'.
insert break or watchpoint (**draft**)	**Z**t,addr,length	t is type: '0' - software breakpoint, '1' - hardware breakpoint, '2' - write watchpoint, '3' - read watchpoint, '4' - access watchpoint; addr is address; length is in bytes. For a software breakpoint, length specifies the size of the instruction to be patched. For hardware breakpoints and watchpoints length specifies the memory region to be monitored. To avoid potential problems with duplicate packets, the operations should be implemented in an idempotent way.
	reply E*NN*	for an error
	reply OK	for success
	''	If not supported.
reserved	<other>	Reserved for future use

The 'C', 'c', 'S', 's' and '?' packets can receive any of the below as a reply. In the case of the 'C', 'c', 'S' and 's' packets, that reply is only returned when the target halts. In the below the exact meaning of 'signal number' is poorly defined. In general one of the UNIX signal numbering conventions is used.

S*AA*	*AA* is the signal number
T*AA*n...:r...;n...:r...;n...:r...;	*AA* = two hex digit signal number; n... = register number (hex), r... = target byte ordered register contents, size defined by REGISTER_RAW_SIZE; n... = 'thread', r... = thread process ID, this is a hex integer; n... = other string not starting with valid hex digit. GDB should ignore this n..., r... pair and go on to the next. This way we can extend the protocol.

WAA	The process exited, and AA is the exit status. This is only applicable for certains sorts of targets.
XAA	The process terminated with signal AA.
NAA;$t...$;$d...$;$b...$ **(obsolete)**	AA = signal number; $t...$ = address of symbol "_start"; $d...$ = base of data section; $b...$ = base of bss section. *Note: only used by Cisco Systems targets. The difference between this reply and the "qOffsets" query is that the 'N' packet may arrive spontaneously whereas the 'qOffsets' is a query initiated by the host debugger.*
O$XX...$	$XX...$ is hex encoding of ASCII data. This can happen at any time while the program is running and the debugger should continue to wait for 'W', 'T', etc.

The following set and query packets have already been defined.

current thread	qC	Return the current thread id.
	reply QC*pid*	Where *pid* is a HEX encoded 16 bit process id.
	reply *	Any other reply implies the old pid.
all thread ids	qfThreadInfo	
	qsThreadInfo	Obtain a list of active thread ids from the target (OS). Since there may be too many active threads to fit into one reply packet, this query works iteratively: it may require more than one query/reply sequence to obtain the entire list of threads. The first query of the sequence will be the qfThreadInfo query; subsequent queries in the sequence will be the qsThreadInfo query. NOTE: replaces the qL query (see below).
	reply m<*id*>	A single thread id
	reply m<*id*>,<*id*>...	a comma-separated list of thread ids
	reply l	(lower case 'el') denotes end of list.

In response to each query, the target will reply with a list of one or more thread ids, in big-endian hex, separated by commas. GDB will respond to each reply with a request for more thread ids (using the qs form of the query), until the target responds with l (lower-case el, for 'last').

extra thread info

qThreadExtraInfo,*id*

Where <*id*> is a thread-id in big-endian hex. Obtain a printable string description of a thread's attributes from the target OS. This string may contain anything that the target OS thinks is interesting for GDB to tell the user about the thread. The string is displayed in GDB's 'info threads' display. Some examples of possible thread extra info strings are "Runnable", or "Blocked on Mutex".

reply *XX...*   Where *XX...* is a hex encoding of ASCII data, comprising the printable string containing the extra information about the thread's attributes.

query *LIST* or *threadLIST* **(deprecated)**

qL*startflag threadcount nextthread*

Obtain thread information from RTOS. Where: *startflag* (one hex digit) is one to indicate the first query and zero to indicate a subsequent query; *threadcount* (two hex digits) is the maximum number of threads the response packet can contain; and *nextthread* (eight hex digits), for subsequent queries (*startflag* is zero), is returned in the response as *argthread*. NOTE: this query is replaced by the qfThreadInfo query (see above).

reply

qM*count done argthread thread...*

Where: *count* (two hex digits) is the number of threads being returned; *done* (one hex digit) is zero to indicate more threads and one indicates no further threads; *argthreadid* (eight hex digits) is *nextthread* from the request packet; *thread...* is a sequence of thread IDs from the target. *threadid* (eight hex digits). See `remote.c:parse_threadlist_response()`.

compute CRC of memory block	`qCRC:`*addr*`,`*length*	
	reply `E`*NN*	An error (such as memory fault)
	reply `C`*CRC32*	A 32 bit cyclic redundancy check of the specified memory region.
query sect offs	`qOffsets`	Get section offsets that the target used when re-locating the downloaded image. *Note: while a* `Bss` *offset is included in the response, GDB ignores this and instead applies the* `Data` *offset to the* `Bss` *section.*
	reply `Text=`*xxx*`;Data=`*yyy*`;Bss=`*zzz*	
thread info request	`qP`*modethreadid*	
		Returns information on *threadid*. Where: *mode* is a hex encoded 32 bit mode; *threadid* is a hex encoded 64 bit thread ID.
	reply `*`	See `remote.c:remote_unpack_thread_info_response()`.
remote command	`qRcmd,`*COMMAND*	
		COMMAND (hex encoded) is passed to the local interpreter for execution. Invalid commands should be reported using the output string. Before the final result packet, the target may also respond with a number of intermediate `O`*OUTPUT* console output packets. *Implementors should note that providing access to a stubs's interpreter may have security implications.*
	reply `OK`	A command response with no output.
	reply `O`*OUTPUT*	A command response with the hex encoded output string *OUTPUT*.
	reply `E`*NN*	Indicate a badly formed request.

	reply ''	When 'q''Rcmd' is not recognized.
symbol lookup	qSymbol::	Notify the target that GDB is prepared to serve symbol lookup requests. Accept requests from the target for the values of symbols.
	reply OK	The target does not need to look up any (more) symbols.
	reply qSymbol:*sym_name*	The target requests the value of symbol *sym_name* (hex encoded). GDB may provide the value by using the qSymbol:*sym_value:sym_name* message, described below.
symbol value	qSymbol:*sym_value:sym_name*	Set the value of SYM_NAME to SYM_VALUE. *sym_name* (hex encoded) is the name of a symbol whose value the target has previously requested. *sym_value* (hex) is the value for symbol *sym_name*. If GDB cannot supply a value for *sym_name*, then this field will be empty.
	reply OK	The target does not need to look up any (more) symbols.
	reply qSymbol:*sym_name*	The target requests the value of a new symbol *sym_name* (hex encoded). GDB will continue to supply the values of symbols (if available), until the target ceases to request them.

The following 'g'/'G' packets have previously been defined. In the below, some thirty-two bit registers are transferred as sixty-four bits. Those registers should be zero/sign extended (which?) to fill the space allocated. Register bytes are transfered in target byte order. The two nibbles within a register byte are transfered most-significant - least-significant.

MIPS32	All registers are transfered as thirty-two bit quantities in the order: 32 general-purpose; sr; lo; hi; bad; cause; pc; 32 floating-point registers; fsr; fir; fp.
MIPS64	All registers are transfered as sixty-four bit quantities (including thirty-two bit registers such as sr). The ordering is the same as MIPS32.

Example sequence of a target being re-started. Notice how the restart does not get any direct output:

```
<- R00
-> +
target restarts
<- ?
-> +
-> T001:1234123412341234
<- +
```

Example sequence of a target being stepped by a single instruction:

```
<- G1445...
-> +
<- s
-> +
time passes
-> T001:1234123412341234
<- +
<- g
-> +
-> 1455...
<- +
```

14.4.1.5 Using the gdbserver program

gdbserver is a control program for Unix-like systems, which allows you to connect your program with a remote GDB via target remote—but without linking in the usual debugging stub.

gdbserver is not a complete replacement for the debugging stubs, because it requires essentially the same operating-system facilities that GDB itself does. In fact, a system that can run gdbserver to connect to a remote GDB could also run GDB locally! gdbserver is sometimes useful nevertheless, because it is a much smaller program than GDB itself. It is also easier to port than all of GDB, so you may be able to get started more quickly on a new system by using gdbserver. Finally, if you develop code for real-time systems, you may find that the tradeoffs involved in real-time operation make it more convenient to do as much development work as possible on another system, for example by cross-compiling. You can use **gdbserver** to make a similar choice for debugging.

GDB and **gdbserver** communicate via either a serial line or a TCP connection, using the standard GDB remote serial protocol.

On the target machine,

you need to have a copy of the program you want to debug. **gdbserver** does not need your program's symbol table, so you can strip the program if necessary to save space. GDB on the host system does all the symbol handling.

To use the server, you must tell it how to communicate with GDB; the name of your program; and the arguments for your program. The syntax is:

```
target> gdbserver comm program [ args ... ]
```

comm is either a device name (to use a serial line) or a TCP hostname and portnumber. For example, to debug Emacs with the argument 'foo.txt' and communicate with GDB over the serial port '/dev/com1':

```
target> gdbserver /dev/com1 emacs foo.txt
```

gdbserver waits passively for the host GDB to communicate with it.

To use a TCP connection instead of a serial line:

```
target> gdbserver host:2345 emacs foo.txt
```

The only difference from the previous example is the first argument, specifying that you are communicating with the host GDB via TCP. The 'host:2345' argument means that **gdbserver** is to expect a TCP connection from machine 'host' to local TCP port 2345. (Currently, the 'host' part is ignored.) You can choose any number you want for the port number as long as it does not conflict with any TCP ports already in use on the target system (for example, 23 is reserved for **telnet**).[1] You must use the same port number with the host GDB **target remote** command.

On the GDB host machine,

you need an unstripped copy of your program, since GDB needs symbols and debugging information. Start up GDB as usual, using the name of the local copy of your program as the first argument. (You may also need the '--baud' option if the serial line is running at anything other than 9600 bps.) After that, use

---

[1] If you choose a port number that conflicts with another service, **gdbserver** prints an error message and exits.

`target remote` to establish communications with `gdbserver`.
Its argument is either a device name (usually a serial device, like
'`/dev/ttyb`'), or a TCP port descriptor in the form *host*:*PORT*.
For example:

```
(gdb) target remote /dev/ttyb
```

communicates with the server via serial line '`/dev/ttyb`', and

```
(gdb) target remote the-target:2345
```

communicates via a TCP connection to port 2345 on host
'`the-target`'. For TCP connections, you must start up
`gdbserver` prior to using the `target remote` command.
Otherwise you may get an error whose text depends on the host
system, but which usually looks something like '`Connection
refused`'.

14.4.1.6 Using the `gdbserve.nlm` program

`gdbserve.nlm` is a control program for NetWare systems, which allows
you to connect your program with a remote GDB via `target remote`.

GDB and `gdbserve.nlm` communicate via a serial line, using the standard
GDB remote serial protocol.

On the target machine,

you need to have a copy of the program you want to debug.
`gdbserve.nlm` does not need your program's symbol table, so
you can strip the program if necessary to save space. GDB on
the host system does all the symbol handling.

To use the server, you must tell it how to communicate with
GDB; the name of your program; and the arguments for your
program. The syntax is:

```
load gdbserve [ BOARD=board ] [ PORT=port ]
              [ BAUD=baud ] program [ args ... ]
```

board and *port* specify the serial line; *baud* specifies the baud
rate used by the connection. *port* and *node* default to 0, *baud*
defaults to 9600 bps.

For example, to debug Emacs with the argument '`foo.txt`'and
communicate with GDB over serial port number 2 or board 1
using a 19200 bps connection:

```
load gdbserve BOARD=1 PORT=2 BAUD=19200 emacs foo.txt
```

On the GDB host machine,

you need an unstripped copy of your program, since GDB
needs symbols and debugging information. Start up GDB as
usual, using the name of the local copy of your program as
the first argument. (You may also need the '`--baud`' option

if the serial line is running at anything other than 9600 bps. After that, use `target remote` to establish communications with `gdbserve.nlm`. Its argument is a device name (usually a serial device, like '`/dev/ttyb`'). For example:

```
(gdb) target remote /dev/ttyb
```

communications with the server via serial line '`/dev/ttyb`'.

14.5 Kernel Object Display

Some targets support kernel object display. Using this facility, GDB communicates specially with the underlying operating system and can display information about operating system-level objects such as mutexes and other synchronization objects. Exactly which objects can be displayed is determined on a per-OS basis.

Use the `set os` command to set the operating system. This tells GDB which kernel object display module to initialize:

```
(gdb) set os cisco
```

If `set os` succeeds, GDB will display some information about the operating system, and will create a new `info` command which can be used to query the target. The `info` command is named after the operating system:

```
(gdb) info cisco
List of Cisco Kernel Objects
Object      Description
any         Any and all objects
```

Further subcommands can be used to query about particular objects known by the kernel.

There is currently no way to determine whether a given operating system is supported other than to try it.

15 Configuration-Specific Information

While nearly all GDB commands are available for all native and cross versions of the debugger, there are some exceptions. This chapter describes things that are only available in certain configurations.

There are three major categories of configurations: native configurations, where the host and target are the same, embedded operating system configurations, which are usually the same for several different processor architectures, and bare embedded processors, which are quite different from each other.

15.1 Native

This section describes details specific to particular native configurations.

15.1.1 HP-UX

On HP-UX systems, if you refer to a function or variable name that begins with a dollar sign, GDB searches for a user or system name first, before it searches for a convenience variable.

15.1.2 SVR4 process information

Many versions of SVR4 provide a facility called '/proc' that can be used to examine the image of a running process using file-system subroutines. If GDB is configured for an operating system with this facility, the command `info proc` is available to report on several kinds of information about the process running your program. `info proc` works only on SVR4 systems that include the `procfs` code. This includes OSF/1 (Digital Unix), Solaris, Irix, and Unixware, but not HP-UX or Linux, for example.

`info proc`   Summarize available information about the process.

`info proc mappings`

> Report on the address ranges accessible in the program, with information on whether your program may read, write, or execute each range.

`info proc times`

> Starting time, user CPU time, and system CPU time for your program and its children.

`info proc id`

> Report on the process IDs related to your program: its own process ID, the ID of its parent, the process group ID, and the session ID.

`info proc status`
> General information on the state of the process. If the process is stopped, this report includes the reason for stopping, and any signal received.

`info proc all`
> Show all the above information about the process.

15.1.3 Features for Debugging DJGPP Programs

DJGPP is the port of GNU development tools to MS-DOS and MS-Windows. DJGPP programs are 32-bit protected-mode programs that use the *DPMI* (DOS Protected-Mode Interface) API to run on top of real-mode DOS systems and their emulations.

GDB supports native debugging of DJGPP programs, and defines a few commands specific to the DJGPP port. This subsection describes those commands.

`info dos`   This is a prefix of DJGPP-specific commands which print information about the target system and important OS structures.

`info dos sysinfo`
> This command displays assorted information about the underlying platform: the CPU type and features, the OS version and flavor, the DPMI version, and the available conventional and DPMI memory.

`info dos gdt`
`info dos ldt`
`info dos idt`
> These 3 commands display entries from, respectively, Global, Local, and Interrupt Descriptor Tables (GDT, LDT, and IDT). The descriptor tables are data structures which store a descriptor for each segment that is currently in use. The segment's selector is an index into a descriptor table; the table entry for that index holds the descriptor's base address and limit, and its attributes and access rights.
>
> A typical DJGPP program uses 3 segments: a code segment, a data segment (used for both data and the stack), and a DOS segment (which allows access to DOS/BIOS data structures and absolute addresses in conventional memory). However, the DPMI host will usually define additional segments in order to support the DPMI environment.
>
> These commands allow to display entries from the descriptor tables. Without an argument, all entries from the specified table are displayed. An argument, which should be an integer expression, means display a single entry whose index is given by

the argument. For example, here's a convenient way to display information about the debugged program's data segment:

```
(gdb) info dos ldt $ds
Ox13f: base=0x11970000 limit=0x0009ffff 32-Bit Data (Read/Write, Exp-up)
```

This comes in handy when you want to see whether a pointer is outside the data segment's limit (i.e. *garbled*).

info dos pde
info dos pte

These two commands display entries from, respectively, the Page Directory and the Page Tables. Page Directories and Page Tables are data structures which control how virtual memory addresses are mapped into physical addresses. A Page Table includes an entry for every page of memory that is mapped into the program's address space; there may be several Page Tables, each one holding up to 4096 entries. A Page Directory has up to 4096 entries, one each for every Page Table that is currently in use.

Without an argument, *info dos pde* displays the entire Page Directory, and *info dos pte* displays all the entries in all of the Page Tables. An argument, an integer expression, given to the *info dos pde* command means display only that entry from the Page Directory table. An argument given to the *info dos pte* command means display entries from a single Page Table, the one pointed to by the specified entry in the Page Directory.

These commands are useful when your program uses *DMA* (Direct Memory Access), which needs physical addresses to program the DMA controller.

These commands are supported only with some DPMI servers.

info dos address-pte *addr*

This command displays the Page Table entry for a specified linear address. The argument linear address *addr* should already have the appropriate segment's base address added to it, because this command accepts addresses which may belong to *any* segment. For example, here's how to display the Page Table entry for the page where the variable i is stored:

```
(gdb) info dos address-pte __djgpp_base_address + (char *)&i
Page Table entry for address 0x11a00d30:
Base=0x02698000 Dirty Acc. Not-Cached Write-Back Usr Read-Write +0xd30
```

This says that i is stored at offset 0xd30 from the page whose physical base address is 0x02698000, and prints all the attributes of that page.

Note that you must cast the addresses of variables to a **char ***, since otherwise the value of **__djgpp_base_address**, the base

address of all variables and functions in a DJGPP program, will be
added using the rules of C pointer arithmetics: if i is declared an
int, GDB will add 4 times the value of __djgpp_base_address
to the address of i.

Here's another example, it displays the Page Table entry for the
transfer buffer:

```
(gdb) info dos address-pte *((unsigned *)&_go32_info_block + 3)
Page Table entry for address 0x29110:
Base=0x00029000 Dirty Acc. Not-Cached Write-Back Usr Read-Write +0x110
```

(The + 3 offset is because the transfer buffer's address is the
3rd member of the _go32_info_block structure.) The output
of this command clearly shows that addresses in conventional
memory are mapped 1:1, i.e. the physical and linear addresses
are identical.

This command is supported only with some DPMI servers.

15.2 Embedded Operating Systems

This section describes configurations involving the debugging of embedded operating systems that are available for several different architectures.

GDB includes the ability to debug programs running on various real-time
operating systems.

15.2.1 Using GDB with VxWorks

target vxworks *machinename*

> A VxWorks system, attached via TCP/IP. The argument *ma-
> chinename* is the target system's machine name or IP address.

On VxWorks, load links *filename* dynamically on the current target system as well as adding its symbols in GDB.

GDB enables developers to spawn and debug tasks running on networked
VxWorks targets from a Unix host. Already-running tasks spawned from the
VxWorks shell can also be debugged. GDB uses code that runs on both the
Unix host and on the VxWorks target. The program gdb is installed and
executed on the Unix host. (It may be installed with the name vxgdb, to
distinguish it from a GDB for debugging programs on the host itself.)

VxWorks-timeout *args*

> All VxWorks-based targets now support the option vxworks-
> timeout. This option is set by the user, and *args* represents the
> number of seconds GDB waits for responses to rpc's. You might
> use this if your VxWorks target is a slow software simulator or
> is on the far side of a thin network line.

The following information on connecting to VxWorks was current when this manual was produced; newer releases of VxWorks may use revised procedures.

To use GDB with VxWorks, you must rebuild your VxWorks kernel to include the remote debugging interface routines in the VxWorks library 'rdb.a'. To do this, define INCLUDE_RDB in the VxWorks configuration file 'configAll.h' and rebuild your VxWorks kernel. The resulting kernel contains 'rdb.a', and spawns the source debugging task tRdbTask when VxWorks is booted. For more information on configuring and remaking VxWorks, see the manufacturer's manual.

Once you have included 'rdb.a' in your VxWorks system image and set your Unix execution search path to find GDB, you are ready to run GDB. From your Unix host, run gdb (or vxgdb, depending on your installation).

GDB comes up showing the prompt:

```
(vxgdb)
```

15.2.1.1 Connecting to VxWorks

The GDB command target lets you connect to a VxWorks target on the network. To connect to a target whose host name is "tt", type:

```
(vxgdb) target vxworks tt
```

GDB displays messages like these:

```
Attaching remote machine across net...
Connected to tt.
```

GDB then attempts to read the symbol tables of any object modules loaded into the VxWorks target since it was last booted. GDB locates these files by searching the directories listed in the command search path (see Section 4.4 [Your program's environment], page 25); if it fails to find an object file, it displays a message such as:

```
prog.o: No such file or directory.
```

When this happens, add the appropriate directory to the search path with the GDB command path, and execute the target command again.

15.2.1.2 VxWorks download

If you have connected to the VxWorks target and you want to debug an object that has not yet been loaded, you can use the GDB load command to download a file from Unix to VxWorks incrementally. The object file given as an argument to the load command is actually opened twice: first by the VxWorks target in order to download the code, then by GDB in order to read the symbol table. This can lead to problems if the current working directories on the two systems differ. If both systems have NFS mounted the same filesystems, you can avoid these problems by using absolute paths. Otherwise, it is simplest to set the working directory on both systems to the

directory in which the object file resides, and then to reference the file by
its name, without any path. For instance, a program 'prog.o' may reside in
'*vxpath*/vw/demo/rdb' in VxWorks and in '*hostpath*/vw/demo/rdb' on the
host. To load this program, type this on VxWorks:

```
-> cd "vxpath/vw/demo/rdb"
```

Then, in GDB, type:

```
(vxgdb) cd hostpath/vw/demo/rdb
(vxgdb) load prog.o
```

GDB displays a response similar to this:

```
Reading symbol data from wherever/vw/demo/rdb/prog.o... done.
```

You can also use the `load` command to reload an object module after
editing and recompiling the corresponding source file. Note that this makes
GDB delete all currently-defined breakpoints, auto-displays, and convenience
variables, and to clear the value history. (This is necessary in order to
preserve the integrity of debugger's data structures that reference the target
system's symbol table.)

15.2.1.3 Running tasks

You can also attach to an existing task using the `attach` command as
follows:

```
(vxgdb) attach task
```

where *task* is the VxWorks hexadecimal task ID. The task can be running
or suspended when you attach to it. Running tasks are suspended at the
time of attachment.

15.3 Embedded Processors

This section goes into details specific to particular embedded configurations.

15.3.1 AMD A29K Embedded

`target adapt` *dev*
> Adapt monitor for A29K.

`target amd-eb` *dev speed PROG*
> Remote PC-resident AMD EB29K board, attached over serial
> lines. *dev* is the serial device, as for `target remote`; *speed* al-
> lows you to specify the linespeed; and *PROG* is the name of the
> program to be debugged, as it appears to DOS on the PC. See
> Section 15.3.1.2 [EBMON protocol for AMD29K], page 175.

15.3.1.1 A29K UDI

GDB supports AMD's UDI ("Universal Debugger Interface") protocol for debugging the a29k processor family. To use this configuration with AMD targets running the MiniMON monitor, you need the program `MONTIP`, available from AMD at no charge. You can also use GDB with the UDI-conformant a29k simulator program `ISSTIP`, also available from AMD.

`target udi` *keyword*

> Select the UDI interface to a remote a29k board or simulator, where *keyword* is an entry in the AMD configuration file 'udi_soc'. This file contains keyword entries which specify parameters used to connect to a29k targets. If the 'udi_soc' file is not in your working directory, you must set the environment variable 'UDICONF' to its pathname.

15.3.1.2 EBMON protocol for AMD29K

AMD distributes a 29K development board meant to fit in a PC, together with a DOS-hosted monitor program called `EBMON`. As a shorthand term, this development system is called the "EB29K". To use GDB from a Unix system to run programs on the EB29K board, you must first connect a serial cable between the PC (which hosts the EB29K board) and a serial port on the Unix system. In the following, we assume you've hooked the cable between the PC's 'COM1' port and '/dev/ttya' on the Unix system.

15.3.1.3 Communications setup

The next step is to set up the PC's port, by doing something like this in DOS on the PC:

```
C:\> MODE com1:9600,n,8,1,none
```

This example—run on an MS DOS 4.0 system—sets the PC port to 9600 bps, no parity, eight data bits, one stop bit, and no "retry" action; you must match the communications parameters when establishing the Unix end of the connection as well.

To give control of the PC to the Unix side of the serial line, type the following at the DOS console:

```
C:\> CTTY com1
```

(Later, if you wish to return control to the DOS console, you can use the command `CTTY con`—but you must send it over the device that had control, in our example over the 'COM1' serial line.)

From the Unix host, use a communications program such as `tip` or `cu` to communicate with the PC; for example,

```
cu -s 9600 -l /dev/ttya
```

The cu options shown specify, respectively, the linespeed and the serial port
to use. If you use tip instead, your command line may look something like
the following:

```
tip -9600 /dev/ttya
```

Your system may require a different name where we show '/dev/ttya' as
the argument to tip. The communications parameters, including which port
to use, are associated with the tip argument in the "remote" descriptions
file—normally the system table '/etc/remote'.

Using the tip or cu connection, change the DOS working directory to
the directory containing a copy of your 29K program, then start the PC
program EBMON (an EB29K control program supplied with your board by
AMD). You should see an initial display from EBMON similar to the one that
follows, ending with the EBMON prompt '#'—

```
C:\> G:

G:\> CD \usr\joe\work29k

G:\USR\JOE\WORK29K> EBMON
Am29000 PC Coprocessor Board Monitor, version 3.0-18
Copyright 1990 Advanced Micro Devices, Inc.
Written by Gibbons and Associates, Inc.

Enter '?' or 'H' for help

PC Coprocessor Type    = EB29K
I/O Base               = 0x208
Memory Base            = 0xd0000

Data Memory Size       = 2048KB
Available I-RAM Range  = 0x8000 to 0x1fffff
Available D-RAM Range  = 0x80002000 to 0x801fffff

PageSize               = 0x400
Register Stack Size    = 0x800
Memory Stack Size      = 0x1800

CPU PRL                = 0x3
Am29027 Available      = No
Byte Write Available   = Yes

# ~.
```

Then exit the cu or tip program (done in the example by typing ~. at
the EBMON prompt). EBMON keeps running, ready for GDB to take over.

For this example, we've assumed what is probably the most convenient way to make sure the same 29K program is on both the PC and the Unix system: a PC/NFS connection that establishes "drive 'G:'" on the PC as a file system on the Unix host. If you do not have PC/NFS or something similar connecting the two systems, you must arrange some other way—perhaps floppy-disk transfer—of getting the 29K program from the Unix system to the PC; GDB does *not* download it over the serial line.

15.3.1.4 EB29K cross-debugging

Finally, `cd` to the directory containing an image of your 29K program on the Unix system, and start GDB—specifying as argument the name of your 29K program:

```
cd /usr/joe/work29k
gdb myfoo
```

Now you can use the `target` command:

```
target amd-eb /dev/ttya 9600 MYFOO
```

In this example, we've assumed your program is in a file called 'myfoo'. Note that the filename given as the last argument to `target amd-eb` should be the name of the program as it appears to DOS. In our example this is simply `MYFOO`, but in general it can include a DOS path, and depending on your transfer mechanism may not resemble the name on the Unix side.

At this point, you can set any breakpoints you wish; when you are ready to see your program run on the 29K board, use the GDB command `run`.

To stop debugging the remote program, use the GDB `detach` command.

To return control of the PC to its console, use `tip` or `cu` once again, after your GDB session has concluded, to attach to `EBMON`. You can then type the command `q` to shut down `EBMON`, returning control to the DOS command-line interpreter. Type *CTTY con* to return command input to the main DOS console, and type ˜. to leave `tip` or `cu`.

15.3.1.5 Remote log

The `target amd-eb` command creates a file 'eb.log' in the current working directory, to help debug problems with the connection. 'eb.log' records all the output from `EBMON`, including echoes of the commands sent to it. Running 'tail -f' on this file in another window often helps to understand trouble with `EBMON`, or unexpected events on the PC side of the connection.

15.3.2 ARM

`target rdi` *dev*
ARM Angel monitor, via RDI library interface to ADP protocol. You may use this target to communicate with both boards

running the Angel monitor, or with the EmbeddedICE JTAG
debug device.

`target rdp` *dev*

ARM Demon monitor.

15.3.3 Hitachi H8/300

`target hms` *dev*

A Hitachi SH, H8/300, or H8/500 board, attached via serial
line to your host. Use special commands `device` and `speed` to
control the serial line and the communications speed used.

`target e7000` *dev*

E7000 emulator for Hitachi H8 and SH.

`target sh3` *dev*
`target sh3e` *dev*

Hitachi SH-3 and SH-3E target systems.

When you select remote debugging to a Hitachi SH, H8/300, or H8/500
board, the `load` command downloads your program to the Hitachi board
and also opens it as the current executable target for GDB on your host
(like the `file` command).

GDB needs to know these things to talk to your Hitachi SH, H8/300, or
H8/500:

1. that you want to use '`target hms`', the remote debugging interface for
   Hitachi microprocessors, or '`target e7000`', the in-circuit emulator for
   the Hitachi SH and the Hitachi 300H. ('`target hms`' is the default when
   GDB is configured specifically for the Hitachi SH, H8/300, or H8/500.)

2. what serial device connects your host to your Hitachi board (the first
   serial device available on your host is the default).

3. what speed to use over the serial device.

15.3.3.1 Connecting to Hitachi boards

Use the special GDB command '`device` *port*' if you need to explicitly set
the serial device. The default *port* is the first available port on your host.
This is only necessary on Unix hosts, where it is typically something like
'`/dev/ttya`'.

GDB has another special command to set the communications speed:
'`speed` *bps*'. This command also is only used from Unix hosts; on DOS hosts,
set the line speed as usual from outside GDB with the DOS `mode` command
(for instance, *mode com2:9600,n,8,1,p* for a 9600 bps connection).

The '`device`' and '`speed`' commands are available only when you use a
Unix host to debug your Hitachi microprocessor programs. If you use a DOS
host, GDB depends on an auxiliary terminate-and-stay-resident program

called `asynctsr` to communicate with the development board through a PC serial port. You must also use the DOS `mode` command to set up the serial port on the DOS side.

The following sample session illustrates the steps needed to start a program under GDB control on an H8/300. The example uses a sample H8/300 program called 't.x'. The procedure is the same for the Hitachi SH and the H8/500.

First hook up your development board. In this example, we use a board attached to serial port `COM2`; if you use a different serial port, substitute its name in the argument of the `mode` command. When you call `asynctsr`, the auxiliary comms program used by the debugger, you give it just the numeric part of the serial port's name; for example, 'asyncstr 2' below runs `asyncstr` on `COM2`.

```
C:\H8300\TEST> asynctsr 2
C:\H8300\TEST> mode com2:9600,n,8,1,p

Resident portion of MODE loaded

COM2: 9600, n, 8, 1, p
```

Warning: We have noticed a bug in PC-NFS that conflicts with `asynctsr`. If you also run PC-NFS on your DOS host, you may need to disable it, or even boot without it, to use `asynctsr` to control your development board.

Now that serial communications are set up, and the development board is connected, you can start up GDB. Call `gdb` with the name of your program as the argument. GDB prompts you, as usual, with the prompt '(gdb)'. Use two special commands to begin your debugging session: 'target hms' to specify cross-debugging to the Hitachi board, and the `load` command to download your program to the board. `load` displays the names of the program's sections, and a '*' for each 2K of data downloaded. (If you want to refresh GDB data on symbols or on the executable file without downloading, use the GDB commands `file` or `symbol-file`. These commands, and `load` itself, are described in Section 13.1 [Commands to specify files], page 135.)

```
(eg-C:\H8300\TEST) gdb t.x
GDB is free software and you are welcome to distribute copies
 of it under certain conditions; type "show copying" to see
 the conditions.
There is absolutely no warranty for GDB; type "show warranty"
for details.
GDB 5.1.1, Copyright 1992 Free Software Foundation, Inc...
(gdb) target hms
Connected to remote H8/300 HMS system.
(gdb) load t.x
```

```
.text    : 0x8000 .. 0xabde ***********
.data    : 0xabde .. 0xad30 *
.stack   : 0xf000 .. 0xf014 *
```

At this point, you're ready to run or debug your program. From here on, you can use all the usual GDB commands. The `break` command sets breakpoints; the `run` command starts your program; `print` or `x` display data; the `continue` command resumes execution after stopping at a breakpoint. You can use the `help` command at any time to find out more about GDB commands.

Remember, however, that *operating system* facilities aren't available on your development board; for example, if your program hangs, you can't send an interrupt—but you can press the RESET switch!

Use the RESET button on the development board

- to interrupt your program (don't use *ctl-C* on the DOS host—it has no way to pass an interrupt signal to the development board); and

- to return to the GDB command prompt after your program finishes normally. The communications protocol provides no other way for GDB to detect program completion.

In either case, GDB sees the effect of a RESET on the development board as a "normal exit" of your program.

15.3.3.2 Using the E7000 in-circuit emulator

You can use the E7000 in-circuit emulator to develop code for either the Hitachi SH or the H8/300H. Use one of these forms of the 'target e7000' command to connect GDB to your E7000:

target e7000 *port speed*

> Use this form if your E7000 is connected to a serial port. The *port* argument identifies what serial port to use (for example, 'com2'). The third argument is the line speed in bits per second (for example, '9600').

target e7000 *hostname*

> If your E7000 is installed as a host on a TCP/IP network, you can just specify its hostname; GDB uses `telnet` to connect.

15.3.3.3 Special GDB commands for Hitachi micros

Some GDB commands are available only for the H8/300:

set machine h8300
set machine h8300h

> Condition GDB for one of the two variants of the H8/300 architecture with 'set machine'. You can use 'show machine' to check which variant is currently in effect.

15.3.4 H8/500

`set memory` *mod*
`show memory`

> Specify which H8/500 memory model (*mod*) you are using with
> 'set memory'; check which memory model is in effect with 'show
> memory'. The accepted values for *mod* are `small`, `big`, `medium`,
> and `compact`.

15.3.5 Intel i960

`target mon960` *dev*

> MON960 monitor for Intel i960.

`target nindy` *devicename*

> An Intel 960 board controlled by a Nindy Monitor. *devicename*
> is the name of the serial device to use for the connection, e.g.
> '/dev/ttya'.

Nindy is a ROM Monitor program for Intel 960 target systems. When
GDB is configured to control a remote Intel 960 using Nindy, you can tell
GDB how to connect to the 960 in several ways:

- Through command line options specifying serial port, version of the
  Nindy protocol, and communications speed;

- By responding to a prompt on startup;

- By using the `target` command at any point during your GDB session.
  See Section 14.2 [Commands for managing targets], page 143.

With the Nindy interface to an Intel 960 board, `load` downloads *filename*
to the 960 as well as adding its symbols in GDB.

15.3.5.1 Startup with Nindy

If you simply start `gdb` without using any command-line options, you are
prompted for what serial port to use, *before* you reach the ordinary GDB
prompt:

> `Attach /dev/ttyNN -- specify NN, or "quit" to quit:`

Respond to the prompt with whatever suffix (after '/dev/tty') identifies the
serial port you want to use. You can, if you choose, simply start up with
no Nindy connection by responding to the prompt with an empty line. If
you do this and later wish to attach to Nindy, use `target` (see Section 14.2
[Commands for managing targets], page 143).

15.3.5.2 Options for Nindy

These are the startup options for beginning your GDB session with a
Nindy-960 board attached:

-r *port*   Specify the serial port name of a serial interface to be used to
               connect to the target system. This option is only available when
               GDB is configured for the Intel 960 target architecture. You may
               specify *port* as any of: a full pathname (e.g. '-r /dev/ttya'),
               a device name in '/dev' (e.g. '-r ttya'), or simply the unique
               suffix for a specific tty (e.g. '-r a').

-O   (An uppercase letter "O", not a zero.) Specify that GDB should
               use the "old" Nindy monitor protocol to connect to the target
               system. This option is only available when GDB is configured
               for the Intel 960 target architecture.

> *Warning:* if you specify '-O', but are actually trying
> to connect to a target system that expects the newer
> protocol, the connection fails, appearing to be a speed
> mismatch. GDB repeatedly attempts to reconnect at
> several different line speeds. You can abort this process
> with an interrupt.

-brk   Specify that GDB should first send a **BREAK** signal to the target
               system, in an attempt to reset it, before connecting to a Nindy
               target.

> *Warning:* Many target systems do not have the hard-
> ware that this requires; it only works with a few boards.

The standard '-b' option controls the line speed used on the serial port.

15.3.5.3 Nindy reset command

reset   For a Nindy target, this command sends a "break" to the remote
               target system; this is only useful if the target has been equipped
               with a circuit to perform a hard reset (or some other interesting
               action) when a break is detected.

15.3.6 Mitsubishi M32R/D

target m32r *dev*
         Mitsubishi M32R/D ROM monitor.

15.3.7 M68k

The Motorola m68k configuration includes ColdFire support, and target
command for the following ROM monitors.

target abug *dev*
         ABug ROM monitor for M68K.

target cpu32bug *dev*
         CPU32BUG monitor, running on a CPU32 (M68K) board.

target dbug *dev*
> dBUG ROM monitor for Motorola ColdFire.

target est *dev*
> EST-300 ICE monitor, running on a CPU32 (M68K) board.

target rom68k *dev*
> ROM 68K monitor, running on an M68K IDP board.

If GDB is configured with **m68*-ericsson-***, it will instead have only a single special target command:

target es1800 *dev*
> ES-1800 emulator for M68K.

[context?]

target rombug *dev*
> ROMBUG ROM monitor for OS/9000.

15.3.8 M88K

target bug *dev*
> BUG monitor, running on a MVME187 (m88k) board.

15.3.9 MIPS Embedded

GDB can use the MIPS remote debugging protocol to talk to a MIPS board attached to a serial line. This is available when you configure GDB with '--target=mips-idt-ecoff'.

Use these GDB commands to specify the connection to your target board:

target mips *port*
> To run a program on the board, start up **gdb** with the name of your program as the argument. To connect to the board, use the command 'target mips *port*', where *port* is the name of the serial port connected to the board. If the program has not already been downloaded to the board, you may use the **load** command to download it. You can then use all the usual GDB commands.
>
> For example, this sequence connects to the target board through a serial port, and loads and runs a program called *prog* through the debugger:
>
> ```
> host$ gdb prog
> GDB is free software and ...
> (gdb) target mips /dev/ttyb
> (gdb) load prog
> (gdb) run
> ```

target mips *hostname:portnumber*

>On some GDB host configurations, you can specify a TCP connection (for instance, to a serial line managed by a terminal concentrator) instead of a serial port, using the syntax '*hostname:portnumber*'.

target pmon *port*

>PMON ROM monitor.

target ddb *port*

>NEC's DDB variant of PMON for Vr4300.

target lsi *port*

>LSI variant of PMON.

target r3900 *dev*

>Densan DVE-R3900 ROM monitor for Toshiba R3900 Mips.

target array *dev*

>Array Tech LSI33K RAID controller board.

GDB also supports these special commands for MIPS targets:

set processor *args*
show processor

>Use the **set processor** command to set the type of MIPS processor when you want to access processor-type-specific registers. For example, **set processor** *r3041* tells GDB to use the CPU registers appropriate for the 3041 chip. Use the **show processor** command to see what MIPS processor GDB is using. Use the **info reg** command to see what registers GDB is using.

set mipsfpu double
set mipsfpu single
set mipsfpu none
show mipsfpu

>If your target board does not support the MIPS floating point coprocessor, you should use the command 'set mipsfpu none' (if you need this, you may wish to put the command in your GDB init file). This tells GDB how to find the return value of functions which return floating point values. It also allows GDB to avoid saving the floating point registers when calling functions on the board. If you are using a floating point coprocessor with only single precision floating point support, as on the R4650 processor, use the command 'set mipsfpu single'. The default double precision floating point coprocessor may be selected using 'set mipsfpu double'.
>
>In previous versions the only choices were double precision or no floating point, so 'set mipsfpu on' will select double precision and 'set mipsfpu off' will select no floating point.

As usual, you can inquire about the `mipsfpu` variable with 'show mipsfpu'.

`set remotedebug` *n*
`show remotedebug`

You can see some debugging information about communications with the board by setting the `remotedebug` variable. If you set it to 1 using 'set remotedebug 1', every packet is displayed. If you set it to 2, every character is displayed. You can check the current value at any time with the command 'show remotedebug'.

`set timeout` *seconds*
`set retransmit-timeout` *seconds*
`show timeout`
`show retransmit-timeout`

You can control the timeout used while waiting for a packet, in the MIPS remote protocol, with the `set timeout` *seconds* command. The default is 5 seconds. Similarly, you can control the timeout used while waiting for an acknowledgement of a packet with the `set retransmit-timeout` *seconds* command. The default is 3 seconds. You can inspect both values with `show timeout` and `show retransmit-timeout`. (These commands are *only* available when GDB is configured for '--target=mips-idt-ecoff'.)

The timeout set by `set timeout` does not apply when GDB is waiting for your program to stop. In that case, GDB waits forever because it has no way of knowing how long the program is going to run before stopping.

15.3.10 PowerPC

`target dink32` *dev*

DINK32 ROM monitor.

`target ppcbug` *dev*
`target ppcbug1` *dev*

PPCBUG ROM monitor for PowerPC.

`target sds` *dev*

SDS monitor, running on a PowerPC board (such as Motorola's ADS).

15.3.11 HP PA Embedded

`target op50n` *dev*

OP50N monitor, running on an OKI HPPA board.

`target w89k` *dev*

W89K monitor, running on a Winbond HPPA board.

15.3.12 Hitachi SH

target hms *dev*
> A Hitachi SH board attached via serial line to your host. Use special commands `device` and `speed` to control the serial line and the communications speed used.

target e7000 *dev*
> E7000 emulator for Hitachi SH.

target sh3 *dev*
target sh3e *dev*
> Hitachi SH-3 and SH-3E target systems.

15.3.13 Tsqware Sparclet

GDB enables developers to debug tasks running on Sparclet targets from a Unix host. GDB uses code that runs on both the Unix host and on the Sparclet target. The program `gdb` is installed and executed on the Unix host.

remotetimeout *args*
> GDB supports the option `remotetimeout`. This option is set by the user, and *args* represents the number of seconds GDB waits for responses.

When compiling for debugging, include the options '`-g`' to get debug information and '`-Ttext`' to relocate the program to where you wish to load it on the target. You may also want to add the options '`-n`' or '`-N`' in order to reduce the size of the sections. Example:

    sparclet-aout-gcc prog.c -Ttext 0x12010000 -g -o prog -N

You can use `objdump` to verify that the addresses are what you intended:

    sparclet-aout-objdump --headers --syms prog

Once you have set your Unix execution search path to find GDB, you are ready to run GDB. From your Unix host, run `gdb` (or `sparclet-aout-gdb`, depending on your installation).

GDB comes up showing the prompt:

    (gdbslet)

15.3.13.1 Setting file to debug

The GDB command `file` lets you choose with program to debug.

    (gdbslet) file prog

GDB then attempts to read the symbol table of 'prog'. GDB locates the file by searching the directories listed in the command search path. If the file was compiled with debug information (option "-g"), source files will be searched as well. GDB locates the source files by searching the directories listed in the directory search path (see Section 4.4 [Your program's environment], page 25). If it fails to find a file, it displays a message such as:

```
prog: No such file or directory.
```

When this happens, add the appropriate directories to the search paths with the GDB commands `path` and `dir`, and execute the `target` command again.

15.3.13.2 Connecting to Sparclet

The GDB command `target` lets you connect to a Sparclet target. To connect to a target on serial port "ttya", type:

```
(gdbslet) target sparclet /dev/ttya
Remote target sparclet connected to /dev/ttya
main () at ../prog.c:3
```

GDB displays messages like these:

```
Connected to ttya.
```

15.3.13.3 Sparclet download

Once connected to the Sparclet target, you can use the GDB `load` command to download the file from the host to the target. The file name and load offset should be given as arguments to the `load` command. Since the file format is aout, the program must be loaded to the starting address. You can use `objdump` to find out what this value is. The load offset is an offset which is added to the VMA (virtual memory address) of each of the file's sections. For instance, if the program 'prog' was linked to text address 0x1201000, with data at 0x12010160 and bss at 0x12010170, in GDB, type:

```
(gdbslet) load prog 0x12010000
Loading section .text, size 0xdb0 vma 0x12010000
```

If the code is loaded at a different address then what the program was linked to, you may need to use the `section` and `add-symbol-file` commands to tell GDB where to map the symbol table.

15.3.13.4 Running and debugging

You can now begin debugging the task using GDB's execution control commands, `b`, `step`, `run`, etc. See the GDB manual for the list of commands.

```
(gdbslet) b main
Breakpoint 1 at 0x12010000: file prog.c, line 3.
```

```
(gdbslet) run
Starting program: prog
Breakpoint 1, main (argc=1, argv=0xeffff21c) at prog.c:3
3          char *symarg = 0;
(gdbslet) step
4          char *execarg = "hello!";
(gdbslet)
```

15.3.14 Fujitsu Sparclite

target sparclite *dev*

> Fujitsu sparclite boards, used only for the purpose of loading. You must use an additional command to debug the program. For example: target remote *dev* using GDB standard remote protocol.

15.3.15 Tandem ST2000

GDB may be used with a Tandem ST2000 phone switch, running Tandem's STDBUG protocol.

To connect your ST2000 to the host system, see the manufacturer's manual. Once the ST2000 is physically attached, you can run:

> target st2000 *dev speed*

to establish it as your debugging environment. *dev* is normally the name of a serial device, such as '/dev/ttya', connected to the ST2000 via a serial line. You can instead specify *dev* as a TCP connection (for example, to a serial line attached via a terminal concentrator) using the syntax *hostname:portnumber*.

The **load** and **attach** commands are *not* defined for this target; you must load your program into the ST2000 as you normally would for standalone operation. GDB reads debugging information (such as symbols) from a separate, debugging version of the program available on your host computer.

These auxiliary GDB commands are available to help you with the ST2000 environment:

st2000 *command*

> Send a *command* to the STDBUG monitor. See the manufacturer's manual for available commands.

connect

> Connect the controlling terminal to the STDBUG command monitor. When you are done interacting with STDBUG, typing either of two character sequences gets you back to the GDB command prompt: (RET)~. (Return, followed by tilde and period) or (RET)~(C-d) (Return, followed by tilde and control-D).

15.3.16 Zilog Z8000

When configured for debugging Zilog Z8000 targets, GDB includes a Z8000 simulator.

For the Z8000 family, 'target sim' simulates either the Z8002 (the unsegmented variant of the Z8000 architecture) or the Z8001 (the segmented variant). The simulator recognizes which architecture is appropriate by inspecting the object code.

target sim *args*

> Debug programs on a simulated CPU. If the simulator supports setup options, specify them via *args*.

After specifying this target, you can debug programs for the simulated CPU in the same style as programs for your host computer; use the `file` command to load a new program image, the `run` command to run your program, and so on.

As well as making available all the usual machine registers (see Section 8.10 [Registers], page 85), the Z8000 simulator provides three additional items of information as specially named registers:

cycles   Counts clock-ticks in the simulator.

insts   Counts instructions run in the simulator.

time   Execution time in 60ths of a second.

You can refer to these values in GDB expressions with the usual conventions; for example, 'b fputc if $cycles>5000' sets a conditional breakpoint that suspends only after at least 5000 simulated clock ticks.

15.4 Architectures

This section describes characteristics of architectures that affect all uses of GDB with the architecture, both native and cross.

15.4.1 A29K

set rstack_high_address *address*

> On AMD 29000 family processors, registers are saved in a separate *register stack*. There is no way for GDB to determine the extent of this stack. Normally, GDB just assumes that the stack is "large enough". This may result in GDB referencing memory locations that do not exist. If necessary, you can get around this problem by specifying the ending address of the register stack with the set rstack_high_address command. The argument should be an address, which you probably want to precede with '0x' to specify in hexadecimal.

`show rstack_high_address`
>Display the current limit of the register stack, on AMD 29000
>family processors.

15.4.2 Alpha

See the following section.

15.4.3 MIPS

Alpha- and MIPS-based computers use an unusual stack frame, which
sometimes requires GDB to search backward in the object code to find the
beginning of a function.

To improve response time (especially for embedded applications, where
GDB may be restricted to a slow serial line for this search) you may want
to limit the size of this search, using one of these commands:

`set heuristic-fence-post` *limit*
>Restrict GDB to examining at most *limit* bytes in its search for
>the beginning of a function. A value of *0* (the default) means
>there is no limit. However, except for *0*, the larger the limit the
>more bytes `heuristic-fence-post` must search and therefore
>the longer it takes to run.

`show heuristic-fence-post`
>Display the current limit.

These commands are available *only* when GDB is configured for debugging
programs on Alpha or MIPS processors.

16 Controlling GDB

You can alter the way GDB interacts with you by using the **set** command. For commands controlling how GDB displays data, see Section 8.7 [Print settings], page 77. Other settings are described here.

16.1 Prompt

GDB indicates its readiness to read a command by printing a string called the *prompt*. This string is normally '**(gdb)**'. You can change the prompt string with the **set prompt** command. For instance, when debugging GDB with GDB, it is useful to change the prompt in one of the GDB sessions so that you can always tell which one you are talking to.

Note: **set prompt** does not add a space for you after the prompt you set. This allows you to set a prompt which ends in a space or a prompt that does not.

set prompt *newprompt*
> Directs GDB to use *newprompt* as its prompt string henceforth.

show prompt
> Prints a line of the form: '**Gdb's prompt is:** *your-prompt*'

16.2 Command editing

GDB reads its input commands via the *readline* interface. This GNU library provides consistent behavior for programs which provide a command line interface to the user. Advantages are GNU Emacs-style or *vi*-style inline editing of commands, **csh**-like history substitution, and a storage and recall of command history across debugging sessions.

You may control the behavior of command line editing in GDB with the command **set**.

set editing
set editing on
> Enable command line editing (enabled by default).

set editing off
> Disable command line editing.

show editing
> Show whether command line editing is enabled.

16.3 Command history

GDB can keep track of the commands you type during your debugging sessions, so that you can be certain of precisely what happened. Use these commands to manage the GDB command history facility.

set history filename *fname*

> Set the name of the GDB command history file to *fname*. This is the file where GDB reads an initial command history list, and where it writes the command history from this session when it exits. You can access this list through history expansion or through the history command editing characters listed below. This file defaults to the value of the environment variable `GDBHISTFILE`, or to '`./.gdb_history`' ('`./_gdb_history`' on MS-DOS) if this variable is not set.

set history save
set history save on

> Record command history in a file, whose name may be specified with the **set history filename** command. By default, this option is disabled.

set history save off

> Stop recording command history in a file.

set history size *size*

> Set the number of commands which GDB keeps in its history list. This defaults to the value of the environment variable `HISTSIZE`, or to 256 if this variable is not set.

History expansion assigns special meaning to the character *!*.

Since *!* is also the logical not operator in C, history expansion is off by default. If you decide to enable history expansion with the **set history expansion on** command, you may sometimes need to follow *!* (when it is used as logical not, in an expression) with a space or a tab to prevent it from being expanded. The readline history facilities do not attempt substitution on the strings *!=* and *!(*, even when history expansion is enabled.

The commands to control history expansion are:

set history expansion on
set history expansion

> Enable history expansion. History expansion is off by default.

set history expansion off

> Disable history expansion.

> The readline code comes with more complete documentation of editing and history expansion features. Users unfamiliar with GNU Emacs or **vi** may wish to read it.

```
show history
show history filename
show history save
show history size
show history expansion
```
These commands display the state of the GDB history parameters. `show history` by itself displays all four states.

```
show commands
```
Display the last ten commands in the command history.

```
show commands n
```
Print ten commands centered on command number *n*.

```
show commands +
```
Print ten commands just after the commands last printed.

16.4 Screen size

Certain commands to GDB may produce large amounts of information output to the screen. To help you read all of it, GDB pauses and asks you for input at the end of each page of output. Type (RET) when you want to continue the output, or `q` to discard the remaining output. Also, the screen width setting determines when to wrap lines of output. Depending on what is being printed, GDB tries to break the line at a readable place, rather than simply letting it overflow onto the following line.

Normally GDB knows the size of the screen from the terminal driver software. For example, on Unix GDB uses the termcap data base together with the value of the TERM environment variable and the `stty rows` and `stty cols` settings. If this is not correct, you can override it with the `set height` and `set width` commands:

```
set height lpp
show height
set width cpl
show width
```
These `set` commands specify a screen height of *lpp* lines and a screen width of *cpl* characters. The associated `show` commands display the current settings.

If you specify a height of zero lines, GDB does not pause during output no matter how long the output is. This is useful if output is to a file or to an editor buffer.

Likewise, you can specify '`set width 0`' to prevent GDB from wrapping its output.

16.5 Numbers

You can always enter numbers in octal, decimal, or hexadecimal in GDB by the usual conventions: octal numbers begin with '0', decimal numbers end with '.', and hexadecimal numbers begin with '0x'. Numbers that begin with none of these are, by default, entered in base 10; likewise, the default display for numbers—when no particular format is specified—is base 10. You can change the default base for both input and output with the `set radix` command.

`set input-radix` *base*

> Set the default base for numeric input. Supported choices for *base* are decimal 8, 10, or 16. *base* must itself be specified either unambiguously or using the current default radix; for example, any of
>
> ```
> set radix 012
> set radix 10.
> set radix 0xa
> ```
>
> sets the base to decimal. On the other hand, '`set radix 10`' leaves the radix unchanged no matter what it was.

`set output-radix` *base*

> Set the default base for numeric display. Supported choices for *base* are decimal 8, 10, or 16. *base* must itself be specified either unambiguously or using the current default radix.

`show input-radix`

> Display the current default base for numeric input.

`show output-radix`

> Display the current default base for numeric display.

16.6 Optional warnings and messages

By default, GDB is silent about its inner workings. If you are running on a slow machine, you may want to use the `set verbose` command. This makes GDB tell you when it does a lengthy internal operation, so you will not think it has crashed.

Currently, the messages controlled by `set verbose` are those which announce that the symbol table for a source file is being read; see `symbol-file` in Section 13.1 [Commands to specify files], page 135.

`set verbose on`

> Enables GDB output of certain informational messages.

`set verbose off`

> Disables GDB output of certain informational messages.

`show verbose`

        Displays whether `set verbose` is on or off.

By default, if GDB encounters bugs in the symbol table of an object file, it is silent; but if you are debugging a compiler, you may find this information useful (see Section 13.2 [Errors reading symbol files], page 139).

`set complaints` *limit*

        Permits GDB to output *limit* complaints about each type of unusual symbols before becoming silent about the problem. Set *limit* to zero to suppress all complaints; set it to a large number to prevent complaints from being suppressed.

`show complaints`

        Displays how many symbol complaints GDB is permitted to produce.

By default, GDB is cautious, and asks what sometimes seems to be a lot of stupid questions to confirm certain commands. For example, if you try to run a program which is already running:

```
(gdb) run
The program being debugged has been started already.
Start it from the beginning? (y or n)
```

If you are willing to unflinchingly face the consequences of your own commands, you can disable this "feature":

`set confirm off`

        Disables confirmation requests.

`set confirm on`

        Enables confirmation requests (the default).

`show confirm`

        Displays state of confirmation requests.

16.7 Optional messages about internal happenings

`set debug arch`

        Turns on or off display of gdbarch debugging info. The default is off

`show debug arch`

        Displays the current state of displaying gdbarch debugging info.

`set debug event`

        Turns on or off display of GDB event debugging info. The default is off.

`show debug event`

> Displays the current state of displaying GDB event debugging info.

`set debug expression`

> Turns on or off display of GDB expression debugging info. The default is off.

`show debug expression`

> Displays the current state of displaying GDB expression debugging info.

`set debug overload`

> Turns on or off display of GDB C++ overload debugging info. This includes info such as ranking of functions, etc. The default is off.

`show debug overload`

> Displays the current state of displaying GDB C++ overload debugging info.

`set debug remote`

> Turns on or off display of reports on all packets sent back and forth across the serial line to the remote machine. The info is printed on the GDB standard output stream. The default is off.

`show debug remote`

> Displays the state of display of remote packets.

`set debug serial`

> Turns on or off display of GDB serial debugging info. The default is off.

`show debug serial`

> Displays the current state of displaying GDB serial debugging info.

`set debug target`

> Turns on or off display of GDB target debugging info. This info includes what is going on at the target level of GDB, as it happens. The default is off.

`show debug target`

> Displays the current state of displaying GDB target debugging info.

`set debug varobj`

> Turns on or off display of GDB variable object debugging info. The default is off.

`show debug varobj`

> Displays the current state of displaying GDB variable object debugging info.

17 Canned Sequences of Commands

Aside from breakpoint commands (see Section 5.1.7 [Breakpoint command lists], page 47), GDB provides two ways to store sequences of commands for execution as a unit: user-defined commands and command files.

17.1 User-defined commands

A *user-defined command* is a sequence of GDB commands to which you assign a new name as a command. This is done with the **define** command. User commands may accept up to 10 arguments separated by whitespace. Arguments are accessed within the user command via *$arg0...$arg9*. A trivial example:

```
define adder
    print $arg0 + $arg1 + $arg2
```

To execute the command use:

```
adder 1 2 3
```

This defines the command **adder**, which prints the sum of its three arguments. Note the arguments are text substitutions, so they may reference variables, use complex expressions, or even perform inferior functions calls.

define *commandname*

> Define a command named *commandname*. If there is already a command by that name, you are asked to confirm that you want to redefine it.
>
> The definition of the command is made up of other GDB command lines, which are given following the **define** command. The end of these commands is marked by a line containing **end**.

if

> Takes a single argument, which is an expression to evaluate. It is followed by a series of commands that are executed only if the expression is true (nonzero). There can then optionally be a line **else**, followed by a series of commands that are only executed if the expression was false. The end of the list is marked by a line containing **end**.

while

> The syntax is similar to **if**: the command takes a single argument, which is an expression to evaluate, and must be followed by the commands to execute, one per line, terminated by an **end**. The commands are executed repeatedly as long as the expression evaluates to true.

document *commandname*

> Document the user-defined command *commandname*, so that it can be accessed by **help**. The command *commandname* must already be defined. This command reads lines of documentation

just as **define** reads the lines of the command definition, ending with **end**. After the **document** command is finished, **help** on command *commandname* displays the documentation you have written.

You may use the **document** command again to change the documentation of a command. Redefining the command with **define** does not change the documentation.

help user-defined

List all user-defined commands, with the first line of the documentation (if any) for each.

show user
show user *commandname*

Display the GDB commands used to define *commandname* (but not its documentation). If no *commandname* is given, display the definitions for all user-defined commands.

When user-defined commands are executed, the commands of the definition are not printed. An error in any command stops execution of the user-defined command.

If used interactively, commands that would ask for confirmation proceed without asking when used inside a user-defined command. Many GDB commands that normally print messages to say what they are doing omit the messages when used in a user-defined command.

17.2 User-defined command hooks

You may define *hooks*, which are a special kind of user-defined command. Whenever you run the command 'foo', if the user-defined command 'hook-foo' exists, it is executed (with no arguments) before that command.

A hook may also be defined which is run after the command you executed. Whenever you run the command 'foo', if the user-defined command 'hookpost-foo' exists, it is executed (with no arguments) after that command. Post-execution hooks may exist simultaneously with pre-execution hooks, for the same command.

It is valid for a hook to call the command which it hooks. If this occurs, the hook is not re-executed, thereby avoiding infinte recursion.

In addition, a pseudo-command, 'stop' exists. Defining ('hook-stop') makes the associated commands execute every time execution stops in your program: before breakpoint commands are run, displays are printed, or the stack frame is printed.

For example, to ignore **SIGALRM** signals while single-stepping, but treat them normally during normal execution, you could define:

```
define hook-stop
handle SIGALRM nopass
```

```
end

define hook-run
handle SIGALRM pass
end

define hook-continue
handle SIGLARM pass
end
```

As a further example, to hook at the begining and end of the **echo** command, and to add extra text to the beginning and end of the message, you could define:

```
define hook-echo
echo <<<---
end

define hookpost-echo
echo --->>>\n
end

(gdb) echo Hello World
<<<---Hello World--->>>
(gdb)
```

You can define a hook for any single-word command in GDB, but not for command aliases; you should define a hook for the basic command name, e.g. **backtrace** rather than **bt**. If an error occurs during the execution of your hook, execution of GDB commands stops and GDB issues a prompt (before the command that you actually typed had a chance to run).

If you try to define a hook which does not match any known command, you get a warning from the **define** command.

17.3 Command files

A command file for GDB is a file of lines that are GDB commands. Comments (lines starting with #) may also be included. An empty line in a command file does nothing; it does not mean to repeat the last command, as it would from the terminal.

When you start GDB, it automatically executes commands from its *init files*. These are files named '.gdbinit' on Unix and 'gdb.ini' on DOS/Windows. During startup, GDB does the following:

1. Reads the init file (if any) in your home directory[1].

2. Processes command line options and operands.

3. Reads the init file (if any) in the current working directory.

4. Reads command files specified by the '-x' option.

The init file in your home directory can set options (such as 'set complaints') that affect subsequent processing of command line options and operands. Init files are not executed if you use the '-nx' option (see Section 2.1.2 [Choosing modes], page 13).

On some configurations of GDB, the init file is known by a different name (these are typically environments where a specialized form of GDB may need to coexist with other forms, hence a different name for the specialized version's init file). These are the environments with special init file names:

- VxWorks (Wind River Systems real-time OS): '.vxgdbinit'

- OS68K (Enea Data Systems real-time OS): '.os68gdbinit'

- ES-1800 (Ericsson Telecom AB M68000 emulator): '.esgdbinit'

You can also request the execution of a command file with the source command:

source *filename*
> Execute the command file *filename*.

The lines in a command file are executed sequentially. They are not printed as they are executed. An error in any command terminates execution of the command file.

Commands that would ask for confirmation if used interactively proceed without asking when used in a command file. Many GDB commands that normally print messages to say what they are doing omit the messages when called from command files.

17.4 Commands for controlled output

During the execution of a command file or a user-defined command, normal GDB output is suppressed; the only output that appears is what is explicitly printed by the commands in the definition. This section describes three commands useful for generating exactly the output you want.

echo *text*   Print *text*. Nonprinting characters can be included in *text* using C escape sequences, such as '\n' to print a newline. **No newline is printed unless you specify one.** In addition to the standard C escape sequences, a backslash followed by a space stands for a space. This is useful for displaying a string with spaces at the beginning or the end, since leading and trailing spaces are

---

[1] On DOS/Windows systems, the home directory is the one pointed to by the HOME environment variable.

otherwise trimmed from all arguments. To print ' and foo = ',
use the command 'echo \ and foo = \ '.

A backslash at the end of *text* can be used, as in C, to continue
the command onto subsequent lines. For example,

```
echo This is some text\n\
which is continued\n\
onto several lines.\n
```

produces the same output as

```
echo This is some text\n
echo which is continued\n
echo onto several lines.\n
```

output *expression*

>Print the value of *expression* and nothing but that value: no
>newlines, no '$*nn* = '. The value is not entered in the value
>history either. See Section 8.1 [Expressions], page 69, for more
>information on expressions.

output/*fmt* *expression*

>Print the value of *expression* in format *fmt*. You can use the
>same formats as for print. See Section 8.4 [Output formats],
>page 73, for more information.

printf *string*, *expressions*. . .

>Print the values of the *expressions* under the control of *string*.
>The *expressions* are separated by commas and may be either
>numbers or pointers. Their values are printed as specified by
>*string*, exactly as if your program were to execute the C subrou-
>tine

>>printf (*string*, *expressions*. . .);

For example, you can print two values in hex like this:

```
printf "foo, bar-foo = 0x%x, 0x%x\n", foo, bar-foo
```

The only backslash-escape sequences that you can use in the format string are the simple ones that consist of backslash followed
by a letter.

18 GDB Text User Interface

The GDB Text User Interface, TUI in short, is a terminal interface which uses the `curses` library to show the source file, the assembly output, the program registers and GDB commands in separate text windows. The TUI is available only when GDB is configured with the `--enable-tui` configure option (see Section B.3 [Configure Options], page 320).

18.1 TUI overview

The TUI has two display modes that can be switched while GDB runs:

- A curses (or TUI) mode in which it displays several text windows on the terminal.
- A standard mode which corresponds to the GDB configured without the TUI.

In the TUI mode, GDB can display several text window on the terminal:

command   This window is the GDB command window with the GDB prompt and the GDB outputs. The GDB input is still managed using readline but through the TUI. The *command* window is always visible.

source   The source window shows the source file of the program. The current line as well as active breakpoints are displayed in this window. The current program position is shown with the '>' marker and active breakpoints are shown with '*' markers.

assembly   The assembly window shows the disassembly output of the program.

register   This window shows the processor registers. It detects when a register is changed and when this is the case, registers that have changed are highlighted.

The source, assembly and register windows are attached to the thread and the frame position. They are updated when the current thread changes, when the frame changes or when the program counter changes. These three windows are arranged by the TUI according to several layouts. The layout defines which of these three windows are visible. The following layouts are available:

- source
- assembly
- source and assembly
- source and registers
- assembly and registers

18.2 TUI Key Bindings

The TUI installs several key bindings in the readline keymaps (see Chapter 23 [Command Line Editing], page 289). They allow to leave or enter in the TUI mode or they operate directly on the TUI layout and windows. The following key bindings are installed for both TUI mode and the GDB standard mode.

C-x C-a
C-x a
C-x A   Enter or leave the TUI mode. When the TUI mode is left, the curses window management is left and GDB operates using its standard mode writing on the terminal directly. When the TUI mode is entered, the control is given back to the curses windows. The screen is then refreshed.

C-x 1   Use a TUI layout with only one window. The layout will either be '`source`' or '`assembly`'. When the TUI mode is not active, it will switch to the TUI mode.

Think of this key binding as the Emacs *C-x 1* binding.

C-x 2   Use a TUI layout with at least two windows. When the current layout shows already two windows, a next layout with two windows is used. When a new layout is chosen, one window will always be common to the previous layout and the new one.

Think of it as the Emacs *C-x 2* binding.

The following key bindings are handled only by the TUI mode:

⟨PgUp⟩   Scroll the active window one page up.

⟨PgDn⟩   Scroll the active window one page down.

⟨Up⟩   Scroll the active window one line up.

⟨Down⟩   Scroll the active window one line down.

⟨Left⟩   Scroll the active window one column left.

⟨Right⟩   Scroll the active window one column right.

⟨C-L⟩   Refresh the screen.

In the TUI mode, the arrow keys are used by the active window for scrolling. This means they are not available for readline. It is necessary to use other readline key bindings such as ⟨C-p⟩, ⟨C-n⟩, ⟨C-b⟩ and ⟨C-f⟩.

18.3 TUI specific commands

The TUI has specific commands to control the text windows. These commands are always available, that is they do not depend on the current terminal mode in which GDB runs. When GDB is in the standard mode, using these commands will automatically switch in the TUI mode.

layout next
> Display the next layout.

layout prev
> Display the previous layout.

layout src
> Display the source window only.

layout asm
> Display the assembly window only.

layout split
> Display the source and assembly window.

layout regs
> Display the register window together with the source or assembly window.

focus next | prev | src | asm | regs | split
> Set the focus to the named window. This command allows to change the active window so that scrolling keys can be affected to another window.

refresh   Refresh the screen. This is similar to using (C-L) key.

update   Update the source window and the current execution point.

winheight *name* +*count*
winheight *name* −*count*
> Change the height of the window *name* by *count* lines. Positive counts increase the height, while negative counts decrease it.

18.4 TUI configuration variables

The TUI has several configuration variables that control the appearance of windows on the terminal.

set tui border-kind *kind*
> Select the border appearance for the source, assembly and register windows. The possible values are the following:
>
> space   Use a space character to draw the border.
>
> ascii   Use ascii characters + - and | to draw the border.

acs   Use the Alternate Character Set to draw the border. The border is drawn using character line graphics if the terminal supports them.

`set tui active-border-mode` *mode*

Select the attributes to display the border of the active window. The possible values are `normal`, `standout`, `reverse`, `half`, `half-standout`, `bold` and `bold-standout`.

`set tui border-mode` *mode*

Select the attributes to display the border of other windows. The *mode* can be one of the following:

normal   Use normal attributes to display the border.

standout   Use standout mode.

reverse   Use reverse video mode.

half   Use half bright mode.

half-standout
                Use half bright and standout mode.

bold   Use extra bright or bold mode.

bold-standout
                Use extra bright or bold and standout mode.

19 Using GDB under GNU Emacs

A special interface allows you to use GNU Emacs to view (and edit) the source files for the program you are debugging with GDB.

To use this interface, use the command *M-x gdb* in Emacs. Give the executable file you want to debug as an argument. This command starts GDB as a subprocess of Emacs, with input and output through a newly created Emacs buffer.

Using GDB under Emacs is just like using GDB normally except for two things:

- All "terminal" input and output goes through the Emacs buffer.

This applies both to GDB commands and their output, and to the input and output done by the program you are debugging.

This is useful because it means that you can copy the text of previous commands and input them again; you can even use parts of the output in this way.

All the facilities of Emacs' Shell mode are available for interacting with your program. In particular, you can send signals the usual way—for example, *C-c C-c* for an interrupt, *C-c C-z* for a stop.

- GDB displays source code through Emacs.

Each time GDB displays a stack frame, Emacs automatically finds the source file for that frame and puts an arrow ('=>') at the left margin of the current line. Emacs uses a separate buffer for source display, and splits the screen to show both your GDB session and the source.

Explicit GDB `list` or search commands still produce output as usual, but you probably have no reason to use them from Emacs.

> *Warning:* If the directory where your program resides is not your current directory, it can be easy to confuse Emacs about the location of the source files, in which case the auxiliary display buffer does not appear to show your source. GDB can find programs by searching your environment's `PATH` variable, so the GDB input and output session proceeds normally; but Emacs does not get enough information back from GDB to locate the source files in this situation. To avoid this problem, either start GDB mode from the directory where your program resides, or specify an absolute file name when prompted for the *M-x gdb* argument.
>
> A similar confusion can result if you use the GDB `file` command to switch to debugging a program in some other location, from an existing GDB buffer in Emacs.

By default, *M-x gdb* calls the program called 'gdb'. If you need to call GDB by a different name (for example, if you keep several configurations around, with different names) you can set the Emacs variable **gdb-command-name**; for example,

```
(setq gdb-command-name "mygdb")
```

(preceded by *M-:* or *ESC :*, or typed in the *scratch* buffer, or in your
'.emacs' file) makes Emacs call the program named "mygdb" instead.

In the GDB I/O buffer, you can use these special Emacs commands in
addition to the standard Shell mode commands:

C-h m   Describe the features of Emacs' GDB Mode.

M-s   Execute to another source line, like the GDB step command;
           also update the display window to show the current file and
           location.

M-n   Execute to next source line in this function, skipping all function
           calls, like the GDB next command. Then update the display
           window to show the current file and location.

M-i   Execute one instruction, like the GDB stepi command; update
           display window accordingly.

M-x gdb-nexti
           Execute to next instruction, using the GDB nexti command;
           update display window accordingly.

C-c C-f   Execute until exit from the selected stack frame, like the GDB
           finish command.

M-c   Continue execution of your program, like the GDB continue
           command.

           Warning: In Emacs v19, this command is *C-c C-p.*

M-u   Go up the number of frames indicated by the numeric argument
           (see section "Numeric Arguments" in *The* GNU *Emacs Manual*),
           like the GDB up command.

           Warning: In Emacs v19, this command is *C-c C-u.*

M-d   Go down the number of frames indicated by the numeric argu-
           ment, like the GDB down command.

           Warning: In Emacs v19, this command is *C-c C-d.*

C-x &   Read the number where the cursor is positioned, and insert it
           at the end of the GDB I/O buffer. For example, if you wish to
           disassemble code around an address that was displayed earlier,
           type *disassemble*; then move the cursor to the address display,
           and pick up the argument for disassemble by typing *C-x &*.

           You can customize this further by defining elements of the list
           gdb-print-command; once it is defined, you can format or oth-
           erwise process numbers picked up by *C-x &* before they are in-
           serted. A numeric argument to *C-x &* indicates that you wish
           special formatting, and also acts as an index to pick an element

of the list. If the list element is a string, the number to be inserted is formatted using the Emacs function `format`; otherwise the number is passed as an argument to the corresponding list element.

In any source file, the Emacs command *C-x SPC* (`gdb-break`) tells GDB to set a breakpoint on the source line point is on.

If you accidentally delete the source-display buffer, an easy way to get it back is to type the command `f` in the GDB buffer, to request a frame display; when you run under Emacs, this recreates the source buffer if necessary to show you the context of the current frame.

The source files displayed in Emacs are in ordinary Emacs buffers which are visiting the source files in the usual way. You can edit the files with these buffers if you wish; but keep in mind that GDB communicates with Emacs in terms of line numbers. If you add or delete lines from the text, the line numbers that GDB knows cease to correspond properly with the code.

20 GDB Annotations

This chapter describes annotations in GDB. Annotations are designed to interface GDB to graphical user interfaces or other similar programs which want to interact with GDB at a relatively high level.

20.1 What is an Annotation?

To produce annotations, start GDB with the `--annotate=2` option.

Annotations start with a newline character, two 'control-z' characters, and the name of the annotation. If there is no additional information associated with this annotation, the name of the annotation is followed immediately by a newline. If there is additional information, the name of the annotation is followed by a space, the additional information, and a newline. The additional information cannot contain newline characters.

Any output not beginning with a newline and two 'control-z' characters denotes literal output from GDB. Currently there is no need for GDB to output a newline followed by two 'control-z' characters, but if there was such a need, the annotations could be extended with an 'escape' annotation which means those three characters as output.

A simple example of starting up GDB with annotations is:

```
$ gdb --annotate=2
GNU GDB 5.0
Copyright 2000 Free Software Foundation, Inc.
GDB is free software, covered by the GNU General Public License,
and you are welcome to change it and/or distribute copies of it
under certain conditions.
Type "show copying" to see the conditions.
There is absolutely no warranty for GDB.  Type "show warranty"
for details.
This GDB was configured as "sparc-sun-sunos4.1.3"

^Z^Zpre-prompt
(gdb)
^Z^Zprompt
quit

^Z^Zpost-prompt
$
```

Here 'quit' is input to GDB; the rest is output from GDB. The three lines beginning '^Z^Z' (where '^Z' denotes a 'control-z' character) are annotations; the rest is output from GDB.

20.2 The Server Prefix

To issue a command to GDB without affecting certain aspects of the state which is seen by users, prefix it with 'server '. This means that this command will not affect the command history, nor will it affect GDB's notion of which command to repeat if (RET) is pressed on a line by itself.

The server prefix does not affect the recording of values into the value history; to print a value without recording it into the value history, use the `output` command instead of the `print` command.

20.3 Values

When a value is printed in various contexts, GDB uses annotations to delimit the value from the surrounding text.

If a value is printed using `print` and added to the value history, the annotation looks like

```
^Z^Zvalue-history-begin history-number value-flags
history-string
^Z^Zvalue-history-value
the-value
^Z^Zvalue-history-end
```

where *history-number* is the number it is getting in the value history, *history-string* is a string, such as '$5 = ', which introduces the value to the user, *the-value* is the output corresponding to the value itself, and *value-flags* is '*' for a value which can be dereferenced and '-' for a value which cannot.

If the value is not added to the value history (it is an invalid float or it is printed with the `output` command), the annotation is similar:

```
^Z^Zvalue-begin value-flags
the-value
^Z^Zvalue-end
```

When GDB prints an argument to a function (for example, in the output from the `backtrace` command), it annotates it as follows:

```
^Z^Zarg-begin
argument-name
^Z^Zarg-name-end
separator-string
^Z^Zarg-value value-flags
the-value
^Z^Zarg-end
```

where *argument-name* is the name of the argument, *separator-string* is text which separates the name from the value for the user's benefit (such as '='), and *value-flags* and *the-value* have the same meanings as in a `value-history-begin` annotation.

When printing a structure, GDB annotates it as follows:

```
^Z^Zfield-begin value-flags
field-name
^Z^Zfield-name-end
separator-string
^Z^Zfield-value
the-value
^Z^Zfield-end
```

where *field-name* is the name of the field, *separator-string* is text which separates the name from the value for the user's benefit (such as '='), and *value-flags* and *the-value* have the same meanings as in a `value-history-begin` annotation.

When printing an array, GDB annotates it as follows:

```
^Z^Zarray-section-begin array-index value-flags
```

where *array-index* is the index of the first element being annotated and *value-flags* has the same meaning as in a `value-history-begin` annotation. This is followed by any number of elements, where is element can be either a single element:

```
',' whitespace          ; omitted for the first element
the-value
^Z^Zelt
```

or a repeated element

```
',' whitespace          ; omitted for the first element
the-value
^Z^Zelt-rep number-of-repititions
repetition-string
^Z^Zelt-rep-end
```

In both cases, *the-value* is the output for the value of the element and *whitespace* can contain spaces, tabs, and newlines. In the repeated case, *number-of-repititons* is the number of consecutive array elements which contain that value, and *repetition-string* is a string which is designed to convey to the user that repitition is being depicted.

Once all the array elements have been output, the array annotation is ended with

```
^Z^Zarray-section-end
```

20.4 Frames

Whenever GDB prints a frame, it annotates it. For example, this applies to frames printed when GDB stops, output from commands such as `backtrace` or `up`, etc.

The frame annotation begins with

`^Z^Zframe-begin` *level address*

level-string

where *level* is the number of the frame (0 is the innermost frame, and other frames have positive numbers), *address* is the address of the code executing in that frame, and *level-string* is a string designed to convey the level to the user. *address* is in the form '`0x`' followed by one or more lowercase hex digits (note that this does not depend on the language). The frame ends with

`^Z^Zframe-end`

Between these annotations is the main body of the frame, which can consist of

-

    `^Z^Zfunction-call`

    function-call-string

    where *function-call-string* is text designed to convey to the user that this frame is associated with a function call made by GDB to a function in the program being debugged.

-

    `^Z^Zsignal-handler-caller`

    signal-handler-caller-string

    where *signal-handler-caller-string* is text designed to convey to the user that this frame is associated with whatever mechanism is used by this operating system to call a signal handler (it is the frame which calls the signal handler, not the frame for the signal handler itself).

- A normal frame.

    This can optionally (depending on whether this is thought of as interesting information for the user to see) begin with

    `^Z^Zframe-address`

    address

    `^Z^Zframe-address-end`

    separator-string

    where *address* is the address executing in the frame (the same address as in the `frame-begin` annotation, but printed in a form which is intended for user consumption—in particular, the syntax varies depending on the language), and *separator-string* is a string intended to separate this address from what follows for the user's benefit.

    Then comes

    `^Z^Zframe-function-name`

    function-name

    `^Z^Zframe-args`

    arguments

    where *function-name* is the name of the function executing in the frame, or '`??`' if not known, and *arguments* are the arguments to the frame, with parentheses around them (each argument is annotated individually as well, see Section 20.3 [Value Annotations], page 214).

If source information is available, a reference to it is then printed:

```
^Z^Zframe-source-begin
```
source-intro-string
```
^Z^Zframe-source-file
```
filename
```
^Z^Zframe-source-file-end
```
:
```
^Z^Zframe-source-line
```
line-number
```
^Z^Zframe-source-end
```

where *source-intro-string* separates for the user's benefit the reference from the text which precedes it, *filename* is the name of the source file, and *line-number* is the line number within that file (the first line is line 1).

If GDB prints some information about where the frame is from (which library, which load segment, etc.; currently only done on the RS/6000), it is annotated with

```
^Z^Zframe-where
```
information

Then, if source is to actually be displayed for this frame (for example, this is not true for output from the **backtrace** command), then a **source** annotation (see Section 20.11 [Source Annotations], page 221) is displayed. Unlike most annotations, this is output instead of the normal text which would be output, not in addition.

20.5 Displays

When GDB is told to display something using the **display** command, the results of the display are annotated:

```
^Z^Zdisplay-begin
```
number
```
^Z^Zdisplay-number-end
```
number-separator
```
^Z^Zdisplay-format
```
format
```
^Z^Zdisplay-expression
```
expression
```
^Z^Zdisplay-expression-end
```
expression-separator
```
^Z^Zdisplay-value
```
value

```
^Z^Zdisplay-end
```

where *number* is the number of the display, *number-separator* is intended to separate the number from what follows for the user, *format* includes information such as the size, format, or other information about how the value is being displayed, *expression* is the expression being displayed, *expression-separator* is intended to separate the expression from the text that follows for the user, and *value* is the actual value being displayed.

20.6 Annotation for GDB Input

When GDB prompts for input, it annotates this fact so it is possible to know when to send output, when the output from a given command is over, etc.

Different kinds of input each have a different *input type*. Each input type has three annotations: a **pre-** annotation, which denotes the beginning of any prompt which is being output, a plain annotation, which denotes the end of the prompt, and then a **post-** annotation which denotes the end of any echo which may (or may not) be associated with the input. For example, the **prompt** input type features the following annotations:

```
^Z^Zpre-prompt
^Z^Zprompt
^Z^Zpost-prompt
```

The input types are

prompt   When GDB is prompting for a command (the main GDB prompt).

commands   When GDB prompts for a set of commands, like in the **commands** command. The annotations are repeated for each command which is input.

overload-choice
            When GDB wants the user to select between various overloaded functions.

query   When GDB wants the user to confirm a potentially dangerous operation.

prompt-for-continue
            When GDB is asking the user to press return to continue. Note: Don't expect this to work well; instead use **set height 0** to disable prompting. This is because the counting of lines is buggy in the presence of annotations.

20.7 Errors

```
^Z^Zquit
```

This annotation occurs right before GDB responds to an interrupt.

`^Z^Zerror`

This annotation occurs right before GDB responds to an error.

Quit and error annotations indicate that any annotations which GDB was in the middle of may end abruptly. For example, if a `value-history-begin` annotation is followed by a `error`, one cannot expect to receive the matching `value-history-end`. One cannot expect not to receive it either, however; an error annotation does not necessarily mean that GDB is immediately returning all the way to the top level.

A quit or error annotation may be preceded by

`^Z^Zerror-begin`

Any output between that and the quit or error annotation is the error message.

Warning messages are not yet annotated.

20.8 Information on Breakpoints

The output from the `info breakpoints` command is annotated as follows:

`^Z^Zbreakpoints-headers`

header-entry

`^Z^Zbreakpoints-table`

where *header-entry* has the same syntax as an entry (see below) but instead of containing data, it contains strings which are intended to convey the meaning of each field to the user. This is followed by any number of entries. If a field does not apply for this entry, it is omitted. Fields may contain trailing whitespace. Each entry consists of:

`^Z^Zrecord`

`^Z^Zfield 0`

number

`^Z^Zfield 1`

type

`^Z^Zfield 2`

disposition

`^Z^Zfield 3`

enable

`^Z^Zfield 4`

address

`^Z^Zfield 5`

what

`^Z^Zfield 6`

frame

`^Z^Zfield 7`

condition

`^Z^Zfield 8`

ignore-count

`^Z^Zfield 9`

commands

Note that *address* is intended for user consumption—the syntax varies depending on the language.

The output ends with

`^Z^Zbreakpoints-table-end`

20.9 Invalidation Notices

The following annotations say that certain pieces of state may have changed.

`^Z^Zframes-invalid`

> The frames (for example, output from the `backtrace` command) may have changed.

`^Z^Zbreakpoints-invalid`

> The breakpoints may have changed. For example, the user just added or deleted a breakpoint.

20.10 Running the Program

When the program starts executing due to a GDB command such as `step` or `continue`,

`^Z^Zstarting`

is output. When the program stops,

`^Z^Zstopped`

is output. Before the `stopped` annotation, a variety of annotations describe how the program stopped.

`^Z^Zexited` *exit-status*

> The program exited, and *exit-status* is the exit status (zero for successful exit, otherwise nonzero).

`^Z^Zsignalled`

> The program exited with a signal. After the `^Z^Zsignalled`, the annotation continues:
>
> *intro-text*
>
> `^Z^Zsignal-name`
>
> *name*
>
> `^Z^Zsignal-name-end`
>
> *middle-text*

> `^Z^Zsignal-string`
>
> *string*
>
> `^Z^Zsignal-string-end`
>
> *end-text*

where *name* is the name of the signal, such as `SIGILL` or `SIGSEGV`, and *string* is the explanation of the signal, such as `Illegal Instruction` or `Segmentation fault`. *intro-text*, *middle-text*, and *end-text* are for the user's benefit and have no particular format.

`^Z^Zsignal`

The syntax of this annotation is just like `signalled`, but GDB is just saying that the program received the signal, not that it was terminated with it.

`^Z^Zbreakpoint` *number*

The program hit breakpoint number *number*.

`^Z^Zwatchpoint` *number*

The program hit watchpoint number *number*.

20.11 Displaying Source

The following annotation is used instead of displaying source code:

> `^Z^Zsource` *filename:line:character:middle:addr*

where *filename* is an absolute file name indicating which source file, *line* is the line number within that file (where 1 is the first line in the file), *character* is the character position within the file (where 0 is the first character in the file) (for most debug formats this will necessarily point to the beginning of a line), *middle* is '`middle`' if *addr* is in the middle of the line, or '`beg`' if *addr* is at the beginning of the line, and *addr* is the address in the target program associated with the source which is being displayed. *addr* is in the form '`0x`' followed by one or more lowercase hex digits (note that this does not depend on the language).

20.12 Annotations We Might Want in the Future

- target-invalid
  the target might have changed (registers, heap contents, or
  execution status). For performance, we might eventually want
  to hit 'registers-invalid' and 'all-registers-invalid' with
  greater precision

- systematic annotation for set/show parameters (including
  invalidation notices).

- similarly, 'info' returns a list of candidates for invalidation
  notices.

21 The GDB/MI Interface

Function and Purpose

GDB/MI is a line based machine oriented text interface to GDB. It is specifically intended to support the development of systems which use the debugger as just one small component of a larger system.

This chapter is a specification of the GDB/MI interface. It is written in the form of a reference manual.

Note that GDB/MI is still under construction, so some of the features described below are incomplete and subject to change.

Notation and Terminology

This chapter uses the following notation:

- | separates two alternatives.
- [*something*] indicates that *something* is optional: it may or may not be given.
- (*group*)* means that *group* inside the parentheses may repeat zero or more times.
- (*group*)+ means that *group* inside the parentheses may repeat one or more times.
- "*string*" means a literal *string*.

Acknowledgments

In alphabetic order: Andrew Cagney, Fernando Nasser, Stan Shebs and Elena Zannoni.

21.1 GDB/MI Command Syntax

21.1.1 GDB/MI Input Syntax

command ↦
> *cli-command* | *mi-command*

cli-command ↦
> [*token*] *cli-command nl*, where *cli-command* is any existing GDB CLI command.

mi-command ↦
> [*token*] "-" *operation* (" " *option*)* [" --"] (" " *parameter*)* *nl*

token ↦   "any sequence of digits"

option ↦   "-" *parameter* [" " *parameter*]

parameter ↦
            non-blank-sequence | *c-string*

operation ↦
            any of the operations described in this chapter

non-blank-sequence ↦
            anything, provided it doesn't contain special characters such as
            "-", nl, """ and of course " "

c-string ↦
            """ *seven-bit-iso-c-string-content* """

nl ↦   CR | CR-LF

Notes:

- The CLI commands are still handled by the MI interpreter; their output is described below.
- The *token*, when present, is passed back when the command finishes.
- Some MI commands accept optional arguments as part of the parameter list. Each option is identified by a leading '-' (dash) and may be followed by an optional argument parameter. Options occur first in the parameter list and can be delimited from normal parameters using '--' (this is useful when some parameters begin with a dash).

  Pragmatics:

- We want easy access to the existing CLI syntax (for debugging).
- We want it to be easy to spot a MI operation.

21.1.2 GDB/MI **Output Syntax**

The output from GDB/MI consists of zero or more out-of-band records followed, optionally, by a single result record. This result record is for the most recent command. The sequence of output records is terminated by '(gdb)'.

If an input command was prefixed with a *token* then the corresponding output for that command will also be prefixed by that same *token*.

output ↦   (*out-of-band-record*)* [*result-record*] "(gdb)" *nl*

result-record ↦
            [*token*] "^" *result-class* ("," *result*)* *nl*

out-of-band-record ↦
            async-record | *stream-record*

async-record ↦
            exec-async-output | *status-async-output* | *notify-async-output*

exec-async-output ↦
> [*token*] "*" *async-output*

status-async-output ↦
> [*token*] "+" *async-output*

notify-async-output ↦
> [*token*] "=" *async-output*

async-output ↦
> *async-class* ("," *result*)* *nl*

result-class ↦
> "done" | "running" | "connected" | "error" | "exit"

async-class ↦
> "stopped" | *others* (where *others* will be added depending on the needs—this is still in development).

result ↦   *variable* "=" *value*

variable ↦
> *string*

value ↦   *const* | *tuple* | *list*

const ↦   *c-string*

tuple ↦   "{}" | "{" *result* ("," *result*)* "}"

list ↦   "[]" | "[" *value* ("," *value*)* "]" | "[" *result* ("," *result*)* "]"

stream-record ↦
> *console-stream-output* | *target-stream-output* | *log-stream-output*

console-stream-output ↦
> "~" *c-string*

target-stream-output ↦
> "@" *c-string*

log-stream-output ↦
> "&" *c-string*

nl ↦   CR | CR-LF

token ↦   *any sequence of digits.*

Notes:

- All output sequences end in a single line containing a period.
- The *token* is from the corresponding request. If an execution command is interrupted by the '-exec-interrupt' command, the *token* associated with the '*stopped' message is the one of the original execution command, not the one of the interrupt command.

- *status-async-output* contains on-going status information about the progress of a slow operation. It can be discarded. All status output is prefixed by '+'.

- *exec-async-output* contains asynchronous state change on the target (stopped, started, disappeared). All async output is prefixed by '*'.

- *notify-async-output* contains supplementary information that the client should handle (e.g., a new breakpoint information). All notify output is prefixed by '='.

- *console-stream-output* is output that should be displayed as is in the console. It is the textual response to a CLI command. All the console output is prefixed by '~'.

- *target-stream-output* is the output produced by the target program. All the target output is prefixed by '@'.

- *log-stream-output* is output text coming from GDB's internals, for instance messages that should be displayed as part of an error log. All the log output is prefixed by '&'.

- New GDB/MI commands should only output *lists* containing *values*.

See Section 21.3.2 [GDB/MI Stream Records], page 228, for more details about the various output records.

21.1.3 Simple Examples of GDB/MI Interaction

This subsection presents several simple examples of interaction using the GDB/MI interface. In these examples, '->' means that the following line is passed to GDB/MI as input, while '<-' means the output received from GDB/MI.

Target Stop

Here's an example of stopping the inferior process:

```
-> -stop
<- (gdb)
```

and later:

```
<- *stop,reason="stop",address="0x123",source="a.c:123"
<- (gdb)
```

Simple CLI Command

Here's an example of a simple CLI command being passed through GDB/MI and on to the CLI.

```
-> print 1+2
<- ~3\n
<- (gdb)
```

Command With Side Effects

```
-> -symbol-file xyz.exe
<- *breakpoint,nr="3",address="0x123",source="a.c:123"
<- (gdb)
```

A Bad Command

Here's what happens if you pass a non-existent command:

```
-> -rubbish
<- error,"Rubbish not found"
<- (gdb)
```

21.2 GDB/MI Compatibility with CLI

To help users familiar with GDB's existing CLI interface, GDB/MI accepts existing CLI commands. As specified by the syntax, such commands can be directly entered into the GDB/MI interface and GDB will respond.

This mechanism is provided as an aid to developers of GDB/MI clients and not as a reliable interface into the CLI. Since the command is being interpreted in an environment that assumes GDB/MI behaviour, the exact output of such commands is likely to end up being an un-supported hybrid of GDB/MI and CLI output.

21.3 GDB/MI Output Records

21.3.1 GDB/MI Result Records

In addition to a number of out-of-band notifications, the response to a GDB/MI command includes one of the following result indications:

`"^done" [ "," results ]`
> The synchronous operation was successful, *results* are the return values.

`"^running"`
> The asynchronous operation was successfully started. The target is running.

`"^error" "," c-string`
> The operation failed. The *c-string* contains the corresponding error message.

21.3.2 GDB/MI **Stream Records**

GDB internally maintains a number of output streams: the console, the target, and the log. The output intended for each of these streams is funneled through the GDB/MI interface using *stream records*.

Each stream record begins with a unique *prefix character* which identifies its stream (see Section 21.1.2 [GDB/MI Output Syntax], page 224). In addition to the prefix, each stream record contains a *string-output*. This is either raw text (with an implicit new line) or a quoted C string (which does not contain an implicit newline).

"~" *string-output*

> The console output stream contains text that should be displayed in the CLI console window. It contains the textual responses to CLI commands.

"@" *string-output*

> The target output stream contains any textual output from the running target.

"&" *string-output*

> The log stream contains debugging messages being produced by GDB's internals.

21.3.3 GDB/MI **Out-of-band Records**

Out-of-band records are used to notify the GDB/MI client of additional changes that have occurred. Those changes can either be a consequence of GDB/MI (e.g., a breakpoint modified) or a result of target activity (e.g., target stopped).

The following is a preliminary list of possible out-of-band records.

"*" "stop"

21.4 GDB/MI **Command Description Format**

The remaining sections describe blocks of commands. Each block of commands is laid out in a fashion similar to this section.

Note the the line breaks shown in the examples are here only for readability. They don't appear in the real output. Also note that the commands with a non-available example (N.A.) are not yet implemented.

Motivation

The motivation for this collection of commands.

Introduction

A brief introduction to this collection of commands as a whole.

Commands

For each command in the block, the following is described:

Synopsis

```
-command args...
```

GDB Command

The corresponding GDB CLI command.

Result

Out-of-band

Notes

Example

21.5 GDB/MI Breakpoint table commands

This section documents GDB/MI commands for manipulating breakpoints.

The -break-after Command

Synopsis

```
-break-after number count
```

The breakpoint number *number* is not in effect until it has been hit *count* times. To see how this is reflected in the output of the '-break-list' command, see the description of the '-break-list' command below.

GDB Command

The corresponding GDB command is 'ignore'.

Example

```
(gdb)
-break-insert main
^done,bkpt={number="1",addr="0x000100d0",file="hello.c",line="5"}
```

```
(gdb)
-break-after 1 3
~
^done
(gdb)
-break-list
^done,BreakpointTable={nr_rows="1",nr_cols="6",
hdr=[{width="3",alignment="-1",col_name="number",colhdr="Num"},
{width="14",alignment="-1",col_name="type",colhdr="Type"},
{width="4",alignment="-1",col_name="disp",colhdr="Disp"},
{width="3",alignment="-1",col_name="enabled",colhdr="Enb"},
{width="10",alignment="-1",col_name="addr",colhdr="Address"},
{width="40",alignment="2",col_name="what",colhdr="What"}],
body=[bkpt={number="1",type="breakpoint",disp="keep",enabled="y",
addr="0x000100d0",func="main",file="hello.c",line="5",times="0",
ignore="3"}]}
(gdb)
```

The -break-condition Command

Synopsis

        -break-condition *number* *expr*

Breakpoint *number* will stop the program only if the condition in *expr*
is true. The condition becomes part of the '-break-list' output (see the
description of the '-break-list' command below).

GDB Command

The corresponding GDB command is 'condition'.

Example

```
(gdb)
-break-condition 1 1
^done
(gdb)
-break-list
^done,BreakpointTable={nr_rows="1",nr_cols="6",
hdr=[{width="3",alignment="-1",col_name="number",colhdr="Num"},
{width="14",alignment="-1",col_name="type",colhdr="Type"},
{width="4",alignment="-1",col_name="disp",colhdr="Disp"},
{width="3",alignment="-1",col_name="enabled",colhdr="Enb"},
{width="10",alignment="-1",col_name="addr",colhdr="Address"},
```

```
{width="40",alignment="2",col_name="what",colhdr="What"}],
body=[bkpt={number="1",type="breakpoint",disp="keep",enabled="y",
addr="0x000100d0",func="main",file="hello.c",line="5",cond="1",
times="0",ignore="3"}]]}
(gdb)
```

The -break-delete Command

Synopsis

```
-break-delete ( breakpoint )+
```

Delete the breakpoint(s) whose number(s) are specified in the argument list. This is obviously reflected in the breakpoint list.

GDB command

The corresponding GDB command is 'delete'.

Example

```
(gdb)
-break-delete 1
^done
(gdb)
-break-list
^done,BreakpointTable={nr_rows="0",nr_cols="6",
hdr=[{width="3",alignment="-1",col_name="number",colhdr="Num"},
{width="14",alignment="-1",col_name="type",colhdr="Type"},
{width="4",alignment="-1",col_name="disp",colhdr="Disp"},
{width="3",alignment="-1",col_name="enabled",colhdr="Enb"},
{width="10",alignment="-1",col_name="addr",colhdr="Address"},
{width="40",alignment="2",col_name="what",colhdr="What"}],
body=[]}
(gdb)
```

The -break-disable Command

Synopsis

```
-break-disable ( breakpoint )+
```

Disable the named breakpoint(s). The field 'enabled' in the break list is now set to 'n' for the named breakpoint(s).

GDB Command

The corresponding GDB command is 'disable'.

Example

```
(gdb)
-break-disable 2
^done
(gdb)
-break-list
^done,BreakpointTable={nr_rows="1",nr_cols="6",
hdr=[{width="3",alignment="-1",col_name="number",colhdr="Num"},
{width="14",alignment="-1",col_name="type",colhdr="Type"},
{width="4",alignment="-1",col_name="disp",colhdr="Disp"},
{width="3",alignment="-1",col_name="enabled",colhdr="Enb"},
{width="10",alignment="-1",col_name="addr",colhdr="Address"},
{width="40",alignment="2",col_name="what",colhdr="What"}],
body=[bkpt={number="2",type="breakpoint",disp="keep",enabled="n",
addr="0x000100d0",func="main",file="hello.c",line="5",times="0"}]]}
(gdb)
```

The -break-enable Command

Synopsis

```
  -break-enable ( breakpoint )+
```
Enable (previously disabled) breakpoint(s).

GDB Command

The corresponding GDB command is 'enable'.

Example

```
(gdb)
-break-enable 2
^done
(gdb)
-break-list
^done,BreakpointTable={nr_rows="1",nr_cols="6",
hdr=[{width="3",alignment="-1",col_name="number",colhdr="Num"},
{width="14",alignment="-1",col_name="type",colhdr="Type"},
{width="4",alignment="-1",col_name="disp",colhdr="Disp"},
{width="3",alignment="-1",col_name="enabled",colhdr="Enb"},
```

```
{width="10",alignment="-1",col_name="addr",colhdr="Address"},
{width="40",alignment="2",col_name="what",colhdr="What"}],
body=[bkpt={number="2",type="breakpoint",disp="keep",enabled="y",
addr="0x000100d0",func="main",file="hello.c",line="5",times="0"}]]}
(gdb)
```

The -break-info Command

Synopsis

> `-break-info` *breakpoint*
> Get information about a single breakpoint.

GDB command

The corresponding GDB command is '`info break` *breakpoint*'.

Example

N.A.

The -break-insert Command

Synopsis

```
-break-insert [ -t ] [ -h ] [ -r ]
    [ -c condition ] [ -i ignore-count ]
    [ -p thread ] [ line | addr ]
```
If specified, *line*, can be one of:

- function
- filename:linenum
- filename:function
- *address

The possible optional parameters of this command are:

'-t'   Insert a tempoary breakpoint.

'-h'   Insert a hardware breakpoint.

'-c *condition*'
            Make the breakpoint conditional on *condition*.

'-i *ignore-count*'
            Initialize the *ignore-count*.

'-r'   Insert a regular breakpoint in all the functions whose names
                        match the given regular expression. Other flags are not applica-
                        ble to regular expresson.

Result

The result is in the form:

```
^done,bkptno="number",func="funcname",
    file="filename",line="lineno"
```

where *number* is the GDB number for this breakpoint, *funcname* is the name
of the function where the breakpoint was inserted, *filename* is the name of
the source file which contains this function, and *lineno* is the source line
number within that file.

Note: this format is open to change.

GDB Command

The corresponding GDB commands are 'break', 'tbreak', 'hbreak',
'thbreak', and 'rbreak'.

Example

```
(gdb)
-break-insert main
^done,bkpt={number="1",addr="0x0001072c",file="recursive2.c",line="4"}
(gdb)
-break-insert -t foo
^done,bkpt={number="2",addr="0x00010774",file="recursive2.c",line="11"}
(gdb)
-break-list
^done,BreakpointTable={nr_rows="2",nr_cols="6",
hdr=[{width="3",alignment="-1",col_name="number",colhdr="Num"},
{width="14",alignment="-1",col_name="type",colhdr="Type"},
{width="4",alignment="-1",col_name="disp",colhdr="Disp"},
{width="3",alignment="-1",col_name="enabled",colhdr="Enb"},
{width="10",alignment="-1",col_name="addr",colhdr="Address"},
{width="40",alignment="2",col_name="what",colhdr="What"}],
body=[bkpt={number="1",type="breakpoint",disp="keep",enabled="y",
addr="0x0001072c", func="main",file="recursive2.c",line="4",times="0"},
bkpt={number="2",type="breakpoint",disp="del",enabled="y",
addr="0x00010774",func="foo",file="recursive2.c",line="11",times="0"}]}
(gdb)
-break-insert -r foo.*
~int foo(int, int);
^done,bkpt={number="3",addr="0x00010774",file="recursive2.c",line="11"}
```

```
(gdb)
```

The -break-list Command

Synopsis

```
-break-list
```
Displays the list of inserted breakpoints, showing the following fields:

'Number'   number of the breakpoint

'Type'   type of the breakpoint: 'breakpoint' or 'watchpoint'

'Disposition'
    should the breakpoint be deleted or disabled when it is hit: 'keep' or 'nokeep'

'Enabled'   is the breakpoint enabled or no: 'y' or 'n'

'Address'   memory location at which the breakpoint is set

'What'   logical location of the breakpoint, expressed by function name, file name, line number

'Times'   number of times the breakpoint has been hit

If there are no breakpoints or watchpoints, the BreakpointTable body field is an empty list.

GDB Command

The corresponding GDB command is 'info break'.

Example

```
(gdb)
-break-list
^done,BreakpointTable={nr_rows="2",nr_cols="6",
hdr=[{width="3",alignment="-1",col_name="number",colhdr="Num"},
{width="14",alignment="-1",col_name="type",colhdr="Type"},
{width="4",alignment="-1",col_name="disp",colhdr="Disp"},
{width="3",alignment="-1",col_name="enabled",colhdr="Enb"},
{width="10",alignment="-1",col_name="addr",colhdr="Address"},
{width="40",alignment="2",col_name="what",colhdr="What"}],
body=[bkpt={number="1",type="breakpoint",disp="keep",enabled="y",
addr="0x000100d0",func="main",file="hello.c",line="5",times="0"},
bkpt={number="2",type="breakpoint",disp="keep",enabled="y",
addr="0x00010114",func="foo",file="hello.c",line="13",times="0"}]}
(gdb)
```
Here's an example of the result when there are no breakpoints:

```
(gdb)
-break-list
^done,BreakpointTable={nr_rows="0",nr_cols="6",
hdr=[{width="3",alignment="-1",col_name="number",colhdr="Num"},
{width="14",alignment="-1",col_name="type",colhdr="Type"},
{width="4",alignment="-1",col_name="disp",colhdr="Disp"},
{width="3",alignment="-1",col_name="enabled",colhdr="Enb"},
{width="10",alignment="-1",col_name="addr",colhdr="Address"},
{width="40",alignment="2",col_name="what",colhdr="What"}],
body=[]}
(gdb)
```

The -break-watch Command

Synopsis

```
-break-watch [ -a | -r ]
```

Create a watchpoint. With the '-a' option it will create an *access* watchpoint, i.e. a watchpoint that triggers either on a read from or on a write to the memory location. With the '-r' option, the watchpoint created is a *read* watchpoint, i.e. it will trigger only when the memory location is accessed for reading. Without either of the options, the watchpoint created is a regular watchpoint, i.e. it will trigger when the memory location is accessed for writing. See Section 5.1.2 [Setting watchpoints], page 40.

Note that '-break-list' will report a single list of watchpoints and breakpoints inserted.

GDB Command

The corresponding GDB commands are 'watch', 'awatch', and 'rwatch'.

Example

Setting a watchpoint on a variable in the main function:

```
(gdb)
-break-watch x
^done,wpt={number="2",exp="x"}
(gdb)
-exec-continue
^running
^done,reason="watchpoint-trigger",wpt={number="2",exp="x"},
value={old="-268439212",new="55"},
frame={func="main",args=[],file="recursive2.c",line="5"}
(gdb)
```

Setting a watchpoint on a variable local to a function. GDB will stop the program execution twice: first for the variable changing value, then for the watchpoint going out of scope.

```
(gdb)
-break-watch C
^done,wpt={number="5",exp="C"}
(gdb)
-exec-continue
^running
^done,reason="watchpoint-trigger",
wpt={number="5",exp="C"},value={old="-276895068",new="3"},
frame={func="callee4",args=[],
file="../../../devo/gdb/testsuite/gdb.mi/basics.c",line="13"}
(gdb)
-exec-continue
^running
^done,reason="watchpoint-scope",wpnum="5",
frame={func="callee3",args=[{name="strarg",
value="0x11940 \"A string argument.\""}],
file="../../../devo/gdb/testsuite/gdb.mi/basics.c",line="18"}
(gdb)
```

Listing breakpoints and watchpoints, at different points in the program execution. Note that once the watchpoint goes out of scope, it is deleted.

```
(gdb)
-break-watch C
^done,wpt={number="2",exp="C"}
(gdb)
-break-list
^done,BreakpointTable={nr_rows="2",nr_cols="6",
hdr=[{width="3",alignment="-1",col_name="number",colhdr="Num"},
{width="14",alignment="-1",col_name="type",colhdr="Type"},
{width="4",alignment="-1",col_name="disp",colhdr="Disp"},
{width="3",alignment="-1",col_name="enabled",colhdr="Enb"},
{width="10",alignment="-1",col_name="addr",colhdr="Address"},
{width="40",alignment="2",col_name="what",colhdr="What"}],
body=[bkpt={number="1",type="breakpoint",disp="keep",enabled="y",
addr="0x00010734",func="callee4",
file="../../../devo/gdb/testsuite/gdb.mi/basics.c",line="8",times="1"},
bkpt={number="2",type="watchpoint",disp="keep",
enabled="y",addr="",what="C",times="0"}]]
(gdb)
-exec-continue
^running
^done,reason="watchpoint-trigger",wpt={number="2",exp="C"},
```

```
value={old="-276895068",new="3"},
frame={func="callee4",args=[],
file="../../../devo/gdb/testsuite/gdb.mi/basics.c",line="13"}
(gdb)
-break-list
^done,BreakpointTable={nr_rows="2",nr_cols="6",
hdr=[{width="3",alignment="-1",col_name="number",colhdr="Num"},
{width="14",alignment="-1",col_name="type",colhdr="Type"},
{width="4",alignment="-1",col_name="disp",colhdr="Disp"},
{width="3",alignment="-1",col_name="enabled",colhdr="Enb"},
{width="10",alignment="-1",col_name="addr",colhdr="Address"},
{width="40",alignment="2",col_name="what",colhdr="What"}],
body=[bkpt={number="1",type="breakpoint",disp="keep",enabled="y",
addr="0x00010734",func="callee4",
file="../../../devo/gdb/testsuite/gdb.mi/basics.c",line="8",times="1"},
bkpt={number="2",type="watchpoint",disp="keep",
enabled="y",addr="",what="C",times="-5"}]]}
(gdb)
-exec-continue
^running
^done,reason="watchpoint-scope",wpnum="2",
frame={func="callee3",args=[{name="strarg",
value="0x11940 \"A string argument.\""}],
file="../../../devo/gdb/testsuite/gdb.mi/basics.c",line="18"}
(gdb)
-break-list
^done,BreakpointTable={nr_rows="1",nr_cols="6",
hdr=[{width="3",alignment="-1",col_name="number",colhdr="Num"},
{width="14",alignment="-1",col_name="type",colhdr="Type"},
{width="4",alignment="-1",col_name="disp",colhdr="Disp"},
{width="3",alignment="-1",col_name="enabled",colhdr="Enb"},
{width="10",alignment="-1",col_name="addr",colhdr="Address"},
{width="40",alignment="2",col_name="what",colhdr="What"}],
body=[bkpt={number="1",type="breakpoint",disp="keep",enabled="y",
addr="0x00010734",func="callee4",
file="../../../devo/gdb/testsuite/gdb.mi/basics.c",line="8",times="1"}]]}
(gdb)
```

21.6 GDB/MI Data Manipulation

This section describes the GDB/MI commands that manipulate data: examine memory and registers, evaluate expressions, etc.

The -data-disassemble Command

Synopsis

```
-data-disassemble
   [ -s start-addr -e end-addr ]
 | [ -f filename -l linenum [ -n lines ] ]
   -- mode
```

Where:

'start-addr'
is the beginning address (or $pc)

'end-addr' is the end address

'filename' is the name of the file to disassemble

'linenum' is the line number to disassemble around

'lines' is the the number of disassembly lines to be produced. If it is -1, the whole function will be disassembled, in case no end-addr is specified. If end-addr is specified as a non-zero value, and lines is lower than the number of disassembly lines between start-addr and end-addr, only lines lines are displayed; if lines is higher than the number of lines between start-addr and end-addr, only the lines up to end-addr are displayed.

'mode' is either 0 (meaning only disassembly) or 1 (meaning mixed source and disassembly).

Result

The output for each instruction is composed of four fields:

- Address
- Func-name
- Offset
- Instruction

Note that whatever included in the instruction field, is not manipulated directely by GDB/MI, i.e. it is not possible to adjust its format.

GDB Command

There's no direct mapping from this command to the CLI.

Example

Disassemble from the current value of $pc to $pc + 20:

```
(gdb)
-data-disassemble -s $pc -e "$pc + 20" -- 0
^done,
asm_insns=[
{address="0x000107c0",func-name="main",offset="4",
inst="mov  2, %o0"},
{address="0x000107c4",func-name="main",offset="8",
inst="sethi  %hi(0x11800), %o2"},
{address="0x000107c8",func-name="main",offset="12",
inst="or  %o2, 0x140, %o1\t! 0x11940 <_lib_version+8>"},
{address="0x000107cc",func-name="main",offset="16",
inst="sethi  %hi(0x11800), %o2"},
{address="0x000107d0",func-name="main",offset="20",
inst="or  %o2, 0x168, %o4\t! 0x11968 <_lib_version+48>"}]
(gdb)
```

Disassemble the whole **main** function. Line 32 is part of **main**.

```
-data-disassemble -f basics.c -l 32 -- 0
^done,asm_insns=[
{address="0x000107bc",func-name="main",offset="0",
inst="save  %sp, -112, %sp"},
{address="0x000107c0",func-name="main",offset="4",
inst="mov  2, %o0"},
{address="0x000107c4",func-name="main",offset="8",
inst="sethi %hi(0x11800), %o2"},
[...]
{address="0x0001081c",func-name="main",offset="96",inst="ret "},
{address="0x00010820",func-name="main",offset="100",inst="restore "}]
(gdb)
```

Disassemble 3 instructions from the start of **main**:

```
(gdb)
-data-disassemble -f basics.c -l 32 -n 3 -- 0
^done,asm_insns=[
{address="0x000107bc",func-name="main",offset="0",
inst="save  %sp, -112, %sp"},
{address="0x000107c0",func-name="main",offset="4",
inst="mov  2, %o0"},
{address="0x000107c4",func-name="main",offset="8",
inst="sethi  %hi(0x11800), %o2"}]
(gdb)
```

Disassemble 3 instructions from the start of **main** in mixed mode:

```
(gdb)
-data-disassemble -f basics.c -l 32 -n 3 -- 1
^done,asm_insns=[
src_and_asm_line={line="31",
file="/kwikemart/marge/ezannoni/flathead-dev/devo/gdb/ \
    testsuite/gdb.mi/basics.c",line_asm_insn=[
{address="0x000107bc",func-name="main",offset="0",
inst="save  %sp, -112, %sp"}]},
src_and_asm_line={line="32",
file="/kwikemart/marge/ezannoni/flathead-dev/devo/gdb/ \
    testsuite/gdb.mi/basics.c",line_asm_insn=[
{address="0x000107c0",func-name="main",offset="4",
inst="mov  2, %o0"},
{address="0x000107c4",func-name="main",offset="8",
inst="sethi  %hi(0x11800), %o2"}]}])
(gdb)
```

The -data-evaluate-expression Command

Synopsis

> -data-evaluate-expression *expr*

Evaluate *expr* as an expression. The expression could contain an inferior function call. The function call will execute synchronously. If the expression contains spaces, it must be enclosed in double quotes.

GDB Command

The corresponding GDB commands are 'print', 'output', and 'call'. In gdbtk only, there's a corresponding 'gdb_eval' command.

Example

In the following example, the numbers that precede the commands are the *tokens* described in Section 21.1 [GDB/MI Command Syntax], page 223. Notice how GDB/MI returns the same tokens in its output.

```
211-data-evaluate-expression A
211^done,value="1"
(gdb)
311-data-evaluate-expression &A
311^done,value="0xefffeb7c"
(gdb)
411-data-evaluate-expression A+3
411^done,value="4"
```

```
(gdb)
511-data-evaluate-expression "A + 3"
511^done,value="4"
(gdb)
```

The -data-list-changed-registers Command

Synopsis

    -data-list-changed-registers
Display a list of the registers that have changed.

GDB Command

GDB doesn't have a direct analog for this command; gdbtk has the corresponding command 'gdb_changed_register_list'.

Example

On a PPC MBX board:
```
(gdb)
-exec-continue
^running

(gdb)
*stopped,reason="breakpoint-hit",bkptno="1",frame={func="main",
args=[],file="try.c",line="5"}
(gdb)
-data-list-changed-registers
^done,changed-registers=["0","1","2","4","5","6","7","8","9",
"10","11","13","14","15","16","17","18","19","20","21","22","23",
"24","25","26","27","28","30","31","64","65","66","67","69"]
(gdb)
```

The -data-list-register-names Command

Synopsis

    -data-list-register-names [(regno)+]
Show a list of register names for the current target. If no arguments are given, it shows a list of the names of all the registers. If integer numbers are given as arguments, it will print a list of the names of the registers corresponding to the arguments. To ensure consistency between a register name and its number, the output list may include empty register names.

GDB Command

GDB does not have a command which corresponds to '-data-list-register-names'. In **gdbtk** there is a corresponding command 'gdb_regnames'.

Example

For the PPC MBX board:

```
(gdb)
-data-list-register-names
^done,register-names=["r0","r1","r2","r3","r4","r5","r6","r7",
"r8","r9","r10","r11","r12","r13","r14","r15","r16","r17","r18",
"r19","r20","r21","r22","r23","r24","r25","r26","r27","r28","r29",
"r30","r31","f0","f1","f2","f3","f4","f5","f6","f7","f8","f9",
"f10","f11","f12","f13","f14","f15","f16","f17","f18","f19","f20",
"f21","f22","f23","f24","f25","f26","f27","f28","f29","f30","f31",
"", "pc","ps","cr","lr","ctr","xer"]
(gdb)
-data-list-register-names 1 2 3
^done,register-names=["r1","r2","r3"]
(gdb)
```

The -data-list-register-values Command

Synopsis

```
-data-list-register-values fmt [ ( regno )*]
```

Display the registers' contents. *fmt* is the format according to which the registers' contents are to be returned, followed by an optional list of numbers specifying the registers to display. A missing list of numbers indicates that the contents of all the registers must be returned.

Allowed formats for *fmt* are:

x   Hexadecimal

o   Octal

t   Binary

d   Decimal

r   Raw

N   Natural

GDB Command

The corresponding GDB commands are 'info reg', 'info all-reg', and (in gdbtk) 'gdb_fetch_registers'.

Example

For a PPC MBX board (note: line breaks are for readability only, they don't appear in the actual output):

```
(gdb)
-data-list-register-values r 64 65
^done,register-values=[{number="64",value="0xfe00a300"},
{number="65",value="0x00029002"}]
(gdb)
-data-list-register-values x
^done,register-values=[{number="0",value="0xfe0043c8"},
{number="1",value="0x3fff88"},{number="2",value="0xfffffffe"},
{number="3",value="0x0"},{number="4",value="0xa"},
{number="5",value="0x3fff68"},{number="6",value="0x3fff58"},
{number="7",value="0xfe011e98"},{number="8",value="0x2"},
{number="9",value="0xfa202820"},{number="10",value="0xfa202808"},
{number="11",value="0x1"},{number="12",value="0x0"},
{number="13",value="0x4544"},{number="14",value="0xffdfffff"},
{number="15",value="0xffffffff"},{number="16",value="0xfffffeff"},
{number="17",value="0xeffffffed"},{number="18",value="0xfffffffe"},
{number="19",value="0xffffffff"},{number="20",value="0xffffffff"},
{number="21",value="0xffffffff"},{number="22",value="0xfffffff7"},
{number="23",value="0xffffffff"},{number="24",value="0xffffffff"},
{number="25",value="0xffffffff"},{number="26",value="0xfffffffb"},
{number="27",value="0xffffffff"},{number="28",value="0xf7bfffff"},
{number="29",value="0x0"},{number="30",value="0xfe010000"},
{number="31",value="0x0"},{number="32",value="0x0"},
{number="33",value="0x0"},{number="34",value="0x0"},
{number="35",value="0x0"},{number="36",value="0x0"},
{number="37",value="0x0"},{number="38",value="0x0"},
{number="39",value="0x0"},{number="40",value="0x0"},
{number="41",value="0x0"},{number="42",value="0x0"},
{number="43",value="0x0"},{number="44",value="0x0"},
{number="45",value="0x0"},{number="46",value="0x0"},
{number="47",value="0x0"},{number="48",value="0x0"},
{number="49",value="0x0"},{number="50",value="0x0"},
{number="51",value="0x0"},{number="52",value="0x0"},
{number="53",value="0x0"},{number="54",value="0x0"},
{number="55",value="0x0"},{number="56",value="0x0"},
```

```
{number="57",value="0x0"},{number="58",value="0x0"},
{number="59",value="0x0"},{number="60",value="0x0"},
{number="61",value="0x0"},{number="62",value="0x0"},
{number="63",value="0x0"},{number="64",value="0xfe00a300"},
{number="65",value="0x29002"},{number="66",value="0x202f04b5"},
{number="67",value="0xfe0043b0"},{number="68",value="0xfe00b3e4"},
{number="69",value="0x20002b03"}]
(gdb)
```

The -data-read-memory Command

Synopsis

```
-data-read-memory [ -o byte-offset ]
    address word-format word-size
    nr-rows nr-cols [ aschar ]
```

where:

'*address*' An expression specifying the address of the first memory word to be read. Complex expressions containing embedded white space should be quoted using the C convention.

'*word-format*'

The format to be used to print the memory words. The notation is the same as for GDB's **print** command (see Section 8.4 [Output formats], page 73).

'*word-size*'

The size of each memory word in bytes.

'*nr-rows*' The number of rows in the output table.

'*nr-cols*' The number of columns in the output table.

'*aschar*' If present, indicates that each row should include an ASCII dump. The value of *aschar* is used as a padding character when a byte is not a member of the printable ASCII character set (printable ASCII characters are those whose code is between 32 and 126, inclusively).

'*byte-offset*'

An offset to add to the *address* before fetching memory.

This command displays memory contents as a table of *nr-rows* by *nr-cols* words, each word being *word-size* bytes. In total, *nr-rows* * *nr-cols* * *word-size* bytes are read (returned as '**total-bytes**'). Should less then the requested number of bytes be returned by the target, the missing words are identified using '**N/A**'. The number of bytes read from the target is returned in '**nr-bytes**' and the starting address used to read memory in '**addr**'.

The address of the next/previous row or page is available in 'next-row' and 'prev-row', 'next-page' and 'prev-page'.

GDB Command

The corresponding GDB command is 'x'. gdbtk has 'gdb_get_mem' memory read command.

Example

Read six bytes of memory starting at bytes+6 but then offset by -6 bytes. Format as three rows of two columns. One byte per word. Display each word in hex.

```
(gdb)
9-data-read-memory -o -6 -- bytes+6 x 1 3 2
9^done,addr="0x00001390",nr-bytes="6",total-bytes="6",
next-row="0x00001396",prev-row="0x0000138e",next-page="0x00001396",
prev-page="0x0000138a",memory=[
{addr="0x00001390",data=["0x00","0x01"]},
{addr="0x00001392",data=["0x02","0x03"]},
{addr="0x00001394",data=["0x04","0x05"]}]
(gdb)
```

Read two bytes of memory starting at address shorts + 64 and display as a single word formatted in decimal.

```
(gdb)
5-data-read-memory shorts+64 d 2 1 1
5^done,addr="0x00001510",nr-bytes="2",total-bytes="2",
next-row="0x00001512",prev-row="0x0000150e",
next-page="0x00001512",prev-page="0x0000150e",memory=[
{addr="0x00001510",data=["128"]}]
(gdb)
```

Read thirty two bytes of memory starting at bytes+16 and format as eight rows of four columns. Include a string encoding with 'x' used as the non-printable character.

```
(gdb)
4-data-read-memory bytes+16 x 1 8 4 x
4^done,addr="0x000013a0",nr-bytes="32",total-bytes="32",
next-row="0x000013c0",prev-row="0x0000139c",
next-page="0x000013c0",prev-page="0x00001380",memory=[
{addr="0x000013a0",data=["0x10","0x11","0x12","0x13"],ascii="xxxx"},
{addr="0x000013a4",data=["0x14","0x15","0x16","0x17"],ascii="xxxx"},
{addr="0x000013a8",data=["0x18","0x19","0x1a","0x1b"],ascii="xxxx"},
{addr="0x000013ac",data=["0x1c","0x1d","0x1e","0x1f"],ascii="xxxx"},
{addr="0x000013b0",data=["0x20","0x21","0x22","0x23"],ascii=" !\"#"},
```

```
{addr="0x000013b4",data=["0x24","0x25","0x26","0x27"],ascii="$%&'"},
{addr="0x000013b8",data=["0x28","0x29","0x2a","0x2b"],ascii="()*+"},
{addr="0x000013bc",data=["0x2c","0x2d","0x2e","0x2f"],ascii=",-./"}]
(gdb)
```

The -display-delete Command

Synopsis

```
-display-delete number
```
Delete the display number.

GDB Command

The corresponding GDB command is 'delete display'.

Example

N.A.

The -display-disable Command

Synopsis

```
-display-disable number
```
Disable display number.

GDB Command

The corresponding GDB command is 'disable display'.

Example

N.A.

The -display-enable Command

Synopsis

```
-display-enable number
```
Enable display number.

GDB Command

The corresponding GDB command is 'enable display'.

Example

N.A.

The -display-insert Command

Synopsis

    -display-insert *expression*
Display *expression* every time the program stops.

GDB Command

The corresponding GDB command is 'display'.

Example

N.A.

The -display-list Command

Synopsis

    -display-list
List the displays. Do not show the current values.

GDB Command

The corresponding GDB command is 'info display'.

Example

N.A.

The -environment-cd Command

Synopsis

    -environment-cd *pathdir*
Set GDB's working directory.

GDB Command

The corresponding GDB command is 'cd'.

Example

```
(gdb)
-environment-cd /kwikemart/marge/ezannoni/flathead-dev/devo/gdb
^done
(gdb)
```

The -environment-directory Command

Synopsis

```
-environment-directory pathdir
```
Add directory *pathdir* to beginning of search path for source files.

GDB Command

The corresponding GDB command is 'dir'.

Example

```
(gdb)
-environment-directory /kwikemart/marge/ezannoni/flathead-dev/devo/gdb
^done
(gdb)
```

The -environment-path Command

Synopsis

```
-environment-path ( pathdir )+
```
Add directories *pathdir* to beginning of search path for object files.

GDB Command

The corresponding GDB command is 'path'.

Example

```
(gdb)
-environment-path /kwikemart/marge/ezannoni/flathead-dev/ppc-eabi/gdb
^done
(gdb)
```

The -environment-pwd Command

Synopsis

```
-environment-pwd
```
Show the current working directory.

GDB command

The corresponding GDB command is 'pwd'.

Example

```
(gdb)
-environment-pwd
~Working directory /kwikemart/marge/ezannoni/flathead-dev/devo/gdb.
^done
(gdb)
```

21.7 GDB/MI Program control

Program termination

As a result of execution, the inferior program can run to completion, if it doesn't encounter any breakpoints. In this case the output will include an exit code, if the program has exited exceptionally.

Examples

Program exited normally:

```
(gdb)
-exec-run
^running
(gdb)
x = 55
*stopped,reason="exited-normally"
(gdb)
```

Program exited exceptionally:

```
(gdb)
-exec-run
^running
(gdb)
x = 55
```

```
*stopped,reason="exited",exit-code="01"
(gdb)
```

Another way the program can terminate is if it receives a signal such as SIGINT. In this case, GDB/MI displays this:

```
(gdb)
*stopped,reason="exited-signalled",signal-name="SIGINT",
signal-meaning="Interrupt"
```

The -exec-abort Command

Synopsis

```
-exec-abort
```
Kill the inferior running program.

GDB Command

The corresponding GDB command is 'kill'.

Example

N.A.

The -exec-arguments Command

Synopsis

```
-exec-arguments args
```
Set the inferior program arguments, to be used in the next '-exec-run'.

GDB Command

The corresponding GDB command is 'set args'.

Example

Don't have one around.

The -exec-continue Command

Synopsis

```
-exec-continue
```

Asynchronous command. Resumes the execution of the inferior program until a breakpoint is encountered, or until the inferior exits.

GDB Command

The corresponding GDB corresponding is 'continue'.

Example

```
-exec-continue
^running
(gdb)
@Hello world
*stopped,reason="breakpoint-hit",bkptno="2",frame={func="foo",args=[],
file="hello.c",line="13"}
(gdb)
```

The -exec-finish Command

Synopsis

```
-exec-finish
```

Asynchronous command. Resumes the execution of the inferior program until the current function is exited. Displays the results returned by the function.

GDB Command

The corresponding GDB command is 'finish'.

Example

Function returning void.

```
-exec-finish
^running
(gdb)
@hello from foo
*stopped,reason="function-finished",frame={func="main",args=[],
file="hello.c",line="7"}
(gdb)
```

Function returning other than void. The name of the internal GDB variable storing the result is printed, together with the value itself.

```
-exec-finish
^running
(gdb)
*stopped,reason="function-finished",frame={addr="0x000107b0",func="foo",
args=[{name="a",value="1"],{name="b",value="9"}},
file="recursive2.c",line="14"},
gdb-result-var="$1",return-value="0"
(gdb)
```

The -exec-interrupt Command

Synopsis

```
-exec-interrupt
```

Asynchronous command. Interrupts the background execution of the target. Note how the token associated with the stop message is the one for the execution command that has been interrupted. The token for the interrupt itself only appears in the '^done' output. If the user is trying to interrupt a non-running program, an error message will be printed.

GDB Command

The corresponding GDB command is 'interrupt'.

Example

```
(gdb)
111-exec-continue
111^running

(gdb)
222-exec-interrupt
222^done
(gdb)
111*stopped,signal-name="SIGINT",signal-meaning="Interrupt",
frame={addr="0x00010140",func="foo",args=[],file="try.c",line="13"}
(gdb)

(gdb)
-exec-interrupt
^error,msg="mi_cmd_exec_interrupt: Inferior not executing."
(gdb)
```

The -exec-next Command

Synopsis

```
-exec-next
```

Asynchronous command. Resumes execution of the inferior program, stopping when the beginning of the next source line is reached.

GDB Command

The corresponding GDB command is 'next'.

Example

```
-exec-next
^running
(gdb)
*stopped,reason="end-stepping-range",line="8",file="hello.c"
(gdb)
```

The -exec-next-instruction Command

Synopsis

```
-exec-next-instruction
```

Asynchronous command. Executes one machine instruction. If the instruction is a function call continues until the function returns. If the program stops at an instruction in the middle of a source line, the address will be printed as well.

GDB Command

The corresponding GDB command is 'nexti'.

Example

```
(gdb)
-exec-next-instruction
^running

(gdb)
*stopped,reason="end-stepping-range",
addr="0x000100d4",line="5",file="hello.c"
(gdb)
```

The -exec-return Command

Synopsis

```
-exec-return
```

Makes current function return immediately. Doesn't execute the inferior. Displays the new current frame.

GDB Command

The corresponding GDB command is 'return'.

Example

```
(gdb)
200-break-insert callee4
200^done,bkpt={number="1",addr="0x00010734",
file="../../../devo/gdb/testsuite/gdb.mi/basics.c",line="8"}
(gdb)
000-exec-run
000^running
(gdb)
000*stopped,reason="breakpoint-hit",bkptno="1",
frame={func="callee4",args=[],
file="../../../devo/gdb/testsuite/gdb.mi/basics.c",line="8"}
(gdb)
205-break-delete
205^done
(gdb)
111-exec-return
111^done,frame={level="0 ",func="callee3",
args=[{name="strarg",
value="0x11940 \"A string argument.\""}],
file="../../../devo/gdb/testsuite/gdb.mi/basics.c",line="18"}
(gdb)
```

The -exec-run Command

Synopsis

```
-exec-run
```

Asynchronous command. Starts execution of the inferior from the beginning. The inferior executes until either a breakpoint is encountered or the program exits.

GDB Command

The corresponding GDB command is 'run'.

Example

```
(gdb)
-break-insert main
^done,bkpt={number="1",addr="0x0001072c",file="recursive2.c",line="4"}
(gdb)
-exec-run
^running
(gdb)
*stopped,reason="breakpoint-hit",bkptno="1",
frame={func="main",args=[],file="recursive2.c",line="4"}
(gdb)
```

The -exec-show-arguments Command

Synopsis

```
-exec-show-arguments
```
Print the arguments of the program.

GDB Command

The corresponding GDB command is 'show args'.

Example

N.A.

The -exec-step Command

Synopsis

```
-exec-step
```
Asynchronous command. Resumes execution of the inferior program, stopping when the beginning of the next source line is reached, if the next source line is not a function call. If it is, stop at the first instruction of the called function.

GDB Command

The corresponding GDB command is 'step'.

Example

Stepping into a function:

```
-exec-step
^running
(gdb)
*stopped,reason="end-stepping-range",
frame={func="foo",args=[{name="a",value="10"},
{name="b",value="0"}],file="recursive2.c",line="11"}
(gdb)
```

Regular stepping:

```
-exec-step
^running
(gdb)
*stopped,reason="end-stepping-range",line="14",file="recursive2.c"
(gdb)
```

The -exec-step-instruction Command

Synopsis

```
-exec-step-instruction
```

Asynchronous command. Resumes the inferior which executes one machine instruction. The output, once GDB has stopped, will vary depending on whether we have stopped in the middle of a source line or not. In the former case, the address at which the program stopped will be printed as well.

GDB Command

The corresponding GDB command is 'stepi'.

Example

```
(gdb)
-exec-step-instruction
^running

(gdb)
*stopped,reason="end-stepping-range",
frame={func="foo",args=[],file="try.c",line="10"}
(gdb)
-exec-step-instruction
^running
```

```
(gdb)
*stopped,reason="end-stepping-range",
frame={addr="0x000100f4",func="foo",args=[],file="try.c",line="10"}
(gdb)
```

The -exec-until Command

Synopsis

```
-exec-until [ location ]
```

Asynchronous command. Executes the inferior until the *location* specified in the argument is reached. If there is no argument, the inferior executes until a source line greater than the current one is reached. The reason for stopping in this case will be '`location-reached`'.

GDB Command

The corresponding GDB command is '`until`'.

Example

```
(gdb)
-exec-until recursive2.c:6
^running
(gdb)
x = 55
*stopped,reason="location-reached",frame={func="main",args=[],
file="recursive2.c",line="6"}
(gdb)
```

The -file-exec-and-symbols Command

Synopsis

```
-file-exec-and-symbols file
```

Specify the executable file to be debugged. This file is the one from which the symbol table is also read. If no file is specified, the command clears the executable and symbol information. If breakpoints are set when using this command with no arguments, GDB will produce error messages. Otherwise, no output is produced, except a completion notification.

GDB Command

The corresponding GDB command is '`file`'.

Example

```
(gdb)
-file-exec-and-symbols /kwikemart/marge/ezannoni/TRUNK/mbx/hello.mbx
^done
(gdb)
```

The -file-exec-file Command

Synopsis

```
-file-exec-file file
```
Specify the executable file to be debugged. Unlike '-file-exec-and-symbols', the symbol table is *not* read from this file. If used without argument, GDB clears the information about the executable file. No output is produced, except a completion notification.

GDB Command

The corresponding GDB command is 'exec-file'.

Example

```
(gdb)
-file-exec-file /kwikemart/marge/ezannoni/TRUNK/mbx/hello.mbx
^done
(gdb)
```

The -file-list-exec-sections Command

Synopsis

```
-file-list-exec-sections
```
List the sections of the current executable file.

GDB Command

The GDB command 'info file' shows, among the rest, the same information as this command. **gdbtk** has a corresponding command 'gdb_load_info'.

Example

N.A.

The `-file-list-exec-source-files` Command

Synopsis

> `-file-list-exec-source-files`
> List the source files for the current executable.

GDB Command

There's no GDB command which directly corresponds to this one. `gdbtk` has an analogous command '`gdb_listfiles`'.

Example

> N.A.

The `-file-list-shared-libraries` Command

Synopsis

> `-file-list-shared-libraries`
> List the shared libraries in the program.

GDB Command

The corresponding GDB command is '`info shared`'.

Example

> N.A.

The `-file-list-symbol-files` Command

Synopsis

> `-file-list-symbol-files`
> List symbol files.

GDB Command

The corresponding GDB command is '`info file`' (part of it).

Example

> N.A.

The -file-symbol-file Command

Synopsis

```
-file-symbol-file file
```
Read symbol table info from the specified *file* argument. When used without arguments, clears GDB's symbol table info. No output is produced, except for a completion notification.

GDB Command

The corresponding GDB command is 'symbol-file'.

Example

```
(gdb)
-file-symbol-file /kwikemart/marge/ezannoni/TRUNK/mbx/hello.mbx
^done
(gdb)
```

21.8 Miscellaneous GDB commands in GDB/MI

The -gdb-exit Command

Synopsis

```
-gdb-exit
```
Exit GDB immediately.

GDB Command

Approximately corresponds to 'quit'.

Example

```
(gdb)
-gdb-exit
```

The -gdb-set Command

Synopsis

```
-gdb-set
```
Set an internal GDB variable.

GDB Command

The corresponding GDB command is 'set'.

Example

```
(gdb)
-gdb-set $foo=3
^done
(gdb)
```

The -gdb-show Command

Synopsis

```
-gdb-show
```
Show the current value of a GDB variable.

GDB command

The corresponding GDB command is 'show'.

Example

```
(gdb)
-gdb-show annotate
^done,value="0"
(gdb)
```

The -gdb-version Command

Synopsis

```
-gdb-version
```
Show version information for GDB. Used mostly in testing.

GDB Command

There's no equivalent GDB command. GDB by default shows this information when you start an interactive session.

Example

```
(gdb)
-gdb-version
```

```
~GNU gdb 5.2.1
~Copyright 2000 Free Software Foundation, Inc.
~GDB is free software, covered by the GNU General Public License, and
~you are welcome to change it and/or distribute copies of it under
~ certain conditions.
~Type "show copying" to see the conditions.
~There is absolutely no warranty for GDB.  Type "show warranty" for
~ details.
~This GDB was configured as
 "--host=sparc-sun-solaris2.5.1 --target=ppc-eabi".
^done
(gdb)
```

21.9 GDB/MI Stack Manipulation Commands

The -stack-info-frame Command

Synopsis

```
-stack-info-frame
```
Get info on the current frame.

GDB Command

The corresponding GDB command is 'info frame' or 'frame' (without arguments).

Example

N.A.

The -stack-info-depth Command

Synopsis

```
-stack-info-depth [ max-depth ]
```
Return the depth of the stack. If the integer argument *max-depth* is specified, do not count beyond *max-depth* frames.

GDB Command

There's no equivalent GDB command.

Example

For a stack with frame levels 0 through 11:

```
(gdb)
-stack-info-depth
^done,depth="12"
(gdb)
-stack-info-depth 4
^done,depth="4"
(gdb)
-stack-info-depth 12
^done,depth="12"
(gdb)
-stack-info-depth 11
^done,depth="11"
(gdb)
-stack-info-depth 13
^done,depth="12"
(gdb)
```

The -stack-list-arguments Command

Synopsis

```
-stack-list-arguments show-values
     [ low-frame high-frame ]
```

Display a list of the arguments for the frames between *low-frame* and *high-frame* (inclusive). If *low-frame* and *high-frame* are not provided, list the arguments for the whole call stack.

The *show-values* argument must have a value of 0 or 1. A value of 0 means that only the names of the arguments are listed, a value of 1 means that both names and values of the arguments are printed.

GDB Command

GDB does not have an equivalent command. gdbtk has a 'gdb_get_args' command which partially overlaps with the functionality of '-stack-list-arguments'.

Example

```
(gdb)
-stack-list-frames
^done,
```

```
stack=[
frame={level="0 ",addr="0x00010734",func="callee4",
file="../../../devo/gdb/testsuite/gdb.mi/basics.c",line="8"},
frame={level="1 ",addr="0x0001076c",func="callee3",
file="../../../devo/gdb/testsuite/gdb.mi/basics.c",line="17"},
frame={level="2 ",addr="0x0001078c",func="callee2",
file="../../../devo/gdb/testsuite/gdb.mi/basics.c",line="22"},
frame={level="3 ",addr="0x000107b4",func="callee1",
file="../../../devo/gdb/testsuite/gdb.mi/basics.c",line="27"},
frame={level="4 ",addr="0x000107e0",func="main",
file="../../../devo/gdb/testsuite/gdb.mi/basics.c",line="32"}]
(gdb)
-stack-list-arguments 0
^done,
stack-args=[
frame={level="0",args=[]},
frame={level="1",args=[name="strarg"]},
frame={level="2",args=[name="intarg",name="strarg"]},
frame={level="3",args=[name="intarg",name="strarg",name="fltarg"]},
frame={level="4",args=[]}]
(gdb)
-stack-list-arguments 1
^done,
stack-args=[
frame={level="0",args=[]},
frame={level="1",
 args=[{name="strarg",value="0x11940 \"A string argument.\""}]},
frame={level="2",args=[
{name="intarg",value="2"},
{name="strarg",value="0x11940 \"A string argument.\""}]},
{frame={level="3",args=[
{name="intarg",value="2"},
{name="strarg",value="0x11940 \"A string argument.\""},
{name="fltarg",value="3.5"}]},
frame={level="4",args=[]}]
(gdb)
-stack-list-arguments 0 2 2
^done,stack-args=[frame={level="2",args=[name="intarg",name="strarg"]}]
(gdb)
-stack-list-arguments 1 2 2
^done,stack-args=[frame={level="2",
args=[{name="intarg",value="2"},
{name="strarg",value="0x11940 \"A string argument.\""}]}]
(gdb)
```

The -stack-list-frames Command

Synopsis

> -stack-list-frames [*low-frame high-frame*]

List the frames currently on the stack. For each frame it displays the following info:

'*level*'	The frame number, 0 being the topmost frame, i.e. the innermost function.
'*addr*'	The $pc value for that frame.
'*func*'	Function name.
'*file*'	File name of the source file where the function lives.
'*line*'	Line number corresponding to the $pc.

If invoked without arguments, this command prints a backtrace for the whole stack. If given two integer arguments, it shows the frames whose levels are between the two arguments (inclusive). If the two arguments are equal, it shows the single frame at the corresponding level.

GDB Command

The corresponding GDB commands are 'backtrace' and 'where'.

Example

Full stack backtrace:

```
(gdb)
-stack-list-frames
^done,stack=
[frame={level="0 ",addr="0x0001076c",func="foo",
  file="recursive2.c",line="11"},
 frame={level="1 ",addr="0x000107a4",func="foo",
  file="recursive2.c",line="14"},
 frame={level="2 ",addr="0x000107a4",func="foo",
  file="recursive2.c",line="14"},
 frame={level="3 ",addr="0x000107a4",func="foo",
  file="recursive2.c",line="14"},
 frame={level="4 ",addr="0x000107a4",func="foo",
  file="recursive2.c",line="14"},
 frame={level="5 ",addr="0x000107a4",func="foo",
  file="recursive2.c",line="14"},
 frame={level="6 ",addr="0x000107a4",func="foo",
  file="recursive2.c",line="14"},
```

```
    frame={level="7 ",addr="0x000107a4",func="foo",
      file="recursive2.c",line="14"},
    frame={level="8 ",addr="0x000107a4",func="foo",
      file="recursive2.c",line="14"},
    frame={level="9 ",addr="0x000107a4",func="foo",
      file="recursive2.c",line="14"},
    frame={level="10",addr="0x000107a4",func="foo",
      file="recursive2.c",line="14"},
    frame={level="11",addr="0x00010738",func="main",
      file="recursive2.c",line="4"}]
(gdb)
```

Show frames between *low_frame* and *high_frame*:

```
(gdb)
-stack-list-frames 3 5
^done,stack=
[frame={level="3 ",addr="0x000107a4",func="foo",
    file="recursive2.c",line="14"},
  frame={level="4 ",addr="0x000107a4",func="foo",
    file="recursive2.c",line="14"},
  frame={level="5 ",addr="0x000107a4",func="foo",
    file="recursive2.c",line="14"}]
(gdb)
```

Show a single frame:

```
(gdb)
-stack-list-frames 3 3
^done,stack=
[frame={level="3 ",addr="0x000107a4",func="foo",
    file="recursive2.c",line="14"}]
(gdb)
```

The -stack-list-locals Command

Synopsis

```
    -stack-list-locals print-values
```

Display the local variable names for the current frame. With an argument of 0 prints only the names of the variables, with argument of 1 prints also their values.

GDB Command

'info locals' in GDB, 'gdb_get_locals' in gdbtk.

Example

```
(gdb)
-stack-list-locals 0
^done,locals=[name="A",name="B",name="C"]
(gdb)
-stack-list-locals 1
^done,locals=[{name="A",value="1"},{name="B",value="2"},
  {name="C",value="3"}]
(gdb)
```

The -stack-select-frame Command

Synopsis

```
-stack-select-frame framenum
```
Change the current frame. Select a different frame *framenum* on the stack.

GDB Command

The corresponding GDB commands are 'frame', 'up', 'down', 'select-frame', 'up-silent', and 'down-silent'.

Example

```
(gdb)
-stack-select-frame 2
^done
(gdb)
```

21.10 GDB/MI Symbol Query Commands

The -symbol-info-address Command

Synopsis

```
-symbol-info-address symbol
```
Describe where *symbol* is stored.

GDB Command

The corresponding GDB command is 'info address'.

Example

N.A.

The -symbol-info-file Command

Synopsis

```
-symbol-info-file
```
Show the file for the symbol.

GDB Command

There's no equivalent GDB command. `gdbtk` has `gdb_find_file`.

Example

N.A.

The -symbol-info-function Command

Synopsis

```
-symbol-info-function
```
Show which function the symbol lives in.

GDB Command

`gdb_get_function` in gdbtk.

Example

N.A.

The -symbol-info-line Command

Synopsis

```
-symbol-info-line
```
Show the core addresses of the code for a source line.

GDB Command

The corresponding GDB comamnd is `info line`. gdbtk has the `gdb_get_line` and `gdb_get_file` commands.

Example

N.A.

The -symbol-info-symbol Command

Synopsis

        -symbol-info-symbol *addr*
Describe what symbol is at location *addr*.

GDB Command

The corresponding GDB command is 'info symbol'.

Example

N.A.

The -symbol-list-functions Command

Synopsis

        -symbol-list-functions
List the functions in the executable.

GDB Command

'info functions' in GDB, 'gdb_listfunc' and 'gdb_search' in gdbtk.

Example

N.A.

The -symbol-list-types Command

Synopsis

        -symbol-list-types
List all the type names.

GDB Command

The corresponding commands are 'info types' in GDB, 'gdb_search' in gdbtk.

Example

N.A.

The -symbol-list-variables Command

Synopsis

```
-symbol-list-variables
```
List all the global and static variable names.

GDB Command

'`info variables`' in GDB, '`gdb_search`' in gdbtk.

Example

N.A.

The -symbol-locate Command

Synopsis

```
-symbol-locate
```

GDB Command

'`gdb_loc`' in gdbtk.

Example

N.A.

The -symbol-type Command

Synopsis

```
-symbol-type variable
```
Show type of *variable*.

GDB Command

The corresponding GDB command is '`ptype`', gdbtk has '`gdb_obj_variable`'.

Example

N.A.

21.11 GDB/MI Target Manipulation Commands

The -target-attach Command

Synopsis

    -target-attach *pid* | *file*
Attach to a process *pid* or a file *file* outside of GDB.

GDB command

The corresponding GDB command is 'attach'.

Example

N.A.

The -target-compare-sections Command

Synopsis

    -target-compare-sections [*section*]
Compare data of section *section* on target to the exec file. Without the
argument, all sections are compared.

GDB Command

The GDB equivalent is 'compare-sections'.

Example

N.A.

The -target-detach Command

Synopsis

    -target-detach
Disconnect from the remote target. There's no output.

GDB command

The corresponding GDB command is 'detach'.

Example

```
(gdb)
-target-detach
^done
(gdb)
```

The -target-download Command

Synopsis

```
-target-download
```

Loads the executable onto the remote target. It prints out an update message every half second, which includes the fields:

'section'   The name of the section.

'section-sent'
            The size of what has been sent so far for that section.

'section-size'
            The size of the section.

'total-sent'
            The total size of what was sent so far (the current and the previous sections).

'total-size'
            The size of the overall executable to download.

Each message is sent as status record (see Section 21.1.2 [GDB/MI Output Syntax], page 224).

In addition, it prints the name and size of the sections, as they are downloaded. These messages include the following fields:

'section'   The name of the section.

'section-size'
            The size of the section.

'total-size'
            The size of the overall executable to download.

At the end, a summary is printed.

GDB Command

The corresponding GDB command is 'load'.

Example

Note: each status message appears on a single line. Here the messages
have been broken down so that they can fit onto a page.

```
(gdb)
-target-download
+download,{section=".text",section-size="6668",total-size="9880"}
+download,{section=".text",section-sent="512",section-size="6668",
total-sent="512",total-size="9880"}
+download,{section=".text",section-sent="1024",section-size="6668",
total-sent="1024",total-size="9880"}
+download,{section=".text",section-sent="1536",section-size="6668",
total-sent="1536",total-size="9880"}
+download,{section=".text",section-sent="2048",section-size="6668",
total-sent="2048",total-size="9880"}
+download,{section=".text",section-sent="2560",section-size="6668",
total-sent="2560",total-size="9880"}
+download,{section=".text",section-sent="3072",section-size="6668",
total-sent="3072",total-size="9880"}
+download,{section=".text",section-sent="3584",section-size="6668",
total-sent="3584",total-size="9880"}
+download,{section=".text",section-sent="4096",section-size="6668",
total-sent="4096",total-size="9880"}
+download,{section=".text",section-sent="4608",section-size="6668",
total-sent="4608",total-size="9880"}
+download,{section=".text",section-sent="5120",section-size="6668",
total-sent="5120",total-size="9880"}
+download,{section=".text",section-sent="5632",section-size="6668",
total-sent="5632",total-size="9880"}
+download,{section=".text",section-sent="6144",section-size="6668",
total-sent="6144",total-size="9880"}
+download,{section=".text",section-sent="6656",section-size="6668",
total-sent="6656",total-size="9880"}
+download,{section=".init",section-size="28",total-size="9880"}
+download,{section=".fini",section-size="28",total-size="9880"}
+download,{section=".data",section-size="3156",total-size="9880"}
+download,{section=".data",section-sent="512",section-size="3156",
total-sent="7236",total-size="9880"}
+download,{section=".data",section-sent="1024",section-size="3156",
total-sent="7748",total-size="9880"}
+download,{section=".data",section-sent="1536",section-size="3156",
total-sent="8260",total-size="9880"}
+download,{section=".data",section-sent="2048",section-size="3156",
total-sent="8772",total-size="9880"}
```

```
+download,{section=".data",section-sent="2560",section-size="3156",
total-sent="9284",total-size="9880"}
+download,{section=".data",section-sent="3072",section-size="3156",
total-sent="9796",total-size="9880"}
^done,address="0x10004",load-size="9880",transfer-rate="6586",
write-rate="429"
(gdb)
```

The -target-exec-status Command

Synopsis

```
-target-exec-status
```
Provide information on the state of the target (whether it is running or not, for instance).

GDB Command

There's no equivalent GDB command.

Example

N.A.

The -target-list-available-targets Command

Synopsis

```
-target-list-available-targets
```
List the possible targets to connect to.

GDB Command

The corresponding GDB command is 'help target'.

Example

N.A.

The -target-list-current-targets Command

Synopsis

> `-target-list-current-targets`
>
> Describe the current target.

GDB Command

The corresponding information is printed by '`info file`' (among other things).

Example

> N.A.

The -target-list-parameters Command

Synopsis

> `-target-list-parameters`

GDB Command

No equivalent.

Example

> N.A.

The -target-select Command

Synopsis

> `-target-select` *type parameters* ...
>
> Connect GDB to the remote target. This command takes two args:

'*type*'   The type of target, for instance '`async`', '`remote`', etc.

'*parameters*'

> Device names, host names and the like. See Section 14.2 [Commands for managing targets], page 143, for more details.

The output is a connection notification, followed by the address at which the target program is, in the following form:

```
^connected,addr="address",func="function name",
   args=[arg list]
```

GDB Command

The corresponding GDB command is 'target'.

Example

```
(gdb)
-target-select async /dev/ttya
^connected,addr="0xfe00a300",func="??",args=[]
(gdb)
```

21.12 GDB/MI Thread Commands

The -thread-info Command

Synopsis

```
-thread-info
```

GDB command

No equivalent.

Example

N.A.

The -thread-list-all-threads Command

Synopsis

```
-thread-list-all-threads
```

GDB Command

The equivalent GDB command is 'info threads'.

Example

N.A.

The -thread-list-ids Command

Synopsis

```
-thread-list-ids
```
Produces a list of the currently known GDB thread ids. At the end of the list it also prints the total number of such threads.

GDB Command

Part of 'info threads' supplies the same information.

Example

No threads present, besides the main process:
```
(gdb)
-thread-list-ids
^done,thread-ids={},number-of-threads="0"
(gdb)
```
Several threads:
```
(gdb)
-thread-list-ids
^done,thread-ids={thread-id="3",thread-id="2",thread-id="1"},
number-of-threads="3"
(gdb)
```

The -thread-select Command

Synopsis

```
-thread-select threadnum
```
Make *threadnum* the current thread. It prints the number of the new current thread, and the topmost frame for that thread.

GDB Command

The corresponding GDB command is 'thread'.

Example

```
(gdb)
-exec-next
^running
(gdb)
*stopped,reason="end-stepping-range",thread-id="2",line="187",
file="../../../devo/gdb/testsuite/gdb.threads/linux-dp.c"
```

```
(gdb)
-thread-list-ids
^done,
thread-ids={thread-id="3",thread-id="2",thread-id="1"},
number-of-threads="3"
(gdb)
-thread-select 3
^done,new-thread-id="3",
frame={level="0 ",func="vprintf",
args=[{name="format",value="0x8048e9c \"%*s%c %d %c\\n\""},
{name="arg",value="0x2"}],file="vprintf.c",line="31"}
(gdb)
```

21.13 GDB/MI Tracepoint Commands

The tracepoint commands are not yet implemented.

21.14 GDB/MI Variable Objects

Motivation for Variable Objects in GDB/MI

For the implementation of a variable debugger window (locals, watched expressions, etc.), we are proposing the adaptation of the existing code used by **Insight**.

The two main reasons for that are:

1. It has been proven in practice (it is already on its second generation).

2. It will shorten development time (needless to say how important it is now).

The original interface was designed to be used by Tcl code, so it was slightly changed so it could be used through GDB/MI. This section describes the GDB/MI operations that will be available and gives some hints about their use.

Note: In addition to the set of operations described here, we expect the GUI implementation of a variable window to require, at least, the following operations:

- -gdb-show output-radix
- -stack-list-arguments
- -stack-list-locals
- -stack-select-frame

Introduction to Variable Objects in GDB/MI

The basic idea behind variable objects is the creation of a named object to represent a variable, an expression, a memory location or even a CPU register. For each object created, a set of operations is available for examining or changing its properties.

Furthermore, complex data types, such as C structures, are represented in a tree format. For instance, the **struct** type variable is the root and the children will represent the struct members. If a child is itself of a complex type, it will also have children of its own. Appropriate language differences are handled for C, C++ and Java.

When returning the actual values of the objects, this facility allows for the individual selection of the display format used in the result creation. It can be chosen among: binary, decimal, hexadecimal, octal and natural. Natural refers to a default format automatically chosen based on the variable type (like decimal for an **int**, hex for pointers, etc.).

The following is the complete set of GDB/MI operations defined to access this functionality:

Operation	Description
-var-create	create a variable object
-var-delete	delete the variable object and its children
-var-set-format	set the display format of this variable
-var-show-format	show the display format of this variable
-var-info-num-children	tells how many children this object has
-var-list-children	return a list of the object's children
-var-info-type	show the type of this variable object
-var-info-expression	print what this variable object represents
-var-show-attributes	is this variable editable? does it exist here?
-var-evaluate-expression	get the value of this variable
-var-assign	set the value of this variable
-var-update	update the variable and its children

In the next subsection we describe each operation in detail and suggest how it can be used.

Description And Use of Operations on Variable Objects

The -var-create Command

Synopsis

```
-var-create {name | "-"}
    {frame-addr | "*"} expression
```

This operation creates a variable object, which allows the monitoring of a variable, the result of an expression, a memory cell or a CPU register.

The *name* parameter is the string by which the object can be referenced. It must be unique. If '-' is specified, the varobj system will generate a string "varNNNNNN" automatically. It will be unique provided that one does not specify *name* on that format. The command fails if a duplicate name is found.

The frame under which the expression should be evaluated can be specified by *frame-addr*. A '*' indicates that the current frame should be used.

expression is any expression valid on the current language set (must not begin with a '*'), or one of the following:

- '*addr*', where *addr* is the address of a memory cell
- '*addr-addr*' — a memory address range (TBD)
- '$regname' — a CPU register name

Result

This operation returns the name, number of children and the type of the object created. Type is returned as a string as the ones generated by the GDB CLI:

```
name="name",numchild="N",type="type"
```

The -var-delete Command

Synopsis

```
-var-delete name
```
Deletes a previously created variable object and all of its children.
Returns an error if the object *name* is not found.

The -var-set-format Command

Synopsis

```
-var-set-format name format-spec
```
Sets the output format for the value of the object *name* to be *format-spec*. The syntax for the *format-spec* is as follows:

```
format-spec ↦
{binary | decimal | hexadecimal | octal | natural}
```

The -var-show-format Command

Synopsis

> `-var-show-format` *name*

Returns the format used to display the value of the object *name*.

> *format* ↦
> *format-spec*

The `-var-info-num-children` Command

Synopsis

> `-var-info-num-children` *name*

Returns the number of children of a variable object *name*:

> `numchild=`*n*

The `-var-list-children` Command

Synopsis

> `-var-list-children` *name*

Returns a list of the children of the specified variable object:

> `numchild=`*n*`,children={{name=`*name*`,`
> `numchild=`*n*`,type=`*type*`},`(repeats N times)`}`

The `-var-info-type` Command

Synopsis

> `-var-info-type` *name*

Returns the type of the specified variable *name*. The type is returned as
a string in the same format as it is output by the GDB CLI:

> `type=`*typename*

The `-var-info-expression` Command

Synopsis

> `-var-info-expression` *name*

Returns what is represented by the variable object *name*:

> `lang=`*lang-spec*`,exp=`*expression*

where *lang-spec* is `{"C" | "C++" | "Java"}`.

The -var-show-attributes Command

Synopsis

> -var-show-attributes *name*

List attributes of the specified variable object *name*:

> status=*attr* [(,*attr*)*]

where *attr* is { { editable | noneditable } | TBD }.

The -var-evaluate-expression Command

Synopsis

> -var-evaluate-expression *name*

Evaluates the expression that is represented by the specified variable object and returns its value as a string in the current format specified for the object:

> value=*value*

The -var-assign Command

Synopsis

> -var-assign *name expression*

Assigns the value of *expression* to the variable object specified by *name*. The object must be 'editable'.

The -var-update Command

Synopsis

> -var-update {*name* | "*"}

Update the value of the variable object *name* by evaluating its expression after fetching all the new values from memory or registers. A '*' causes all existing variable objects to be updated.

22 Reporting Bugs in GDB

Your bug reports play an essential role in making GDB reliable.

Reporting a bug may help you by bringing a solution to your problem, or it may not. But in any case the principal function of a bug report is to help the entire community by making the next version of GDB work better. Bug reports are your contribution to the maintenance of GDB.

In order for a bug report to serve its purpose, you must include the information that enables us to fix the bug.

22.1 Have you found a bug?

If you are not sure whether you have found a bug, here are some guidelines:

- If the debugger gets a fatal signal, for any input whatever, that is a GDB bug. Reliable debuggers never crash.

- If GDB produces an error message for valid input, that is a bug. (Note that if you're cross debugging, the problem may also be somewhere in the connection to the target.)

- If GDB does not produce an error message for invalid input, that is a bug. However, you should note that your idea of "invalid input" might be our idea of "an extension" or "support for traditional practice".

- If you are an experienced user of debugging tools, your suggestions for improvement of GDB are welcome in any case.

22.2 How to report bugs

A number of companies and individuals offer support for GNU products. If you obtained GDB from a support organization, we recommend you contact that organization first.

You can find contact information for many support companies and individuals in the file 'etc/SERVICE' in the GNU Emacs distribution.

In any event, we also recommend that you send bug reports for GDB to this addresses:

    bug-gdb@gnu.org

Do not send bug reports to 'info-gdb', or to 'help-gdb', or to any newsgroups. Most users of GDB do not want to receive bug reports. Those that do have arranged to receive 'bug-gdb'.

The mailing list 'bug-gdb' has a newsgroup 'gnu.gdb.bug' which serves as a repeater. The mailing list and the newsgroup carry exactly the same messages. Often people think of posting bug reports to the newsgroup instead of mailing them. This appears to work, but it has one problem which can be crucial: a newsgroup posting often lacks a mail path back to the sender. Thus, if we need to ask for more information, we may be unable to reach you. For this reason, it is better to send bug reports to the mailing list.

As a last resort, send bug reports on paper to:

```
GNU Debugger Bugs
Free Software Foundation Inc.
59 Temple Place - Suite 330
Boston, MA 02111-1307
USA
```

The fundamental principle of reporting bugs usefully is this: **report all the facts**. If you are not sure whether to state a fact or leave it out, state it!

Often people omit facts because they think they know what causes the problem and assume that some details do not matter. Thus, you might assume that the name of the variable you use in an example does not matter. Well, probably it does not, but one cannot be sure. Perhaps the bug is a stray memory reference which happens to fetch from the location where that name is stored in memory; perhaps, if the name were different, the contents of that location would fool the debugger into doing the right thing despite the bug. Play it safe and give a specific, complete example. That is the easiest thing for you to do, and the most helpful.

Keep in mind that the purpose of a bug report is to enable us to fix the bug. It may be that the bug has been reported previously, but neither you nor we can know that unless your bug report is complete and self-contained.

Sometimes people give a few sketchy facts and ask, "Does this ring a bell?" Those bug reports are useless, and we urge everyone to *refuse to respond to them* except to chide the sender to report bugs properly.

To enable us to fix the bug, you should include all these things:

- The version of GDB. GDB announces it if you start with no arguments; you can also print it at any time using `show version`.

  Without this, we will not know whether there is any point in looking for the bug in the current version of GDB.

- The type of machine you are using, and the operating system name and version number.

- What compiler (and its version) was used to compile GDB—e.g. "gcc–2.8.1".

- What compiler (and its version) was used to compile the program you are debugging—e.g. "gcc–2.8.1", or "HP92453-01 A.10.32.03 HP C Compiler". For GCC, you can say `gcc --version` to get this information; for other compilers, see the documentation for those compilers.

- The command arguments you gave the compiler to compile your example and observe the bug. For example, did you use '-O'? To guarantee you will not omit something important, list them all. A copy of the Makefile (or the output from make) is sufficient.

If we were to try to guess the arguments, we would probably guess wrong and then we might not encounter the bug.

- A complete input script, and all necessary source files, that will reproduce the bug.

- A description of what behavior you observe that you believe is incorrect. For example, "It gets a fatal signal."

  Of course, if the bug is that GDB gets a fatal signal, then we will certainly notice it. But if the bug is incorrect output, we might not notice unless it is glaringly wrong. You might as well not give us a chance to make a mistake.

  Even if the problem you experience is a fatal signal, you should still say so explicitly. Suppose something strange is going on, such as, your copy of GDB is out of synch, or you have encountered a bug in the C library on your system. (This has happened!) Your copy might crash and ours would not. If you told us to expect a crash, then when ours fails to crash, we would know that the bug was not happening for us. If you had not told us to expect a crash, then we would not be able to draw any conclusion from our observations.

- If you wish to suggest changes to the GDB source, send us context diffs. If you even discuss something in the GDB source, refer to it by context, not by line number.

  The line numbers in our development sources will not match those in your sources. Your line numbers would convey no useful information to us.

Here are some things that are not necessary:

- A description of the envelope of the bug.

  Often people who encounter a bug spend a lot of time investigating which changes to the input file will make the bug go away and which changes will not affect it.

  This is often time consuming and not very useful, because the way we will find the bug is by running a single example under the debugger with breakpoints, not by pure deduction from a series of examples. We recommend that you save your time for something else.

  Of course, if you can find a simpler example to report *instead* of the original one, that is a convenience for us. Errors in the output will be easier to spot, running under the debugger will take less time, and so on.

  However, simplification is not vital; if you do not want to do this, report the bug anyway and send us the entire test case you used.

- A patch for the bug.

  A patch for the bug does help us if it is a good one. But do not omit the necessary information, such as the test case, on the assumption that a patch is all we need. We might see problems with your patch and decide to fix the problem another way, or we might not understand it at all.

Sometimes with a program as complicated as GDB it is very hard to construct an example that will make the program follow a certain path through the code. If you do not send us the example, we will not be able to construct one, so we will not be able to verify that the bug is fixed.

And if we cannot understand what bug you are trying to fix, or why your patch should be an improvement, we will not install it. A test case will help us to understand.

- A guess about what the bug is or what it depends on.

  Such guesses are usually wrong. Even we cannot guess right about such things without first using the debugger to find the facts.

23 Command Line Editing

This chapter describes the basic features of the GNU command line editing interface.

23.1 Introduction to Line Editing

The following paragraphs describe the notation used to represent keystrokes.

The text *C-k* is read as 'Control-K' and describes the character produced when the Ⓚ key is pressed while the Control key is depressed.

The text *M-k* is read as 'Meta-K' and describes the character produced when the Meta key (if you have one) is depressed, and the Ⓚ key is pressed. The Meta key is labeled (ALT) on many keyboards. On keyboards with two keys labeled (ALT) (usually to either side of the space bar), the (ALT) on the left side is generally set to work as a Meta key. The (ALT) key on the right may also be configured to work as a Meta key or may be configured as some other modifier, such as a Compose key for typing accented characters.

If you do not have a Meta or (ALT) key, or another key working as a Meta key, the identical keystroke can be generated by typing (ESC) *first*, and then typing Ⓚ. Either process is known as *metafying* the Ⓚ key.

The text *M-C-k* is read as 'Meta-Control-k' and describes the character produced by *metafying* *C-k*.

In addition, several keys have their own names. Specifically, (DEL), (ESC), (LFD), (SPC), (RET), and (TAB) all stand for themselves when seen in this text, or in an init file (see Section 23.3 [Readline Init File], page 292). If your keyboard lacks a (LFD) key, typing (C-j) will produce the desired character. The (RET) key may be labeled (Return) or (Enter) on some keyboards.

23.2 Readline Interaction

Often during an interactive session you type in a long line of text, only to notice that the first word on the line is misspelled. The Readline library gives you a set of commands for manipulating the text as you type it in, allowing you to just fix your typo, and not forcing you to retype the majority of the line. Using these editing commands, you move the cursor to the place that needs correction, and delete or insert the text of the corrections. Then, when you are satisfied with the line, you simply press (RET). You do not have to be at the end of the line to press (RET); the entire line is accepted regardless of the location of the cursor within the line.

23.2.1 Readline Bare Essentials

In order to enter characters into the line, simply type them. The typed character appears where the cursor was, and then the cursor moves one space to the right. If you mistype a character, you can use your erase character to back up and delete the mistyped character.

Sometimes you may mistype a character, and not notice the error until you have typed several other characters. In that case, you can type `C-b` to move the cursor to the left, and then correct your mistake. Afterwards, you can move the cursor to the right with `C-f`.

When you add text in the middle of a line, you will notice that characters to the right of the cursor are 'pushed over' to make room for the text that you have inserted. Likewise, when you delete text behind the cursor, characters to the right of the cursor are 'pulled back' to fill in the blank space created by the removal of the text. A list of the bare essentials for editing the text of an input line follows.

`C-b`   Move back one character.

`C-f`   Move forward one character.

(DEL) or (Backspace)
                Delete the character to the left of the cursor.

`C-d`   Delete the character underneath the cursor.

Printing characters
                Insert the character into the line at the cursor.

`C-_` or `C-x C-u`
                Undo the last editing command. You can undo all the way back to an empty line.

(Depending on your configuration, the (Backspace) key be set to delete the character to the left of the cursor and the (DEL) key set to delete the character underneath the cursor, like `C-d`, rather than the character to the left of the cursor.)

23.2.2 Readline Movement Commands

The above table describes the most basic keystrokes that you need in order to do editing of the input line. For your convenience, many other commands have been added in addition to `C-b`, `C-f`, `C-d`, and (DEL). Here are some commands for moving more rapidly about the line.

`C-a`   Move to the start of the line.

`C-e`   Move to the end of the line.

`M-f`   Move forward a word, where a word is composed of letters and digits.

`M-b`   Move backward a word.

`C-l`   Clear the screen, reprinting the current line at the top.

Notice how *C-f* moves forward a character, while *M-f* moves forward a word. It is a loose convention that control keystrokes operate on characters while meta keystrokes operate on words.

23.2.3 Readline Killing Commands

Killing text means to delete the text from the line, but to save it away for later use, usually by *yanking* (re-inserting) it back into the line. ('Cut' and 'paste' are more recent jargon for 'kill' and 'yank'.)

If the description for a command says that it 'kills' text, then you can be sure that you can get the text back in a different (or the same) place later.

When you use a kill command, the text is saved in a *kill-ring*. Any number of consecutive kills save all of the killed text together, so that when you yank it back, you get it all. The kill ring is not line specific; the text that you killed on a previously typed line is available to be yanked back later, when you are typing another line.

Here is the list of commands for killing text.

C-k   Kill the text from the current cursor position to the end of the line.

M-d   Kill from the cursor to the end of the current word, or, if between words, to the end of the next word. Word boundaries are the same as those used by *M-f*.

M-⟨DEL⟩   Kill from the cursor the start of the previous word, or, if between words, to the start of the previous word. Word boundaries are the same as those used by *M-b*.

C-w   Kill from the cursor to the previous whitespace. This is different than *M-⟨DEL⟩* because the word boundaries differ.

Here is how to *yank* the text back into the line. Yanking means to copy the most-recently-killed text from the kill buffer.

C-y   Yank the most recently killed text back into the buffer at the cursor.

M-y   Rotate the kill-ring, and yank the new top. You can only do this if the prior command is *C-y* or *M-y*.

23.2.4 Readline Arguments

You can pass numeric arguments to Readline commands. Sometimes the argument acts as a repeat count, other times it is the *sign* of the argument that is significant. If you pass a negative argument to a command which normally acts in a forward direction, that command will act in a backward direction. For example, to kill text back to the start of the line, you might type 'M-- C-k'.

The general way to pass numeric arguments to a command is to type meta digits before the command. If the first 'digit' typed is a minus sign ('-'), then the sign of the argument will be negative. Once you have typed one meta digit to get the argument started, you can type the remainder of the digits, and then the command. For example, to give the *C-d* command an argument of 10, you could type 'M-1 0 C-d', which will delete the next ten characters on the input line.

23.2.5 Searching for Commands in the History

Readline provides commands for searching through the command history for lines containing a specified string. There are two search modes: *incremental* and *non-incremental*.

Incremental searches begin before the user has finished typing the search string. As each character of the search string is typed, Readline displays the next entry from the history matching the string typed so far. An incremental search requires only as many characters as needed to find the desired history entry. To search backward in the history for a particular string, type *C-r*. Typing *C-s* searches forward through the history. The characters present in the value of the `isearch-terminators` variable are used to terminate an incremental search. If that variable has not been assigned a value, the (ESC) and *C-J* characters will terminate an incremental search. *C-g* will abort an incremental search and restore the original line. When the search is terminated, the history entry containing the search string becomes the current line.

To find other matching entries in the history list, type *C-r* or *C-s* as appropriate. This will search backward or forward in the history for the next entry matching the search string typed so far. Any other key sequence bound to a Readline command will terminate the search and execute that command. For instance, a (RET) will terminate the search and accept the line, thereby executing the command from the history list. A movement command will terminate the search, make the last line found the current line, and begin editing.

Non-incremental searches read the entire search string before starting to search for matching history lines. The search string may be typed by the user or be part of the contents of the current line.

23.3 Readline Init File

Although the Readline library comes with a set of Emacs-like keybindings installed by default, it is possible to use a different set of keybindings. Any user can customize programs that use Readline by putting commands in an *inputrc* file, conventionally in his home directory. The name of this file is taken from the value of the environment variable `INPUTRC`. If that variable is unset, the default is '~/.inputrc'.

When a program which uses the Readline library starts up, the init file is read, and the key bindings are set.

In addition, the `C-x C-r` command re-reads this init file, thus incorporating any changes that you might have made to it.

23.3.1 Readline Init File Syntax

There are only a few basic constructs allowed in the Readline init file. Blank lines are ignored. Lines beginning with a '#' are comments. Lines beginning with a '$' indicate conditional constructs (see Section 23.3.2 [Conditional Init Constructs], page 297). Other lines denote variable settings and key bindings.

Variable Settings

You can modify the run-time behavior of Readline by altering the values of variables in Readline using the **set** command within the init file. The syntax is simple:

set *variable value*

Here, for example, is how to change from the default Emacs-like key binding to use **vi** line editing commands:

set editing-mode vi

Variable names and values, where appropriate, are recognized without regard to case.

A great deal of run-time behavior is changeable with the following variables.

bell-style

Controls what happens when Readline wants to ring the terminal bell. If set to 'none', Readline never rings the bell. If set to 'visible', Readline uses a visible bell if one is available. If set to 'audible' (the default), Readline attempts to ring the terminal's bell.

comment-begin

The string to insert at the beginning of the line when the insert-comment command is executed. The default value is "#".

completion-ignore-case

If set to 'on', Readline performs filename matching and completion in a case-insensitive fashion. The default value is 'off'.

completion-query-items

The number of possible completions that determines when the user is asked whether he wants to see the list of possibilities. If the number of possible completions is greater than this value, Readline will ask the user whether or not he wishes to view them; otherwise, they are simply listed. This variable must be set to an integer value greater than or equal to 0. The default limit is 100.

`convert-meta`

If set to 'on', Readline will convert characters with the eighth bit set to an ASCII key sequence by stripping the eighth bit and prefixing an (ESC) character, converting them to a meta-prefixed key sequence. The default value is 'on'.

`disable-completion`

If set to 'On', Readline will inhibit word completion. Completion characters will be inserted into the line as if they had been mapped to `self-insert`. The default is 'off'.

`editing-mode`

The `editing-mode` variable controls which default set of key bindings is used. By default, Readline starts up in Emacs editing mode, where the keystrokes are most similar to Emacs. This variable can be set to either 'emacs' or 'vi'.

`enable-keypad`

When set to 'on', Readline will try to enable the application keypad when it is called. Some systems need this to enable the arrow keys. The default is 'off'.

`expand-tilde`

If set to 'on', tilde expansion is performed when Readline attempts word completion. The default is 'off'.

`horizontal-scroll-mode`

This variable can be set to either 'on' or 'off'. Setting it to 'on' means that the text of the lines being edited will scroll horizontally on a single screen line when they are longer than the width of the screen, instead of wrapping onto a new screen line. By default, this variable is set to 'off'.

`input-meta`

If set to 'on', Readline will enable eight-bit input (it will not clear the eighth bit in the characters it reads), regardless of what the terminal claims it

can support. The default value is 'off'. The name
`meta-flag` is a synonym for this variable.

`isearch-terminators`

> The string of characters that should terminate an
> incremental search without subsequently executing
> the character as a command (see Section 23.2.5
> [Searching], page 292). If this variable has not been
> given a value, the characters (ESC) and *C-J* will ter-
> minate an incremental search.

`keymap`   Sets Readline's idea of the current keymap for key
binding commands. Acceptable `keymap` names are
`emacs`, `emacs-standard`, `emacs-meta`, `emacs-ctlx`,
`vi`, `vi-move`, `vi-command`, and `vi-insert`. `vi` is
equivalent to `vi-command`; `emacs` is equivalent to
`emacs-standard`. The default value is `emacs`. The
value of the `editing-mode` variable also affects the
default keymap.

`mark-directories`

> If set to 'on', completed directory names have a slash
> appended. The default is 'on'.

`mark-modified-lines`

> This variable, when set to 'on', causes Readline to
> display an asterisk ('*') at the start of history lines
> which have been modified. This variable is 'off' by
> default.

`output-meta`

> If set to 'on', Readline will display characters with
> the eighth bit set directly rather than as a meta-
> prefixed escape sequence. The default is 'off'.

`print-completions-horizontally`

> If set to 'on', Readline will display completions with
> matches sorted horizontally in alphabetical order,
> rather than down the screen. The default is 'off'.

`show-all-if-ambiguous`

> This alters the default behavior of the completion
> functions. If set to 'on', words which have more
> than one possible completion cause the matches to
> be listed immediately instead of ringing the bell.
> The default value is 'off'.

`visible-stats`

> If set to 'on', a character denoting a file's type is
> appended to the filename when listing possible com-
> pletions. The default is 'off'.

Key Bindings

The syntax for controlling key bindings in the init file is simple.
First you need to find the name of the command that you want
to change. The following sections contain tables of the command
name, the default keybinding, if any, and a short description of
what the command does.

Once you know the name of the command, simply place on a
line in the init file the name of the key you wish to bind the
command to, a colon, and then the name of the command. The
name of the key can be expressed in different ways, depending
on what you find most comfortable.

In addition to command names, readline allows keys to be bound
to a string that is inserted when the key is pressed (a *macro*).

keyname: *function-name* or *macro*

keyname is the name of a key spelled out in English.
For example:

```
Control-u: universal-argument
Meta-Rubout: backward-kill-word
Control-o: "> output"
```

In the above example, *C-u* is bound to the function
universal-argument, *M-DEL* is bound to the function **backward-kill-word**, and *C-o* is bound to run
the macro expressed on the right hand side (that is,
to insert the text '> output' into the line).

A number of symbolic character names are rec-
ognized while processing this key binding syntax:
*DEL, ESC, ESCAPE, LFD, NEWLINE, RET, RE-
TURN, RUBOUT, SPACE, SPC,* and *TAB.*

"*keyseq*": *function-name* or *macro*

keyseq differs from *keyname* above in that strings
denoting an entire key sequence can be specified, by
placing the key sequence in double quotes. Some
GNU Emacs style key escapes can be used, as in the
following example, but the special character names
are not recognized.

```
"\C-u": universal-argument
"\C-x\C-r": re-read-init-file
"\e[11~": "Function Key 1"
```

In the above example, *C-u* is again bound to the
function **universal-argument** (just as it was in
the first example), '*C-x C-r*' is bound to the function **re-read-init-file**, and '(ESC) ⟨⟩ ⟨1⟩ ⟨1⟩ ⟨~⟩' is
bound to insert the text 'Function Key 1'.

The following GNU Emacs style escape sequences are available when specifying key sequences:

\C-	control prefix
\M-	meta prefix
\e	an escape character
\\	backslash
\"	(''), a double quotation mark
\'	(), a single quote or apostrophe

In addition to the GNU Emacs style escape sequences, a second set of backslash escapes is available:

\a	alert (bell)
\b	backspace
\d	delete
\f	form feed
\n	newline
\r	carriage return
\t	horizontal tab
\v	vertical tab
\\nnn	the character whose ASCII code is the octal value nnn (one to three digits)
\x$nnn$	the character whose ASCII code is the hexadecimal value nnn (one to three digits)

When entering the text of a macro, single or double quotes must be used to indicate a macro definition. Unquoted text is assumed to be a function name. In the macro body, the backslash escapes described above are expanded. Backslash will quote any other character in the macro text, including '"' and '''. For example, the following binding will make 'C-x \' insert a single '\' into the line:

```
"\C-x\\": "\\"
```

23.3.2 Conditional Init Constructs

Readline implements a facility similar in spirit to the conditional compilation features of the C preprocessor which allows key bindings and variable settings to be performed as the result of tests. There are four parser directives used.

$if   The $if construct allows bindings to be made based on the
             editing mode, the terminal being used, or the application using
             Readline. The text of the test extends to the end of the line; no
             characters are required to isolate it.

             mode   The mode= form of the $if directive is used to test
                         whether Readline is in emacs or vi mode. This may
                         be used in conjunction with the 'set keymap' com-
                         mand, for instance, to set bindings in the emacs-
                         standard and emacs-ctlx keymaps only if Readline
                         is starting out in emacs mode.

             term   The term= form may be used to include terminal-
                         specific key bindings, perhaps to bind the key se-
                         quences output by the terminal's function keys. The
                         word on the right side of the '=' is tested against
                         both the full name of the terminal and the portion
                         of the terminal name before the first '-'. This allows
                         sun to match both sun and sun-cmd, for instance.

             application
                         The application construct is used to include
                         application-specific settings. Each program using
                         the Readline library sets the application name,
                         and you can test for a particular value. This could
                         be used to bind key sequences to functions useful
                         for a specific program. For instance, the following
                         command adds a key sequence that quotes the
                         current or previous word in Bash:

                         ```
                         $if Bash
                         # Quote the current or previous word
                         "\C-xq": "\eb\"\ef\""
                         $endif
                         ```

$endif   This command, as seen in the previous example, terminates an
             $if command.

$else   Commands in this branch of the $if directive are executed if
             the test fails.

$include   This directive takes a single filename as an argument and reads
             commands and bindings from that file. For example, the follow-
             ing directive reads from '/etc/inputrc':

                         ```
                         $include /etc/inputrc
                         ```

23.3.3 Sample Init File

Here is an example of an inputrc file. This illustrates key binding, variable
assignment, and conditional syntax.

```
# This file controls the behaviour of line input editing for
# programs that use the Gnu Readline library.  Existing
# programs include FTP, Bash, and Gdb.
#
# You can re-read the inputrc file with C-x C-r.
# Lines beginning with '#' are comments.
#
# First, include any systemwide bindings and variable
# assignments from /etc/Inputrc
$include /etc/Inputrc


#
# Set various bindings for emacs mode.

set editing-mode emacs

$if mode=emacs

Meta-Control-h:  backward-kill-word Text here is ignored


#
# Arrow keys in keypad mode
#
#"\M-OD":        backward-char
#"\M-OC":        forward-char
#"\M-OA":        previous-history
#"\M-OB":        next-history
#
# Arrow keys in ANSI mode
#
"\M-[D":        backward-char
"\M-[C":        forward-char
"\M-[A":        previous-history
"\M-[B":        next-history
#
# Arrow keys in 8 bit keypad mode
#
#"\M-\C-OD":        backward-char
#"\M-\C-OC":        forward-char
#"\M-\C-OA":        previous-history
#"\M-\C-OB":        next-history
#
# Arrow keys in 8 bit ANSI mode
```

```
#
#"\M-\C-[D":        backward-char
#"\M-\C-[C":        forward-char
#"\M-\C-[A":        previous-history
#"\M-\C-[B":        next-history

C-q: quoted-insert

$endif

# An old-style binding.  This happens to be the default.
TAB: complete

# Macros that are convenient for shell interaction
$if Bash
# edit the path
"\C-xp": "PATH=${PATH}\e\C-e\C-a\ef\C-f"
# prepare to type a quoted word -- insert open and close
# double quotes and move to just after the open quote
"\C-x\"": "\"\"\C-b"
# insert a backslash (testing backslash escapes in sequences
# and macros)
"\C-x\\": "\\"
# Quote the current or previous word
"\C-xq": "\eb\"\ef\""
# Add a binding to refresh the line, which is unbound
"\C-xr": redraw-current-line
# Edit variable on current line.
"\M-\C-v": "\C-a\C-k$\C-y\M-\C-e\C-a\C-y="
$endif

# use a visible bell if one is available
set bell-style visible

# don't strip characters to 7 bits when reading
set input-meta on

# allow iso-latin1 characters to be inserted rather than
# converted to prefix-meta sequences
set convert-meta off

# display characters with the eighth bit set directly
# rather than as meta-prefixed characters
set output-meta on
```

```
# if there are more than 150 possible completions for a
# word, ask the user if he wants to see all of them
set completion-query-items 150

# For FTP
$if Ftp
"\C-xg": "get \M-?"
"\C-xt": "put \M-?"
"\M-.": yank-last-arg
$endif
```

23.4 Bindable Readline Commands

This section describes Readline commands that may be bound to key sequences. Command names without an accompanying key sequence are unbound by default.

In the following descriptions, *point* refers to the current cursor position, and *mark* refers to a cursor position saved by the set-mark command. The text between the point and mark is referred to as the *region*.

23.4.1 Commands For Moving

beginning-of-line (C-a)
> Move to the start of the current line.

end-of-line (C-e)
> Move to the end of the line.

forward-char (C-f)
> Move forward a character.

backward-char (C-b)
> Move back a character.

forward-word (M-f)
> Move forward to the end of the next word. Words are composed of letters and digits.

backward-word (M-b)
> Move back to the start of the current or previous word. Words are composed of letters and digits.

clear-screen (C-l)
> Clear the screen and redraw the current line, leaving the current line at the top of the screen.

`redraw-current-line ()`

> Refresh the current line. By default, this is unbound.

23.4.2 Commands For Manipulating The History

`accept-line (Newline or Return)`

> Accept the line regardless of where the cursor is. If this line is non-empty, it may be added to the history list for future recall with `add_history()`. If this line is a modified history line, the history line is restored to its original state.

`previous-history (C-p)`

> Move 'back' through the history list, fetching the previous command.

`next-history (C-n)`

> Move 'forward' through the history list, fetching the next command.

`beginning-of-history (M-<)`

> Move to the first line in the history.

`end-of-history (M->)`

> Move to the end of the input history, i.e., the line currently being entered.

`reverse-search-history (C-r)`

> Search backward starting at the current line and moving 'up' through the history as necessary. This is an incremental search.

`forward-search-history (C-s)`

> Search forward starting at the current line and moving 'down' through the the history as necessary. This is an incremental search.

`non-incremental-reverse-search-history (M-p)`

> Search backward starting at the current line and moving 'up' through the history as necessary using a non-incremental search for a string supplied by the user.

`non-incremental-forward-search-history (M-n)`

> Search forward starting at the current line and moving 'down' through the the history as necessary using a non-incremental search for a string supplied by the user.

`history-search-forward ()`

> Search forward through the history for the string of characters between the start of the current line and the point. This is a non-incremental search. By default, this command is unbound.

`history-search-backward ()`

> Search backward through the history for the string of characters between the start of the current line and the point. This is a non-incremental search. By default, this command is unbound.

`yank-nth-arg (M-C-y)`

> Insert the first argument to the previous command (usually the second word on the previous line) at point. With an argument *n*, insert the *n*th word from the previous command (the words in the previous command begin with word 0). A negative argument inserts the *n*th word from the end of the previous command.

`yank-last-arg (M-. or M-_)`

> Insert last argument to the previous command (the last word of the previous history entry). With an argument, behave exactly like `yank-nth-arg`. Successive calls to `yank-last-arg` move back through the history list, inserting the last argument of each line in turn.

23.4.3 Commands For Changing Text

`delete-char (C-d)`

> Delete the character at point. If point is at the beginning of the line, there are no characters in the line, and the last character typed was not bound to `delete-char`, then return EOF.

`backward-delete-char (Rubout)`

> Delete the character behind the cursor. A numeric argument means to kill the characters instead of deleting them.

`forward-backward-delete-char ()`

> Delete the character under the cursor, unless the cursor is at the end of the line, in which case the character behind the cursor is deleted. By default, this is not bound to a key.

`quoted-insert (C-q or C-v)`

> Add the next character typed to the line verbatim. This is how to insert key sequences like *C-q*, for example.

`tab-insert (M-⟨TAB⟩)`

> Insert a tab character.

`self-insert (a, b, A, 1, !, ...)`

> Insert yourself.

`transpose-chars (C-t)`

> Drag the character before the cursor forward over the character at the cursor, moving the cursor forward as well. If the insertion

point is at the end of the line, then this transposes the last two
characters of the line. Negative arguments have no effect.

transpose-words (M-t)
> Drag the word before point past the word after point, moving
> point past that word as well.

upcase-word (M-u)
> Uppercase the current (or following) word. With a negative
> argument, uppercase the previous word, but do not move the
> cursor.

downcase-word (M-l)
> Lowercase the current (or following) word. With a negative
> argument, lowercase the previous word, but do not move the
> cursor.

capitalize-word (M-c)
> Capitalize the current (or following) word. With a negative ar-
> gument, capitalize the previous word, but do not move the cur-
> sor.

23.4.4 Killing And Yanking

kill-line (C-k)
> Kill the text from point to the end of the line.

backward-kill-line (C-x Rubout)
> Kill backward to the beginning of the line.

unix-line-discard (C-u)
> Kill backward from the cursor to the beginning of the current
> line.

kill-whole-line ()
> Kill all characters on the current line, no matter where point is.
> By default, this is unbound.

kill-word (M-d)
> Kill from point to the end of the current word, or if between
> words, to the end of the next word. Word boundaries are the
> same as `forward-word`.

backward-kill-word (M-⟨DEL⟩)
> Kill the word behind point. Word boundaries are the same as
> `backward-word`.

unix-word-rubout (C-w)
> Kill the word behind point, using white space as a word bound-
> ary. The killed text is saved on the kill-ring.

`delete-horizontal-space ()`
> Delete all spaces and tabs around point. By default, this is unbound.

`kill-region ()`
> Kill the text in the current region. By default, this command is unbound.

`copy-region-as-kill ()`
> Copy the text in the region to the kill buffer, so it can be yanked right away. By default, this command is unbound.

`copy-backward-word ()`
> Copy the word before point to the kill buffer. The word boundaries are the same as `backward-word`. By default, this command is unbound.

`copy-forward-word ()`
> Copy the word following point to the kill buffer. The word boundaries are the same as `forward-word`. By default, this command is unbound.

`yank (C-y)`
> Yank the top of the kill ring into the buffer at point.

`yank-pop (M-y)`
> Rotate the kill-ring, and yank the new top. You can only do this if the prior command is `yank` or `yank-pop`.

23.4.5 Specifying Numeric Arguments

`digit-argument (M-0, M-1, ... M--)`
> Add this digit to the argument already accumulating, or start a new argument. `M--` starts a negative argument.

`universal-argument ()`
> This is another way to specify an argument. If this command is followed by one or more digits, optionally with a leading minus sign, those digits define the argument. If the command is followed by digits, executing `universal-argument` again ends the numeric argument, but is otherwise ignored. As a special case, if this command is immediately followed by a character that is neither a digit or minus sign, the argument count for the next command is multiplied by four. The argument count is initially one, so executing this function the first time makes the argument count four, a second time makes the argument count sixteen, and so on. By default, this is not bound to a key.

23.4.6 Letting Readline Type For You

complete (⟨TAB⟩)

> Attempt to perform completion on the text before point. The actual completion performed is application-specific. The default is filename completion.

possible-completions (M-?)

> List the possible completions of the text before point.

insert-completions (M-*)

> Insert all completions of the text before point that would have been generated by possible-completions.

menu-complete ()

> Similar to complete, but replaces the word to be completed with a single match from the list of possible completions. Repeated execution of menu-complete steps through the list of possible completions, inserting each match in turn. At the end of the list of completions, the bell is rung (subject to the setting of bell-style) and the original text is restored. An argument of *n* moves *n* positions forward in the list of matches; a negative argument may be used to move backward through the list. This command is intended to be bound to ⟨TAB⟩, but is unbound by default.

delete-char-or-list ()

> Deletes the character under the cursor if not at the beginning or end of the line (like delete-char). If at the end of the line, behaves identically to possible-completions. This command is unbound by default.

23.4.7 Keyboard Macros

start-kbd-macro (C-x ()

> Begin saving the characters typed into the current keyboard macro.

end-kbd-macro (C-x))

> Stop saving the characters typed into the current keyboard macro and save the definition.

call-last-kbd-macro (C-x e)

> Re-execute the last keyboard macro defined, by making the characters in the macro appear as if typed at the keyboard.

23.4.8 Some Miscellaneous Commands

re-read-init-file (C-x C-r)
> Read in the contents of the *inputrc* file, and incorporate any
> bindings or variable assignments found there.

abort (C-g)
> Abort the current editing command and ring the terminal's bell
> (subject to the setting of **bell-style**).

do-uppercase-version (M-a, M-b, M-x, ...)
> If the metafied character x is lowercase, run the command that
> is bound to the corresponding uppercase character.

prefix-meta (ESC)
> Metafy the next character typed. This is for keyboards without
> a meta key. Typing 'ESC f' is equivalent to typing M-f.

undo (C-_ or C-x C-u)
> Incremental undo, separately remembered for each line.

revert-line (M-r)
> Undo all changes made to this line. This is like executing the
> **undo** command enough times to get back to the beginning.

tilde-expand (M-~)
> Perform tilde expansion on the current word.

set-mark (C-@)
> Set the mark to the point. If a numeric argument is supplied,
> the mark is set to that position.

exchange-point-and-mark (C-x C-x)
> Swap the point with the mark. The current cursor position is
> set to the saved position, and the old cursor position is saved as
> the mark.

character-search (C-])
> A character is read and point is moved to the next occurrence
> of that character. A negative count searches for previous occur-
> rences.

character-search-backward (M-C-])
> A character is read and point is moved to the previous occur-
> rence of that character. A negative count searches for subse-
> quent occurrences.

insert-comment (M-#)
> The value of the **comment-begin** variable is inserted at the be-
> ginning of the current line, and the line is accepted as if a newline
> had been typed.

dump-functions ()

> Print all of the functions and their key bindings to the Readline output stream. If a numeric argument is supplied, the output is formatted in such a way that it can be made part of an *inputrc* file. This command is unbound by default.

dump-variables ()

> Print all of the settable variables and their values to the Readline output stream. If a numeric argument is supplied, the output is formatted in such a way that it can be made part of an *inputrc* file. This command is unbound by default.

dump-macros ()

> Print all of the Readline key sequences bound to macros and the strings they output. If a numeric argument is supplied, the output is formatted in such a way that it can be made part of an *inputrc* file. This command is unbound by default.

23.5 Readline vi Mode

While the Readline library does not have a full set of **vi** editing functions, it does contain enough to allow simple editing of the line. The Readline **vi** mode behaves as specified in the POSIX 1003.2 standard.

In order to switch interactively between **emacs** and **vi** editing modes, use the command *M-C-j* (bound to emacs-editing-mode when in **vi** mode and to vi-editing-mode in **emacs** mode). The Readline default is **emacs** mode.

When you enter a line in **vi** mode, you are already placed in 'insertion' mode, as if you had typed an 'i'. Pressing (ESC) switches you into 'command' mode, where you can edit the text of the line with the standard **vi** movement keys, move to previous history lines with 'k' and subsequent lines with 'j', and so forth.

24 Using History Interactively

This chapter describes how to use the GNU History Library interactively, from a user's standpoint. It should be considered a user's guide.

24.1 History Expansion

The History library provides a history expansion feature that is similar to the history expansion provided by `csh`. This section describes the syntax used to manipulate the history information.

History expansions introduce words from the history list into the input stream, making it easy to repeat commands, insert the arguments to a previous command into the current input line, or fix errors in previous commands quickly.

History expansion takes place in two parts. The first is to determine which line from the history list should be used during substitution. The second is to select portions of that line for inclusion into the current one. The line selected from the history is called the *event*, and the portions of that line that are acted upon are called *words*. Various *modifiers* are available to manipulate the selected words. The line is broken into words in the same fashion that Bash does, so that several words surrounded by quotes are considered one word. History expansions are introduced by the appearance of the history expansion character, which is '!' by default.

24.1.1 Event Designators

An event designator is a reference to a command line entry in the history list.

!	Start a history substitution, except when followed by a space, tab, the end of the line, '=' or '('.
!*n*	Refer to command line *n*.
!-*n*	Refer to the command *n* lines back.
!!	Refer to the previous command. This is a synonym for '!-1'.
!*string*	Refer to the most recent command starting with *string*.
!?*string*[?]	
	Refer to the most recent command containing *string*. The trailing '?' may be omitted if the *string* is followed immediately by a newline.
^*string1*^*string2*^	
	Quick Substitution. Repeat the last command, replacing *string1* with *string2*. Equivalent to !!:s/*string1*/*string2*/.
!#	The entire command line typed so far.

24.1.2 Word Designators

Word designators are used to select desired words from the event. A
':' separates the event specification from the word designator. It may be
omitted if the word designator begins with a '^', '$', '*', '-', or '%'. Words are
numbered from the beginning of the line, with the first word being denoted
by 0 (zero). Words are inserted into the current line separated by single
spaces.

For example,

`!!`	designates the preceding command. When you type this, the preceding command is repeated in toto.
`!!:$`	designates the last argument of the preceding command. This may be shortened to `!$`.
`!fi:2`	designates the second argument of the most recent command starting with the letters `fi`.

Here are the word designators:

`0 (zero)`	The 0th word. For many applications, this is the command word.
n	The *n*th word.
`^`	The first argument; that is, word 1.
`$`	The last argument.
`%`	The word matched by the most recent '?*string*?' search.
x-y	A range of words; '*-y*' abbreviates '0-*y*'.
`*`	All of the words, except the 0th. This is a synonym for '1-$'. It is not an error to use '*' if there is just one word in the event; the empty string is returned in that case.
x*	Abbreviates '*x*-$'
x-	Abbreviates '*x*-$' like '*x**', but omits the last word.

If a word designator is supplied without an event specification, the previous command is used as the event.

24.1.3 Modifiers

After the optional word designator, you can add a sequence of one or
more of the following modifiers, each preceded by a ':'.

`h`	Remove a trailing pathname component, leaving only the head.
`t`	Remove all leading pathname components, leaving the tail.
`r`	Remove a trailing suffix of the form '.*suffix*', leaving the base-name.

e   Remove all but the trailing suffix.

p   Print the new command but do not execute it.

s/*old*/*new*/

Substitute *new* for the first occurrence of *old* in the event line. Any delimiter may be used in place of '/'. The delimiter may be quoted in *old* and *new* with a single backslash. If '&' appears in *new*, it is replaced by *old*. A single backslash will quote the '&'. The final delimiter is optional if it is the last character on the input line.

&   Repeat the previous substitution.

g   Cause changes to be applied over the entire event line. Used in conjunction with 's', as in gs/*old*/*new*/, or with '&'.

Appendix A Formatting Documentation

The GDB 4 release includes an already-formatted reference card, ready for printing with PostScript or Ghostscript, in the 'gdb' subdirectory of the main source directory[1]. If you can use PostScript or Ghostscript with your printer, you can print the reference card immediately with 'refcard.ps'.

The release also includes the source for the reference card. You can format it, using TeX, by typing:

```
make refcard.dvi
```

The GDB reference card is designed to print in *landscape* mode on US "letter" size paper; that is, on a sheet 11 inches wide by 8.5 inches high. You will need to specify this form of printing as an option to your DVI output program.

All the documentation for GDB comes as part of the machine-readable distribution. The documentation is written in Texinfo format, which is a documentation system that uses a single source file to produce both on-line information and a printed manual. You can use one of the Info formatting commands to create the on-line version of the documentation and TeX (or `texi2roff`) to typeset the printed version.

GDB includes an already formatted copy of the on-line Info version of this manual in the 'gdb' subdirectory. The main Info file is 'gdb-5.1.1/gdb/gdb.info', and it refers to subordinate files matching 'gdb.info*' in the same directory. If necessary, you can print out these files, or read them with any editor; but they are easier to read using the `info` subsystem in GNU Emacs or the standalone `info` program, available as part of the GNU Texinfo distribution.

If you want to format these Info files yourself, you need one of the Info formatting programs, such as `texinfo-format-buffer` or `makeinfo`.

If you have `makeinfo` installed, and are in the top level GDB source directory ('gdb-5.1.1', in the case of version 5.1.1), you can make the Info file by typing:

```
cd gdb
make gdb.info
```

If you want to typeset and print copies of this manual, you need TeX, a program to print its DVI output files, and 'texinfo.tex', the Texinfo definitions file.

TeX is a typesetting program; it does not print files directly, but produces output files called DVI files. To print a typeset document, you need a program to print DVI files. If your system has TeX installed, chances are it has such a program. The precise command to use depends on your system; *lpr -d* is common; another (for PostScript devices) is *dvips*. The DVI print command may require a file name without any extension or a '.dvi' extension.

---

[1] In 'gdb-5.1.1/gdb/refcard.ps' of the version 5.1.1 release.

TEX also requires a macro definitions file called 'texinfo.tex'. This file tells TEX how to typeset a document written in Texinfo format. On its own, TEX cannot either read or typeset a Texinfo file. 'texinfo.tex' is distributed with GDB and is located in the 'gdb-*version-number*/texinfo' directory.

If you have TEX and a DVI printer program installed, you can typeset and print this manual. First switch to the the 'gdb' subdirectory of the main source directory (for example, to 'gdb-5.1.1/gdb') and type:

    make gdb.dvi

Then give 'gdb.dvi' to your DVI printing program.

Appendix B Installing GDB

GDB comes with a `configure` script that automates the process of preparing GDB for installation; you can then use `make` to build the `gdb` program.[1]

The GDB distribution includes all the source code you need for GDB in a single directory, whose name is usually composed by appending the version number to 'gdb'.

For example, the GDB version 5.1.1 distribution is in the 'gdb-5.1.1' directory. That directory contains:

`gdb-5.1.1/configure` (and supporting files)
        script for configuring GDB and all its supporting libraries

`gdb-5.1.1/gdb`
        the source specific to GDB itself

`gdb-5.1.1/bfd`
        source for the Binary File Descriptor library

`gdb-5.1.1/include`
        GNU include files

`gdb-5.1.1/libiberty`
        source for the '-liberty' free software library

`gdb-5.1.1/opcodes`
        source for the library of opcode tables and disassemblers

`gdb-5.1.1/readline`
        source for the GNU command-line interface

`gdb-5.1.1/glob`
        source for the GNU filename pattern-matching subroutine

`gdb-5.1.1/mmalloc`
        source for the GNU memory-mapped malloc package

The simplest way to configure and build GDB is to run `configure` from the 'gdb-*version-number*' source directory, which in this example is the 'gdb-5.1.1' directory.

First switch to the 'gdb-*version-number*' source directory if you are not already in it; then run `configure`. Pass the identifier for the platform on which GDB will run as an argument.

For example:

---

[1] If you have a more recent version of GDB than 5.1.1, look at the 'README' file in the sources; we may have improved the installation procedures since publishing this manual.

```
cd gdb-5.1.1
./configure host
make
```

where *host* is an identifier such as 'sun4' or 'decstation', that identifies the platform where GDB will run. (You can often leave off *host*; configure tries to guess the correct value by examining your system.)

Running 'configure *host*' and then running make builds the 'bfd', 'readline', 'mmalloc', and 'libiberty' libraries, then gdb itself. The configured source files, and the binaries, are left in the corresponding source directories.

configure is a Bourne-shell (/bin/sh) script; if your system does not recognize this automatically when you run a different shell, you may need to run sh on it explicitly:

```
sh configure host
```

If you run configure from a directory that contains source directories for multiple libraries or programs, such as the 'gdb-5.1.1' source directory for version 5.1.1, configure creates configuration files for every directory level underneath (unless you tell it not to, with the '--norecursion' option).

You can run the configure script from any of the subordinate directories in the GDB distribution if you only want to configure that subdirectory, but be sure to specify a path to it.

For example, with version 5.1.1, type the following to configure only the bfd subdirectory:

```
cd gdb-5.1.1/bfd
../configure host
```

You can install gdb anywhere; it has no hardwired paths. However, you should make sure that the shell on your path (named by the 'SHELL' environment variable) is publicly readable. Remember that GDB uses the shell to start your program—some systems refuse to let GDB debug child processes whose programs are not readable.

B.1 Compiling GDB in another directory

If you want to run GDB versions for several host or target machines, you need a different gdb compiled for each combination of host and target. configure is designed to make this easy by allowing you to generate each configuration in a separate subdirectory, rather than in the source directory. If your make program handles the 'VPATH' feature (GNU make does), running make in each of these directories builds the gdb program specified there.

To build gdb in a separate directory, run configure with the '--srcdir' option to specify where to find the source. (You also need to specify a path to find configure itself from your working directory. If the path to configure would be the same as the argument to '--srcdir', you can leave out the '--srcdir' option; it is assumed.)

For example, with version 5.1.1, you can build GDB in a separate directory for a Sun 4 like this:

```
cd gdb-5.1.1
mkdir ../gdb-sun4
cd ../gdb-sun4
../gdb-5.1.1/configure sun4
make
```

When `configure` builds a configuration using a remote source directory, it creates a tree for the binaries with the same structure (and using the same names) as the tree under the source directory. In the example, you'd find the Sun 4 library 'libiberty.a' in the directory 'gdb-sun4/libiberty', and GDB itself in 'gdb-sun4/gdb'.

One popular reason to build several GDB configurations in separate directories is to configure GDB for cross-compiling (where GDB runs on one machine—the *host*—while debugging programs that run on another machine—the *target*). You specify a cross-debugging target by giving the '--target=*target*' option to `configure`.

When you run `make` to build a program or library, you must run it in a configured directory—whatever directory you were in when you called `configure` (or one of its subdirectories).

The `Makefile` that `configure` generates in each source directory also runs recursively. If you type `make` in a source directory such as 'gdb-5.1.1' (or in a separate configured directory configured with '--srcdir=*dirname*/gdb-5.1.1'), you will build all the required libraries, and then build GDB.

When you have multiple hosts or targets configured in separate directories, you can run `make` on them in parallel (for example, if they are NFS-mounted on each of the hosts); they will not interfere with each other.

B.2 Specifying names for hosts and targets

The specifications used for hosts and targets in the `configure` script are based on a three-part naming scheme, but some short predefined aliases are also supported. The full naming scheme encodes three pieces of information in the following pattern:

> *architecture-vendor-os*

For example, you can use the alias `sun4` as a *host* argument, or as the value for *target* in a `--target=`*target* option. The equivalent full name is 'sparc-sun-sunos4'.

The `configure` script accompanying GDB does not provide any query facility to list all supported host and target names or aliases. `configure` calls the Bourne shell script `config.sub` to map abbreviations to full names; you can read the script, if you wish, or you can use it to test your guesses on abbreviations—for example:

```
% sh config.sub i386-linux
i386-pc-linux-gnu
% sh config.sub alpha-linux
alpha-unknown-linux-gnu
% sh config.sub hp9k700
hppa1.1-hp-hpux
% sh config.sub sun4
sparc-sun-sunos4.1.1
% sh config.sub sun3
m68k-sun-sunos4.1.1
% sh config.sub i986v
Invalid configuration 'i986v': machine 'i986v' not recognized
```

config.sub is also distributed in the GDB source directory ('gdb-5.1.1', for version 5.1.1).

B.3 configure options

Here is a summary of the configure options and arguments that are most often useful for building GDB. configure also has several other options not listed here. See Info file 'configure.info', node 'What Configure Does', for a full explanation of configure.

```
configure [--help]
          [--prefix=dir]
          [--exec-prefix=dir]
          [--srcdir=dirname]
          [--norecursion] [--rm]
          [--target=target]
          host
```

You may introduce options with a single '-' rather than '--' if you prefer; but you may abbreviate option names if you use '--'.

--help   Display a quick summary of how to invoke configure.

--prefix=dir
            Configure the source to install programs and files under directory 'dir'.

--exec-prefix=dir
            Configure the source to install programs under directory 'dir'.

--srcdir=*dirname*

> **Warning: using this option requires** GNU make, **or another** make **that implements the** VPATH **feature.**
>
> Use this option to make configurations in directories separate from the GDB source directories. Among other things, you can use this to build (or maintain) several configurations simultaneously, in separate directories. configure writes configuration specific files in the current directory, but arranges for them to use the source in the directory *dirname*. configure creates directories under the working directory in parallel to the source directories below *dirname*.

--norecursion

> Configure only the directory level where configure is executed; do not propagate configuration to subdirectories.

--target=*target*

> Configure GDB for cross-debugging programs running on the specified *target*. Without this option, GDB is configured to debug programs that run on the same machine (*host*) as GDB itself.
>
> There is no convenient way to generate a list of all available targets.

host ...

> Configure GDB to run on the specified *host*.
>
> There is no convenient way to generate a list of all available hosts.

There are many other options available as well, but they are generally needed for special purposes only.

Appendix C GNU Free Documentation License

Version 1.1, March 2000

Copyright (C) 2000 Free Software Foundation, Inc.
59 Temple Place, Suite 330, Boston, MA 02111-1307 USA

0. PREAMBLE

The purpose of this License is to make a manual, textbook, or other
written document "free" in the sense of freedom: to assure everyone the
effective freedom to copy and redistribute it, with or without modifying
it, either commercially or noncommercially. Secondarily, this License
preserves for the author and publisher a way to get credit for their
work, while not being considered responsible for modifications made by
others.

This License is a kind of "copyleft", which means that derivative works
of the document must themselves be free in the same sense. It com-
plements the GNU General Public License, which is a copyleft license
designed for free software.

We have designed this License in order to use it for manuals for free software, because free software needs free documentation: a free program
should come with manuals providing the same freedoms that the software does. But this License is not limited to software manuals; it can
be used for any textual work, regardless of subject matter or whether it
is published as a printed book. We recommend this License principally
for works whose purpose is instruction or reference.

1. APPLICABILITY AND DEFINITIONS

This License applies to any manual or other work that contains a notice
placed by the copyright holder saying it can be distributed under the
terms of this License. The "Document", below, refers to any such manual or work. Any member of the public is a licensee, and is addressed
as "you."

A "Modified Version" of the Document means any work containing the
Document or a portion of it, either copied verbatim, or with modifications and/or translated into another language.

A "Secondary Section" is a named appendix or a front-matter section
of the Document that deals exclusively with the relationship of the publishers or authors of the Document to the Document's overall subject
(or to related matters) and contains nothing that could fall directly
within that overall subject. (For example, if the Document is in part

a textbook of mathematics, a Secondary Section may not explain any mathematics.) The relationship could be a matter of historical connection with the subject or with related matters, or of legal, commercial, philosophical, ethical or political position regarding them.

The "Invariant Sections" are certain Secondary Sections whose titles are designated, as being those of Invariant Sections, in the notice that says that the Document is released under this License.

The "Cover Texts" are certain short passages of text that are listed, as Front-Cover Texts or Back-Cover Texts, in the notice that says that the Document is released under this License.

A "Transparent" copy of the Document means a machine-readable copy, represented in a format whose specification is available to the general public, whose contents can be viewed and edited directly and straightforwardly with generic text editors or (for images composed of pixels) generic paint programs or (for drawings) some widely available drawing editor, and that is suitable for input to text formatters or for automatic translation to a variety of formats suitable for input to text formatters. A copy made in an otherwise Transparent file format whose markup has been designed to thwart or discourage subsequent modification by readers is not Transparent. A copy that is not "Transparent" is called "Opaque."

Examples of suitable formats for Transparent copies include plain ASCII without markup, Texinfo input format, LaTeX input format, SGML or XML using a publicly available DTD, and standard-conforming simple HTML designed for human modification. Opaque formats include PostScript, PDF, proprietary formats that can be read and edited only by proprietary word processors, SGML or XML for which the DTD and/or processing tools are not generally available, and the machine-generated HTML produced by some word processors for output purposes only.

The "Title Page" means, for a printed book, the title page itself, plus such following pages as are needed to hold, legibly, the material this License requires to appear in the title page. For works in formats which do not have any title page as such, "Title Page" means the text near the most prominent appearance of the work's title, preceding the beginning of the body of the text.

2. VERBATIM COPYING

You may copy and distribute the Document in any medium, either commercially or noncommercially, provided that this License, the copyright notices, and the license notice saying this License applies to the Document are reproduced in all copies, and that you add no other conditions whatsoever to those of this License. You may not use technical measures to obstruct or control the reading or further copying of the copies you make or distribute. However, you may accept compensation in exchange for copies. If you distribute a large enough number of copies you must also follow the conditions in section 3.

You may also lend copies, under the same conditions stated above, and you may publicly display copies.

3. COPYING IN QUANTITY

If you publish printed copies of the Document numbering more than 100, and the Document's license notice requires Cover Texts, you must enclose the copies in covers that carry, clearly and legibly, all these Cover Texts: Front-Cover Texts on the front cover, and Back-Cover Texts on the back cover. Both covers must also clearly and legibly identify you as the publisher of these copies. The front cover must present the full title with all words of the title equally prominent and visible. You may add other material on the covers in addition. Copying with changes limited to the covers, as long as they preserve the title of the Document and satisfy these conditions, can be treated as verbatim copying in other respects.

If the required texts for either cover are too voluminous to fit legibly, you should put the first ones listed (as many as fit reasonably) on the actual cover, and continue the rest onto adjacent pages.

If you publish or distribute Opaque copies of the Document numbering more than 100, you must either include a machine-readable Transparent copy along with each Opaque copy, or state in or with each Opaque copy a publicly-accessible computer-network location containing a complete Transparent copy of the Document, free of added material, which the general network-using public has access to download anonymously at no charge using public-standard network protocols. If you use the latter option, you must take reasonably prudent steps, when you begin distribution of Opaque copies in quantity, to ensure that this Transparent copy will remain thus accessible at the stated location until at least one year after the last time you distribute an Opaque copy (directly or through your agents or retailers) of that edition to the public.

It is requested, but not required, that you contact the authors of the Document well before redistributing any large number of copies, to give them a chance to provide you with an updated version of the Document.

4. MODIFICATIONS

You may copy and distribute a Modified Version of the Document under the conditions of sections 2 and 3 above, provided that you release the Modified Version under precisely this License, with the Modified Version filling the role of the Document, thus licensing distribution and modification of the Modified Version to whoever possesses a copy of it. In addition, you must do these things in the Modified Version:

A. Use in the Title Page (and on the covers, if any) a title distinct from that of the Document, and from those of previous versions (which should, if there were any, be listed in the History section of the Document). You may use the same title as a previous version if the original publisher of that version gives permission.

B. List on the Title Page, as authors, one or more persons or entities responsible for authorship of the modifications in the Modified Version, together with at least five of the principal authors of the Document (all of its principal authors, if it has less than five).

C. State on the Title page the name of the publisher of the Modified Version, as the publisher.

D. Preserve all the copyright notices of the Document.

E. Add an appropriate copyright notice for your modifications adjacent to the other copyright notices.

F. Include, immediately after the copyright notices, a license notice giving the public permission to use the Modified Version under the terms of this License, in the form shown in the Addendum below.

G. Preserve in that license notice the full lists of Invariant Sections and required Cover Texts given in the Document's license notice.

H. Include an unaltered copy of this License.

I. Preserve the section entitled "History", and its title, and add to it an item stating at least the title, year, new authors, and publisher of the Modified Version as given on the Title Page. If there is no section entitled "History" in the Document, create one stating the title, year, authors, and publisher of the Document as given on its Title Page, then add an item describing the Modified Version as stated in the previous sentence.

J. Preserve the network location, if any, given in the Document for public access to a Transparent copy of the Document, and likewise the network locations given in the Document for previous versions it was based on. These may be placed in the "History" section. You may omit a network location for a work that was published at least four years before the Document itself, or if the original publisher of the version it refers to gives permission.

K. In any section entitled "Acknowledgements" or "Dedications", preserve the section's title, and preserve in the section all the substance and tone of each of the contributor acknowledgements and/or dedications given therein.

L. Preserve all the Invariant Sections of the Document, unaltered in their text and in their titles. Section numbers or the equivalent are not considered part of the section titles.

M. Delete any section entitled "Endorsements." Such a section may not be included in the Modified Version.

N. Do not retitle any existing section as "Endorsements" or to conflict in title with any Invariant Section.

If the Modified Version includes new front-matter sections or appendices that qualify as Secondary Sections and contain no material copied from the Document, you may at your option designate some or all of these sections as invariant. To do this, add their titles to the list of Invariant Sections in the Modified Version's license notice. These titles must be distinct from any other section titles.

You may add a section entitled "Endorsements", provided it contains nothing but endorsements of your Modified Version by various parties—for example, statements of peer review or that the text has been approved by an organization as the authoritative definition of a standard.

You may add a passage of up to five words as a Front-Cover Text, and a passage of up to 25 words as a Back-Cover Text, to the end of the list of Cover Texts in the Modified Version. Only one passage of Front-Cover Text and one of Back-Cover Text may be added by (or through arrangements made by) any one entity. If the Document already includes a cover text for the same cover, previously added by you or by arrangement made by the same entity you are acting on behalf of, you may not add another; but you may replace the old one, on explicit permission from the previous publisher that added the old one.

The author(s) and publisher(s) of the Document do not by this License give permission to use their names for publicity for or to assert or imply endorsement of any Modified Version.

5. COMBINING DOCUMENTS

You may combine the Document with other documents released under this License, under the terms defined in section 4 above for modified versions, provided that you include in the combination all of the Invariant Sections of all of the original documents, unmodified, and list them all as Invariant Sections of your combined work in its license notice.

The combined work need only contain one copy of this License, and multiple identical Invariant Sections may be replaced with a single copy. If there are multiple Invariant Sections with the same name but different contents, make the title of each such section unique by adding at the end of it, in parentheses, the name of the original author or publisher of that section if known, or else a unique number. Make the same adjustment to the section titles in the list of Invariant Sections in the license notice of the combined work.

In the combination, you must combine any sections entitled "History" in the various original documents, forming one section entitled "History"; likewise combine any sections entitled "Acknowledgements", and any sections entitled "Dedications." You must delete all sections entitled "Endorsements."

6. COLLECTIONS OF DOCUMENTS

You may make a collection consisting of the Document and other documents released under this License, and replace the individual copies of this License in the various documents with a single copy that is included in the collection, provided that you follow the rules of this License for verbatim copying of each of the documents in all other respects.

You may extract a single document from such a collection, and distribute it individually under this License, provided you insert a copy of this License into the extracted document, and follow this License in all other respects regarding verbatim copying of that document.

7. AGGREGATION WITH INDEPENDENT WORKS

A compilation of the Document or its derivatives with other separate and independent documents or works, in or on a volume of a storage or distribution medium, does not as a whole count as a Modified Version of the Document, provided no compilation copyright is claimed for the compilation. Such a compilation is called an "aggregate", and this License does not apply to the other self-contained works thus compiled with the Document, on account of their being thus compiled, if they are not themselves derivative works of the Document.

If the Cover Text requirement of section 3 is applicable to these copies of the Document, then if the Document is less than one quarter of the entire aggregate, the Document's Cover Texts may be placed on covers that surround only the Document within the aggregate. Otherwise they must appear on covers around the whole aggregate.

8. TRANSLATION

Translation is considered a kind of modification, so you may distribute translations of the Document under the terms of section 4. Replacing Invariant Sections with translations requires special permission from their copyright holders, but you may include translations of some or all Invariant Sections in addition to the original versions of these Invariant Sections. You may include a translation of this License provided that you also include the original English version of this License. In case of a disagreement between the translation and the original English version of this License, the original English version will prevail.

9. TERMINATION

You may not copy, modify, sublicense, or distribute the Document except as expressly provided for under this License. Any other attempt to copy, modify, sublicense or distribute the Document is void, and will automatically terminate your rights under this License. However, parties who have received copies, or rights, from you under this License will not have their licenses terminated so long as such parties remain in full compliance.

10. FUTURE REVISIONS OF THIS LICENSE

The Free Software Foundation may publish new, revised versions of the GNU Free Documentation License from time to time. Such new versions will be similar in spirit to the present version, but may differ in detail to address new problems or concerns. See http://www.gnu.org/copyleft/.

Each version of the License is given a distinguishing version number. If the Document specifies that a particular numbered version of this License "or any later version" applies to it, you have the option of following the terms and conditions either of that specified version or of any later version that has been published (not as a draft) by the Free Software Foundation. If the Document does not specify a version number of this License, you may choose any version ever published (not as a draft) by the Free Software Foundation.

ADDENDUM: How to use this License for your documents

To use this License in a document you have written, include a copy of the License in the document and put the following copyright and license notices just after the title page:

```
Copyright (C)  year   your name.
Permission is granted to copy, distribute and/or modify this document
under the terms of the GNU Free Documentation License, Version 1.1
or any later version published by the Free Software Foundation;
with the Invariant Sections being list their titles, with the
Front-Cover Texts being list, and with the Back-Cover Texts being list.
A copy of the license is included in the section entitled "GNU
Free Documentation License."
```

If you have no Invariant Sections, write "with no Invariant Sections" instead of saying which ones are invariant. If you have no Front-Cover Texts, write "no Front-Cover Texts" instead of "Front-Cover Texts being list"; likewise for Back-Cover Texts.

If your document contains nontrivial examples of program code, we recommend releasing these examples in parallel under your choice of free software license, such as the GNU General Public License, to permit their use in free software.

Index

.

/

:

@

^

'

{

U

V

W

X